BANNER OF LIBERTY SERIES

Book 2

THE THREAT OF ANARCHY LEADS TO THE CONSTIUTION

(With Study Guide CD)

Written By:

Mary Mostert

E-Mail: Mary@bannerofliberty.com

To access Banner of Liberty online Footnotes go to:
http://www.bannerofliberty.com/Action/8-16-2003ftnt.html

Published by CTR Publishing Incorporated
3904 Foothill Drive
Provo, UT 84604

ISBN 0-9753851-4-3

Cover Art:
The Prayer at Valley Forge by Arnold Friberg.
For more information on this painting and other works by Arnold Friberg, please visit www.fribergfineart.com or Call 1-800-545-5460.

Table of Contents

Chapter 1
A Decisive Battle and a Stumbling Hero

Military historians John K. Robertson and Bob McDonald in *A Brief Profile of the Continental Army – The Army of 1777 through 1780* described how the experiences of George Washington and the haphazard nature of the Continental Army changed military thinking by the end of 1777.

> "Based on Congressional decisions made in September and early October of 1776, precisely as Washington's army was being driven entirely from Manhattan into Westchester County, the fundamental nature of the Continental Army was defined for 1777 and, with minor modifications, for the remainder of the war." [1]

Finally, the idealistic notion of short-term enlistments of Patriot citizen soldiers gave way to the realistic requirements of a trained and dependable army. Two important resolutions of the Second Continental Congress began finally to authorize the kind of army it would take to win freedom. One was called the "Eight-Eight Battalion Resolution of the Continental Congress Authorizing an Expanded Continental Army To Serve for the Duration of the War, 16 September 1776."

This resolution, for the very first time, implemented a quota of regiments, based on each colony's population, which each colony was required to furnish the new national army.[2] The total number of regiments authorized was 88.[3] The six most populous states, Virginia, Massachusetts, Pennsylvania, North Carolina, Connecticut and Maryland were to furnish sixty-seven battalions; and the states with smaller populations, South Carolina, New York, New Jersey, New Hampshire, Rhode Island, Georgia and Delaware were to furnish the other 21 battalions.

The second important resolution in building an effective army was called "Resolutions of the Continental Congress

---

[1] The Revolutionary War – RevWar75 Resource Library - http://www.revwar75.com/ob/army1777.htm

[2] U.S. Army Military – Revolutionary years - http://www.army.mil/cmh-pg/books/RevWar/ss/revdoc.htm

[3] September 1776 –Continental Congress' "88 Battalion Resolution - http://www.army.mil/cmh-pg/books/RevWar/ss/revdoc.htm#rev6

Expanding the Continental Army and Extending Emergency Powers to Washington, 27 December 1776."[4] This resolution was passed by Congress immediately following the Battle of Trenton as the British army marched to capture Philadelphia and the members of Congress. The resolution stated:

> "The very existence of civil liberty now depends on the right execution of military powers, and the vigorous, decisive conduct of these, being impossible to distant, numerous, and deliberative bodies":

It authorized General Washington:

> 'to raise and collect together, in the most speedy and effectual manner, from any or all of these United States, 16 battalions of infantry, in addition to those already voted by Congress; to appoint officers for the said battalions; to raise, officer, and equip three thousand light horse; three regiments of artillery, and a corps of engineers, and to establish their pay; to apply to any of the states for such aid of the militia as he shall judge necessary; to form such magazines of provisions, and in such places, as he shall think proper; to displace and appoint all officers under the rank of brigadier general, and to fill up all vacancies in every other department in the American armies; to take, wherever he may be, whatever he may want for the use of the army, if the inhabitants will not sell it, allowing a reasonable price for the same; to arrest and confine persons who refuse to take the continental currency, or are otherwise disaffected to the American cause; and return to the states of which they are citizens, their names, and the nature of their offences, together with the witnesses to prove them."

In effect, faced with the impending capture of Philadelphia, the Continental Congress that had micromanaged everything Washington was trying to do, dumped the entire conduct of the war into his lap and left town.

On January 19, 1777, Washington reported in a letter to Congress from Winter Quarters in Morris Town:

---

[4] U.S. Army Military – 181- http://www.army.mil/cmh-pg/books/RevWar/ss/revdoc.htm

"The fluctuating state of an Army, composed chiefly of militia, bids fair to reduce us to the situation in which we were some little time ago, that is, of scarce having any Army at all, except Reinforcements speedily arrive. One of the battalions from the City of Philadelphia goes home today, and the other two only remain a few days longer upon courtesy. The time, for which a county brigade under General Mifflin came out, is expired, and they stay from day to day, by dint of solicitation. Their numbers much reduced by desertions....

"Thus, you have a sketch of our present Army, with which we are obliged to keep up appearances, before an enemy already double to us in Numbers. ... I have ordered away every Officer that could be spared, some to recruit and some to collect the scattered Men of the different Regiments, who are dispersed almost over the Continent." [5]

From January through the spring and early summer, Washington continued a concentrated effort to raise and train his army, evading several efforts on the part of General Howe to lure him out of his safe quarters in Morristown.

On August 24, 1777, General William Howe, made a move. Arriving by ship, he landed 13,000 British and 5,000 Hessian troops at Head of Elk, Maryland, for his second attempt to seize Philadelphia and, hopefully, the Congress that met there.

There were considerable supplies in the area where Howe landed, but Washington was able to send in some of his soldiers to remove them before Howe's army got organized to stop them. However, Howe's troops greatly outnumbered those of Washington's.

By September 9, Howe's army was at Kennett Square, Pennsylvania, six miles west of the Chadd's Ford Crossing of Brandywine Creek. Facing him from the east side of Chadd's Ford, about five miles downstream, was George Washington with 11,000

---

[5] George Washington's January 19, 1777 letter to Congress – need for enlistments - http://etext.lib.virginia.edu/etcbin/toccer-new2?id=WasFi07.xml&images=images/modeng&data=/texts/english/modeng/parsed&tag=public&part=30&division=div1

American soldiers and a few foreign soldiers who had come to help the Americans.

Map – Brandywine Creek, Chadd's Fort[6]

One of the foreign soldiers was 20-year-old Frenchman, Marquis Gilbert Motier de Lafayette, who had arrived in America with his friend Johann DeKalb to help the American cause. The young nobleman's eagerness to help the cause of liberty at his own expense, prompted General Washington to choose the young man as one of his aide-de-camps.

On September 11, 1777, the Battle of Brandywine Creek in Pennsylvania took place between Washington and Howe's army. At midnight Washington wrote a report to the President of the Congress stating:

> "I am sorry to inform you, that in this day's engagement, we have been obliged to leave the enemy masters of the field. Unfortunately the intelligence received of the enemy's advancing up the Brandywine, and crossing at a ford about six

---

[6] Map - Pennsylvania Historical and Museum Commission
http://www.phmc.state.pa.us/ppet/brandywine/page1.asp?secid=31

miles above us, was uncertain and contradictory, notwithstanding all my pains to get the best."[7]

Congress' response was to attempt to find someone to blame and chose General John Sullivan. They sent an order to Washington demanding that Sullivan be "recalled from the Army" until an inquiry could be made. Washington replied:[8]

> "Our Situation at this time is critical and delicate, and nothing should be done to add to its embarrassments. We are now most probably on the point of another Action, and to derange the Army by withdrawing so many General Officers from it, may and must be attended with many disagreeable, if not ruinous, Consequences. Such a proceeding at another time, might not produce any bad effects, but How can the Army be possibly conducted with a prospect of Success, if the General Officers are taken off, in the moment of Battle? Congress may rely upon it, such a measure will not promote, but injure the service."

Despite bad intelligence information and being outnumbered, Washington had fewer casualties than the British and thwarted Howe's plan to totally crush the Americans. Lafayette, however, who fought valiantly at the Battle of Brandywine was wounded with a bullet through his left leg.[9]

After the defeat at Brandywine, Washington moved his army away from the British, placing them Northwest of the city so he could protect both Philadelphia and Reading, where his supplies were. General Howe did not immediately pursue Washington but when he learned from Tory spies that he was only about ten miles away, Howe marched his army out to destroy Washington.

---

[7] Washington's Letter to Congress, Sept. 11, 1777- http://etext.lib.virginia.edu/etcbin/toccer-ew2?id=WasFi09.xml&images=images/modeng&data=/texts/english/modeng/parsed&tag=public&part=192&division=div1

[8] Washington's Letter to Congress defending Gen. Sullivan-Sept. 15, 2003 - http://wyllie.lib.virginia.edu:8086/perl/toccer-new?id=WasFi09.xml&images=images/modeng&data=/texts/english/modeng/parsed&tag=public&part=215&division=div1

[9] Marquis of LaFayette at Brandywine- http://www.ushistory.org/brandywine/lafayette.htm

When the British army arrived in the valley to confront Washington's troops on September 16, suddenly a torrential rainstorm moved in. The battle, later called the "Battle of the Clouds," was, in effect, called off due to the downpour which prevented the soldiers from loading their muskets with gunpowder.

On September 19, 1777, the Continental Congress fled Philadelphia for York, Pennsylvania about 100 miles Southwest.

General Anthony Wayne[10]

The following day, on September 20, 1777, as most of Washington's army marched to Reading Forge to replenish their ammunition, General Anthony Wayne, with a force of about 1500 men, were a few miles south of Valley Forge at Paoli. When General William Howe learned they were there, he ordered General Sir Charles Grey to attack the Rebels with 5000 men under his command.

Around midnight Grey, guided by Tory spies, led a surprise bayonet attack on Wayne's 1500 troops, killing 53 and wounding more than 100.[11]

On September 26, Howe occupied Philadelphia with nearly 20,000 soldiers who needed to be fed; and his supplies were on ships anchored in the Chesapeake Bay.

Letters to General Howe that had been intercepted by the Americans alerted General Washington to the fact that Howe "had

---

[10] Wayne Township – General Anthony Wayne http://www.waynetownship.com/index.htm?hisgen.htm&2

[11] British Broadcasting Company (BBC) The Paoli Massacre - http://www.bbc.co.uk/dna/h2g2/alabaster/A482410

detached a part of his force for the purpose of reducing Billingsport (New Jersey) and the Forts on Delaware." Now that Howe had captured Philadelphia, he needed to get control of the Delaware River to bring in supplies. And, Washington's army had control of the Delaware River forts.

Washington, on the other hand, was determined to prevent Howe from being able to control the Delaware River, and on October 4, 1777, he attacked the British forces at General Howe's

Cliveden House – Germantown, Pennsylvania[12]

Cliveden House headquarters in Germantown, near Philadelphia. The day was so foggy that, Washington reported to Congress,

> "it was impossible to discover their (the British) movements or firing on account of a thick, heavy Fog which prevented our seeing more than Fifty Yards." [13]

One prong of Washington's attack in the Battle of Germantown, in fact, got lost in the fog the Americans failed to rout the British from Cliveden House. Washington wrote that because of the fog some of his men mistook "one another for the enemy." Several of his soldiers were accidentally shot and killed in the American army's first "friendly fire" incident.

By October 1777, Congress' resolutions that allowed Washington to strengthen and train a standing army had begun to

---

[12] Cliveden House Battle - Germantown, PA – http://www.cliveden.org/Pages/battle.htm

[13] Washington's Letter to Congress on Germantown Battle - October 5, 1777 - http://wyllie.lib.virginia.edu:8086/perl/toccer-new?id=WasFi09.xml&images=images/modeng&data=/texts/english/modeng/parsed&tag=public&part=295&division=div1

bear fruit, such as the spectacular defeat Britain's General John Burgoyne at Saratoga, New York on October 7, 1777.

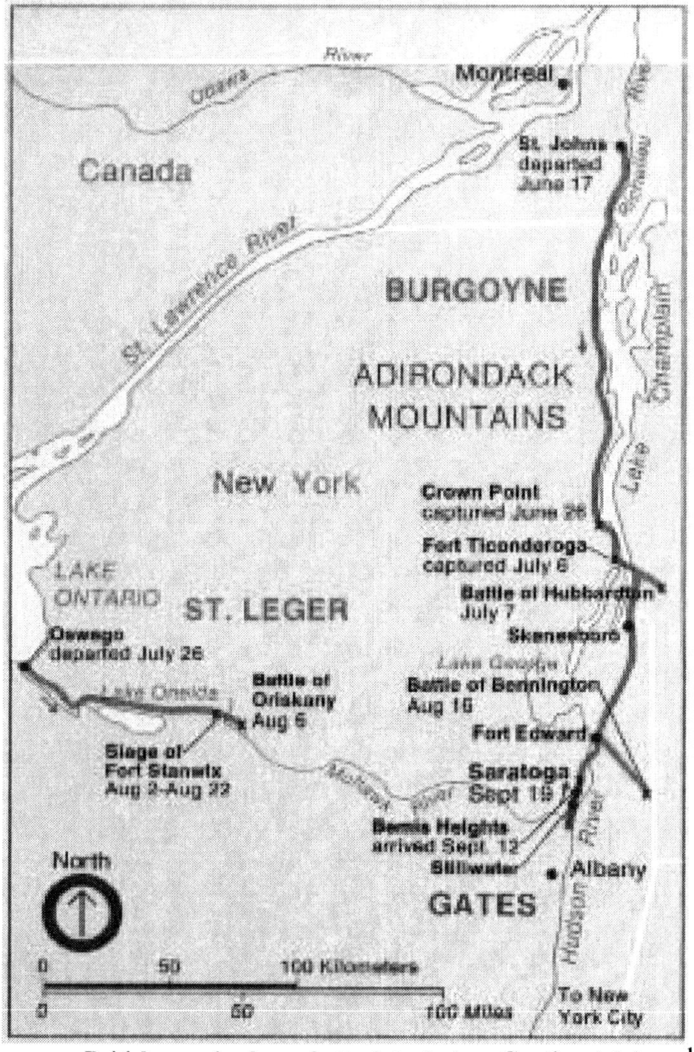

British army's planned attack to destroy Continental Army[14]

Instead of an untrained, poorly supplied and temporary fighting force, Washington was able to put 20,000 soldiers into New York, for the first time outnumbering the British forces.[15]

---

[14] American Revolution- Map -Battle of Saratoga
http://www.americanrevolution.com/BattleofSaratoga.htm

[15] American Revolution – Freeman's Farm , Saratoga, NY
http://theamericanrevolution.org/battles/bat_sara.asp

In the British Campaign of 1777, Major General Burgoyne planned a three-column attack to isolate and destroy the Continental forces of New England.[16] He led the main column, which moved southward along the Hudson River.

A second column under General Barry St. Leger would serve as a diversionary attack, moving eastward from Canada along the Mohawk River. General Howe would be expected to direct the third element of the attack. According to the plan, Howe would direct General Henry Clinton to move northward along the Hudson River and link up with Burgoyne in Albany.

Nineteenth century British Historian Sir Edward Creasy described the Battle of Saratoga, which Burgoyne lost, as one of the *Fifteen Decisive Battles of the World.* Creasy described the Battle of Saratoga and its impact on world history as follows:

Burgoyne Surrenders at Saratoga by John Trumbull[17]

> "Burgoyne now took up his last position on the heights near Saratoga; and hemmed in by the enemy, who refused any encounter, and baffled in all his attempts at finding a path of

[16] WPI-Military Science –Battle of Saratoga - http://www.wpi.edu/Academics/Depts/MilSci/BTSI/abs_sara.html

[17] Burgoyne Surrenders at Saratoga by John Trumbull - http://www.americanrevolution.org/burgone.html

escape, he there lingered until famine compelled him to capitulate. The fortitude of the British army during this melancholy period has been justly eulogized by many native historians.

"The articles of capitulation were settled on October 15th, and on that very evening a messenger arrived from Clinton with an account of his successes, and with the tidings that part of his force had penetrated as far as Esopus, within fifty miles of Burgoyne's camp. But it was too late. The public faith was pledged; and the army was indeed too debilitated by fatigue and hunger to resist an attack, if made; and Gates certainly would have made it if the convention had been broken off. Accordingly, on the 17th, the Convention of Saratoga was carried into effect."[18]

Creasy ranked the British defeat in the Battle of Saratoga with Napoleon's defeat at Waterloo in 1815[19], and the sinking of the Spanish Armada[20] which prevented Spain's invasion of England to restore Catholicism in 1588.

The Battle of Saratoga also changed politics worldwide. France realized for the first time that the Americans could win, with a little help. Benjamin Franklin and his fellow Americans in Paris began to find more doors open to them for wider discussions. In a secret 50-50 partnership with Spain, France had been supplying the Americans with arms, cannons, guns, and other support. After the British defeat at Saratoga, France and other nations decided to openly support the colonies which would soon turn the American Revolution against their King into a world war.

One of the American generals responsible for the victory at Saratoga was Benedict Arnold, whose heroism in several key battles has been long forgotten. Because of bad choices he made later, the very name of Benedict Arnold became synonymous with treachery. Early in the conflict, however, Benedict Arnold distinguished himself in helping Ethan Allen seize Fort

---

[18] Great Epochs in History – The Defeat of Burgoyne at Saratoga http://www.usgennet.org/usa/topic/preservation/epochs/vol3/pg155.htm

[19] BBC- Napoleon's Defeat at Waterloo - http://www.bbc.co.uk/history/war/waterloo/waterloo.shtml

[20] History Buff-Defeat of Spanish Armada- http://www.historybuff.com/library/refspain.html

Ticonderoga, thereby providing the cannons that General Washington used in New York and in a naval battle on Lake Champlain.

At Saratoga, Benedict Arnold,[21] who had a daring and impetuous nature, argued with his cautious superior, General Gates, over tactics. Gates relieved Arnold of any command, but it was, in the end, the daring of Benedict Arnold that actually won the Battle of Saratoga. Seeing an opening, and without orders, Arnold led a charge into the ranks of the Hessian soldiers that was the decisive moment of the battle and led to the defeat of the British troops. However, It almost cost Benedict Arnold his leg. A Hessian soldier shot him in the same leg he had nearly lost in Quebec. Then his horse fell on him when it was shot and killed. The leg eventually healed, but it was two inches shorter than his other leg.

Arnold's contentious disposition and resentment at not being honored or, he believed, properly appreciated for his daring, had caused Congress to pass him up in appointing five new major generals in 1777, all of them younger than he. When Benedict Arnold threatened to resign, George Washington urged him to stay in the army.

Arnold's bold move so badly wounded the British forces that Burgoyne surrendered days later at Saratoga, setting in motion events that would bring victory to the Americans. General Gates, however, after trying to stop Benedict Arnold's bold move, then claimed entire credit for the success of the battle.

Congress did vote to thank Arnold and promoted him to major general, but his resentment continued to fester. According to The University of Michigan's Spy Letters of the American Revolution:

> "In 1778 Washington appointed Arnold the military commander of Philadelphia after the British evacuated (the city.) In Philadelphia, Patriots accused him of using public wagons for private profit and for making money for himself after he closed all the shops down in Philadelphia. Patriots also

---

[21] American History.com – Benedict Arnold – Making of a Traitor - http://americanhistory.about.com/library/prm/blbenedictarnold1.htm

accused him of being too friendly with Loyalists. After all, the British had just evacuated Philadelphia, and tensions were high between Loyalists and Patriots. Arnold then faced a court martial for corruption and resigned his post on March 19, 1779."[22]

Benedict Arnold and some members of Congress, appeared to be more motivated by a desire for personal glory and a place in history, than saving their country. George Washington, on the other hand, patiently, and without criticism or rancor, endured hardships, petty jealousies, the criticism of others, failure on the part of the Congress, treachery among his generals, and the refusal of states to provide adequate food, munitions, clothing and tents for their soldiers. He never seemed to lose sight of the goal – freedom for America.

The Battle of Saratoga also ignited a smoldering jealousy and resentment among some members of both the Continental Congress and the army to challenge the popularity and power of George Washington's position as Commander-in-Chief. A faction in the Continental Congress began a campaign to elevate General Horatio Gates, who led the American forces against Burgoyne, to be commander-in-chief. An Irish soldier of fortune named Thomas Conway, who had been appointed a brigadier general by the Congress in May of 1777, led what was called the "Conway Cabal" to remove Washington as Commaner in Chief.

General Sullivan wrote a letter praising Conway's "knowledge of military matters," adding, in a veiled criticism of Washington, that his knowledge "far exceeds any officer we have." Puffed up by the praise and the victory, Conway wrote a boastful letter to Congress asking for a promotion to major general, while disparaging Washington in his conversations. He was heard to say that Washington's "talents for the command of an army were miserable indeed."

---

[22] Univ. of Michigan – Spy Letters of the American Revolution – Benedict Arnold - http://www.si.umich.edu/spies/people.html#arnold

On October 17, 1777 Washington wrote to Richard Henry Lee in Congress concerning reports he had heard that Conway was about to be elevated to a major general: [23]

"If there is any truth in a report which has been handed to me; Vizt., that Congress hath appointed, or, as others say, are about to appoint, Brigadier Conway a Major General in this Army, it will be as unfortunate a measure as ever was adopted. I may add (and I think with truth) that it will give a fatal blow to the existence of the Army.

"Upon so interesting a subject, I must speak plain: The duty I owe my Country; the Ardent desire I have to promote its true Interests, and justice to Individuals requires this of me. General Conway's merit, then, as an Officer, and his importance in this Army, exists more in his own imagination, than in reality: For it is a maxim with him, to leave no service of his own untold, nor to want any thing which is to be obtained by importunity.

"...I would ask, why the Youngest Brigadier in the service (for I believe he is so) should be put over the heads of all the Eldest? and thereby take Rank, and Command Gentlemen, who but Yesterday, were his Seniors; Gentlemen, who, I will be bold to say (in behalf of some of them at least) of sound judgment and unquestionable Bravery?

"...To Sum up the whole, I have been a Slave to the service: I have undergone more than most Men are aware of, to harmonize so many discordant parts; but it will be impossible for me to be of any further service, if such insuperable difficulties are thrown in my way.

"You may believe me, my good Sir, that I have no Earthly views, but the public good, in what I have said. I have no prejudice against General Conway, nor desire to serve any other Brigadier, further than I think the cause will be benefited by it; to bring which to a speedy and happy conclusion, is the most fervent wish of my Soul."

---

[23] Washington's Letter to Richard Henry Lee about Thomas Conway appointment - http://etext.lib.virginia.edu/etcbin/toccer-new2?id=WasFi09.xml&images=images/modeng&data=/texts/english/modeng/parsed&tag=public&part=358&division=div1

Although Lee responded to Washington's letter assuring him "No such appointment has been made, nor do I believe it will," on December 13, 1777 Congress created the Office of Inspector General of the Army to review the troops, "see that officers and soldiers were instructed in exercise maneuvers established by the Board of War, ensure that discipline be strictly observed and ensure that officers command properly and treat soldiers with justice."

The person appointed for that position was Thomas Conway.

Chapter 2
Articles of Confederation – An Imperfect Union

Adopting a confederation among the states was part of a resolution introduced by Richard Henry Lee on June 7, 1776, declaring independence for each of the colonies:

> "That these United Colonies are, and of right ought to be, free and independent States: that they are absolved from all allegiance to the British Crown; and that all political connection between them and the State of Great Britain is, and ought to be, totally dissolved; that measures should be immediately taken for procuring the assistance of foreign powers, and a Confederation be formed to bind the colonies more closely together."[24]

The committee chosen to write the Articles of Confederation was made up of one person from each colony.[25] The chairman was James Dickinson[26] of Pennsylvania. Dickinson at the time opposed the Declaration of Independence, but had been writing about the rights of the colonists for nearly ten years. In fact, many of his views were expressed the year before when he wrote the "Declaration of the United Colonies of North America,"[27] which Congress adopted the previous year on June 9, 1775. It was basically a call for a form of civil disobedience.

Dickenson's document declared that the Parliament that altered the Massachusetts-Bay Charter, and any governor or lieutenant governor who failed to respect the people's rights in that original Charter were to be simply ignored, or treated as if the offices they held were "vacant." However, believing that

---

[24]Colonial Hall- Signers of the Articles of Confederation http://www.colonialhall.com/bioaoc.asp

[25] Articles of Confederation Committee - http://www.cr.nps.gov/history/online_books/dube/inde3.htm

[26] James Dickinson Biography and writings - http://www.colonialhall.com/dickinson/dickinson.asp

[27] Declaration of the United Colonies of North America –June 9, 1775- http://www.americanrevolution.com/DeclarationOfTheCauses.htm

compromise was still practicable, he felt that his countrymen were not yet ripe for a complete separation from Great Britain.

The Articles of Confederation, written with the hope that eventually Britain would recognize the rights of the colonists, made it clear in the first three articles that each state would retain the sovereignty it enjoyed as a colony while cooperating for the common defense, security and welfare of all the states:

> **I.** The Stile of this Confederacy shall be "The United States of America".
>
> **II.** Each state retains its sovereignty, freedom, and independence, and every power, jurisdiction, and right, which is not by this Confederation expressly delegated to the United States, in Congress assembled.
>
> **III.** The said States hereby severally enter into a firm league of friendship with each other, for their common defense, the security of their liberties, and their mutual and general welfare, binding themselves to assist each other, against all force offered to, or attacks made upon them, or any of them, on account of religion, sovereignty, trade, or any other pretense whatever.

The great weakness of the Articles of Confederation, as George Washington discovered in trying to maintain an army and fight a war, was that while the Congress had the authority to print money and incur debt, there was no taxing authority to enable the new government to pay its debts and no executive wing of the government to make needed decisions. Decisions were made, if made at all, by a committee composed of a representative from all 13 colonies or the War Board Committee.

The sovereign states quite often were under no obligation to a federal power to actually execute anything Congress voted on. There was no federal executive or judicial branch with the power or authority to enforce legislation passed by the Continental Congress.

Article IV gave freedom of movement between the states "to secure and perpetuate mutual friendship and intercourse." It also stated that "Full faith and credit shall be given in each of these States to the records, acts, and judicial proceedings of the courts and magistrates of every other State," which later became Article IV Section I of the Constitution of the United States.

Freedom of speech and debate were guaranteed by **Article V and Article VI** of the Articles of Confederation. The Continental Congress, rather than the States, were given the authority to "send any embassy to, or receive any embassy from, or enter into any conference, agreement, alliance or treaty with any King, Prince or State" and to enter into treaties for all 13 states. States were not allowed to maintain warships or engage in war "without the consent of the United States in Congress assembled, unless such State be actually invaded by enemies."

All officers for the land forces raised by the states under the rank of colonel were appointed by the state legislatures in **Article VII.**

Article VIII called for a "common treasury" to pay for the "common defense or general welfare" by means of Congress deciding what was needed but the "taxes for paying that proportion" had to be "levied by the authority and direction of the legislatures of the several States within the time agreed upon by the United States in Congress assembled.

Article IX gave the Continental Congress "the sole and exclusive right and power of determining on peace and war," but allowed the states to impose "such imposts and duties on foreigners, as their own people are subjected to" and to prohibit "the exportation or importation of any species of goods or commodities whatsoever."

Congress was designated as "the last resort on appeal in all disputes and differences" between two or more States concerning boundary, jurisdiction or any other causes whatever and the Congress was designated to "appoint by joint consent, commissioners or judges to constitute a court for hearing and determining the matter in question." If no agreement was reached, Congress would make a list of 3 persons from each state to act as final judge with an elimination process that reduced the number to 13 persons, and then choose a 7 to 9 judges to hear and determine the matter.

Article X authorized any 9 of the states, when Congress was recessed, to decide matters and **Article XI** enabled Canada to be entitled to "be admitted into, and entitled to all the advantages of this Union; but no other colony shall be admitted into the same, unless such admission be agreed to by nine States."

Article XII made Congress responsible for "bills of credit emitted, monies borrowed, and debts contracted" by the United States by vote of the Continental Congress and **Article XIII** required every state in the Union to "abide by the determination of the United States in Congress assembled, on all questions which by this confederation are submitted to them." It also declared "the Union shall be perpetual" and required that any alteration in the Articles of Confederation "be agreed to in a Congress of the United States, and be afterwards confirmed by the legislatures of every State."

The Articles of Confederation[28] were agreed to by Congress on November 15, 1777, and declared in force after ratification by Maryland, March 1, 1781, nearly 5 years after being introduced in June of 1776.

[28] Articles of Confederation - http://www.yale.edu/lawweb/avalon/artconf.htm>

26 Chapter Three
The Ordeal of Winter Quarters at Valley Forge

Hungry, cold, discouraged American soldiers in the winter of 1777-1778 at Valley Forge[29]

George Washington arrived with 12,000 men at winter quarters at Valley Forge, Pennsylvania, on December 19, 1777. Valley Forge was approximately 23 miles Northwest of Philadelphia. On December 22, 1777, Washington wrote to Congress, which was meeting in York, Pennsylvania, about 75 miles West of Valley Forge.

> "It is with infinite pain and concern, that I transmit Congress the enclosed copies of sundry letters respecting the state of the Commissary's department. If these matters are not exaggerated, I do not know from what cause, this alarming deficiency or rather total failure of supplies arises; but unless more vigorous exertions and better regulations take place in that line, and immediately, this Army must dissolve.
>
> "I have done all in my power, by remonstrating, by writing to, by ordering the Commissaries on this Head, from time to time; but without any good effect, or obtaining more than a present scanty relief. Owing to this, the march of the Army has been delayed upon more than one interesting

[29] From Newberry Library in Chicago –Ayer Collection – From 1953 World Book Encyclopedia-Valley Forge

occasion, in the course of the present Campaign, and had a Body of the Enemy crossed Schuylkill this Morning, as I had reason to expect from the intelligence I received at Four O'clock last night, the Divisions which I ordered to be in readiness to march and meet them, could not have moved. It is unnecessary for me to add more upon the subject." [30]

Washington and his men at Valley Forge[31]

In that same letter to Congress, Washington forwarded a letter from Brigadier General Jedidiah Huntington of Connecticut, in which he said,:

"I received an order to hold my Brigade in readiness to march; fighting will be by far preferable to starving; my Brigade are out of provisions nor can the Brigade Commissary

[30] Washington's Letter to Congress, December 22, 1777 from Valley Forge - http://etext.lib.virginia.edu/etcbin/toccer-new2?id=WasFi10.xml&images=images/modeng&data=/texts/english/modeng/parsed&tag=public&part=177&division=div1

[31] U.S. Army Quartermaster Museum-Washington at Valley Forge with his men January 1777 – http://www.qmmuseum.lee.army.mil/historyweek/1-7Jan.html

obtain any meat, it has several times been the case before though the Failure has generally been in flour. I am exceedingly unhappy in being the bearer of complaints to Headquarters. I have used every argument my imagination could invent to make the soldiers easy, but I despair of being able to do it much longer."

The Isaac Potts' home, - Washington's headquarters at Valley Forge[32]

A combination of factors caused the lack of food and clothing at Valley Forge in the winter of 1777-1778. A major cause was inaction on the part of Congress to appoint a new Quartermaster General after General Mifflin resigned in September 1777.[33]

The much larger British army occupying Philadelphia was not the problem, although food and clothing were also in short supply, and expensive, in Philadelphia. Transportation problems due to a shortage of wagons, bad weather and the lack of roads were factors, along with political opposition and the lack of an executive in the Continental government. By February of 1778, deaths from illness, starvation and freezing, along with desertions, had reduced the numbers of men at Valley Forge to about 8,000 (from 12,000.)

---

[32] Home of Isaac Potts, Washington's Headquarters at Valley Forge - http://www.nps.gov/vafo/structures/gwhq.html

[33] Nathanael Greene and the Supply of the Continental Army - http://www.qmfound.com/greene.htm

It was during the depths of that winter that an event occurred which was later memorialized in paintings by several artists. The pictures are based on a story told by Isaac Potts, the owner of the stone building that was Washington's headquarters. Isaac Watts was a Quaker who believed that all war was wrong, and, therefore, he did not support the Revolution.

There were several accounts of this event; one of them by The Reverend Nathaniel Randolph Snowden, a Princeton College graduate and an ordained Presbyterian minister. Isaac Potts told Snowden the story which he recorded in his diary:

George Washington in Prayer at Valley Forge [34] by H. Brueckner

"I knew personally the celebrated Quaker Potts who saw Gen'l Washington alone in the woods at prayer. I got it from himself, myself. Weems mentioned it in his history of Washington, but I got it from the man myself, as follows:

[34]Library of Congress - The Prayer at Valley Forge / painted by H. Brueckner-engraved by John C. McRae
http://www.ushistoricalarchive.com/presidents/2.html

"I was riding with him (Mr. Potts) in Montgomery County, Pennsylvania, near to the Valley Forge, where the army lay during the war of ye Revolution. Mr. Potts was a Senator in our State and a Whig. I told him I was agreeably surprised to find him a friend to his country as the Quakers were mostly Tories.

"He said, 'It was so and I was a rank Tory once, for I never believed that America could proceed against Great Britain whose fleets and armies covered the land and ocean, but something very extraordinary converted me to the Good Faith!"

"'What was that,' I inquired?

"'Do you see that woods, and that plain?' It was about a quarter of a mile off from the place we were riding, as it happened. 'There,' said he, 'laid the army of Washington. It was a most distressing time of ye war, and all were for giving up the Ship but that great and good man. In that woods pointing to a close in view, I heard a plaintive sound as, of a man at prayer. I tied my horse to a sapling and went quietly into the woods and to my astonishment I saw the great George Washington on his knees alone, with his sword on one side and his cocked hat on the other. He was at Prayer to the God of the Armies, beseeching to interpose with his Divine aid, as it was ye Crisis, and the cause of the country, of humanity and of the world.

"'Such a prayer I never heard from the lips of man. I left him alone praying. I went home & told my wife. I saw a sight and heard today what I never saw or heard before, and just related to her what I had seen and heard and observed. We never thought a man could be a soldier and a Christian, but if there is one in the world, it is Washington. She also was astonished. We thought it was the cause of God, and America could prevail.' "He then to me put out his right hand and said 'I turned right about and became a Whig.'"[35]

In spite of the hardships and the deaths at Valley Forge, according to Worchester Polytechnic Institute's Military Science, it was there that

---

[35] U.S. History.org website – Excerpt from Snowden's Diary - http://personal.pitnet.net/primarysources/valleyforge_html.html

"Washington and the Continental Army endured and gained much hardiness due to both the hardships and the arrival of Friedrich Wilhem von Steuben. Steuben arrived in February of 1778 from Prussia where he had been a Captain under Frederick the Great. Washington saw the need for uniform training and organization in his command and gave von Steuben a chance to manifest those goals." [36]

Baron von Steuben teaching Continental Army drill discipline[37]

It was at Valley Forge under the training of Baron von Steuben that the Continental Army truly became an army. Even to this very day, the U.S. Army Study Guide praises the "good sense and humanity" of Baron Von Steuben's drill regulations.

"Von Steuben also stressed the importance of discipline and the daily routine; he went minutely into field and company administration. He prescribed that platoons should camp by battalions. He allowed sumps (latrines) to be dug no nearer to occupied tents than 300 feet. He charged field officers with seeing that their camps were pitched regularly and properly, especially that kitchens and sumps were put in sanitary places.

---

[36] Worchester Polytechnic Institute (WPI) Military Science –Winter at Valley Forge - http://www.wpi.edu/Academics/Depts/MilSci/BTSI/abs_valley.html>

[37] Baron Von Steuben trains the troops at Valley Forge-picture/Bio - http://www.americanrevwar.homestead.com/files/VONSTUB.HTM

He outlined methods of getting wood and water by means of an organized system of signals and formations." [38]

The Army Study Guide outlines von Steuben's training as follows:

"The lieutenant was to be zealous in regard to the 'health and convenience' of the soldier, and the ensign in regard to 'neatness and cleanliness'. Von Steuben here discreetly laid emphasis on the development of self-respect and pride, qualities, which are the lading strings of success. Then he capped this by setting a check upon ill treatment, which arises through 'pique or resentment'. Understanding how partiality and prejudice may be the ruin of discipline he closed his instructions by putting a special guard on that sort of justice.

"Von Steuben spent much time in developing a keen sense of responsibility in the company officer in comparison to that of the field and general officer. He knew that if the individual soldier had affection and regard for his immediate leaders, the higher commands would take care of themselves. He realized that the pride and bearing of the rank and file were the keynotes to achievements in the field, as was demonstrated many times in World War. Could any set of instructions more grippingly embrace the essentials of discipline?"

Marquis Gilbert Motier de Lafayette[39]

---

[38] U.S. Army Study Guide - on Von Stueben training - http://www.armystudyguide.com/history/von-stuben.htm

Von Steuben's training showed almost immediate results. His improved sanitation requirements rapidly reduced sickness among the men and many lives were saved in battle because they learned from von Steuben the importance of obeying orders from their battlefield commanders quickly and in unison. In May of 1778, General Washington gave twenty-year-old Marquis LaFayette a secret mission:

> "The detachment under your command with which you will immediately march toward the enemy's lines is designed to answer the following purposes: to be a security to this camp and a cover to the country between the Delaware and Schuylkill, to interrupt the communication with Philadelphia, obstruct the incursions of the enemy's parties, and obtain intelligence of their motions and designs. This last is a matter of very interesting moment, and ought to claim your particular attention. You will endeavor to procure trusty and intelligent spies, who will advise you faithfully of whatever may be passing in the city; and you will without delay communicate to me every piece of material information you obtain.
>
> "A variety of concurring accounts make it probable the enemy are preparing to evacuate Philadelphia. This is a point, which it is of the utmost importance to ascertain; and if possible the place of their future destination."[40]

Lafayette's reconnaissance left Valley Forge on May 18, and marched about ten miles, camping at Barren Hill, approximately half-way between Valley Forge and British Headquarters in Philadelphia.

Just as the young major general prepared to send a woman spy into the enemy camp, a Loyalist spy who had learned the details of Lafayette's mission, gave the information to the senior British commander, General Sir William Howe. The Loyalist alerted the British of the movement of Lafayette and his 2200 men, which prompted Howe to send 8000 men to capture Lafayette.

---

[39] Picture Marquis Gilbert Motier de Lafayette – Ridpath History Volume XIV The Age of Revolution – War of American Independence-page 604

[40] Washington Letter to Lafayette containing his orders on purpose the secret mission - http://etext.lib.virginia.edu/etcbin/toccer-new2?id=WasFi11.xml&images=images/modeng&data=/texts/english/modeng/parsed&tag=public&part=389&division=div1

The American Friends of Lafayette describe on their website[41] The American Friends of Lafayette – 27 reasons why we should honor Lafayette - how the outnumbered and surrounded Lafayette, combining the lessons of von Steuben with his natural tactical military genius, escaped the trap that five of Britain's finest and most experienced generals set for him:

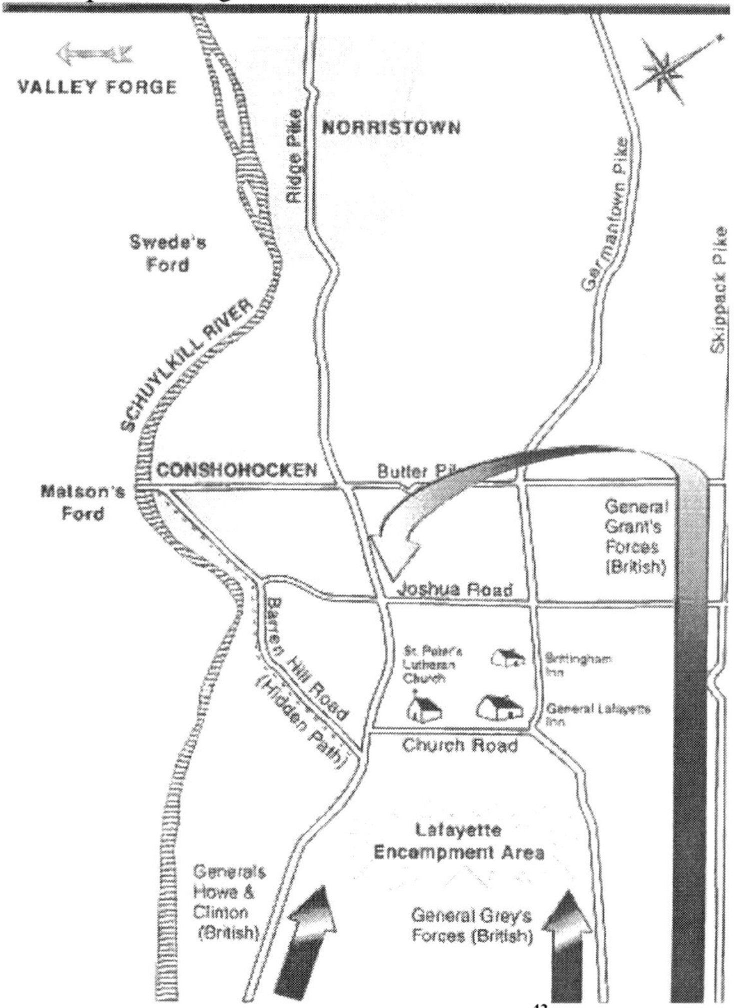

Map of Barren Hill Battle [42]

---

[41] The American Friends of Lafayette- 27 reasons why we should honor Lafayette - http://friendsoflafayette.org/data/barrenhill.html

[42] The American Friends of Lafayette- Map of Barren Hill Battle - http://www.friendsoflafayette.org/data/map519.html

"On May 19 the British and Hessians began their maneuver to capture Lafayette. Eight thousand of their elite troops marched twenty miles in a wide flanking movement and cut off Lafayette's rear escape route; four thousand marched along Germantown Pike and cut off his left flank; and four thousand moved along Ridge Pike past Roxborough and cut off his right flank and frontal position.

"On May 20 a surprised Lafayette saw that he and his entire detachment were completely surrounded by the five generals and their awesome forces poised for a final strike. A cry of panic went up among some of his men, but with the instinct of a born tactician and the coolness of an unruffled, super bowl quarterback, the young lion gathered several hundred picked troops at the churchyard of Saint Peter's Lutheran Church, reversed his front and marched them against the British army to his rear. British General James Grant halted his advance and gathered his officers for an assessment of this bold counterattack.. This was the hesitation Lafayette badly needed.

"He quickly retrieved his men away from this feint and followed behind the soldiers from the main encampment area led by his two generals, Enoch Poor and James Varnum. They navigated down a hidden path towards Conshohocken and across the Schuylkill River at Matson's Ford to the safety of the high ground into present day West Conshohocken.

"General Grant resumed his maneuver and believed he and General Grey had Lafayette trapped at the churchyard. By the time he moved in for the snare Lafayette was gone! He had outfoxed the generals and their formidable army. Howe's forces - once keyed up and confidently poised for a quick, devastating blow - were reduced to a weary and disappointed array of soldiers.

"Realizing that the 'boy' as they called him had pulled off one of the most spectacular escapes in the annals of military history, they marched back to Philadelphia disappointed without their quarry."[43]

Shortly after this embarrassing defeat, Parliament recalled General William Howe and conducted an inquiry[44] into his conduct as commander of the British forces in America. After testimony from fellow officers that he "did not have sufficient forces to win," he was acquitted. Britain's next commander in chief, General Sir Henry Clinton, eliminated from his memoirs, *The American Rebellion: 1775-1782*, the report of how the 20-year-old Lafayette outwitted five seasoned British generals.

---

[43] The American Friends of Lafayette - General Lafayette: Washington's "Superbowl Quarterback." By Ruday Cusumano - http://friendsoflafayette.org/data/barrenhill.html

[44] Biography of William Howe – British General http://www.virtualology.com/virtualwarmuseum.com/revolutionarywarhall/WILLIAMHOWE.COM/

Chapter Four
A Search for Wisdom, Skill and Good Policies

In February, 1778, France formally acknowledged the United States as a "free and Independent Country," rather than a group of little British colonies, and ceded to the United States "all the Territory formerly ceded by them to Great Britain." The territories France ceded to Britain in the 1763 Treaty of Paris ending the French and Indian War included all of Canada, Cape Breton, and all the islands and coasts in the gulf and coasts of the St. Lawrence River.[45]

In May of 1778, word reached Valley Forge that both General Howe and Admiral Howe were returning to Britain.

On July 10, 1778, France declared war on Britain in support of the United States. In 1779, Spain, as an ally to France, also declared war on Britain. In 1780, the Dutch Republic joined the cause against Britain. The War for Independence in America had become a world war.

The far-sighted Washington predicted in a letter to his brother, Augustine Washington, it would be, "One of the most important periods that ever America saw."[46]

It would be a period in which America would need its finest minds in the Congress, because, Washington observed it:

> "Will require all the skill, the wisdom, and policy, of the first abilities of these States, to manage the helm, and steer with judgment to the haven of our wishes through so many Shelves and Rocks, as will be thrown in our way."

Many states were not even sending representatives to Congress, he noted, but now was the time for the "first characters" (best men) in every state be sent.

In the same letter, Washington also noted he had gotten word that:

---

[45] Treaty of Paris, 1763, France Cedes Canada to Britain – http://www.yale.edu/lawweb/avalon/paris763.htm

[46] George Washington's Letter to Augustine Washington – an "important period" - http://etext.lib.virginia.edu/etcbin/toccer-new2?id=WasFi11.xml&images=images/modeng&data=/texts/english/modeng/parsed&tag=public&part=466&division=div1

"France having declared the United States free and Independent, and guaranteeing to them all the Territory formerly ceded by them to Great Britain ... must put the Independency of America out of all manner of dispute."

This was the result of a formal treaty of alliance, and another treaty of amity (friendship) and commerce that were signed on February 6, 1778, by Franklin, Silas Deane, and Arthur Lee for the United States, and by Conrad Alexandre Gerard for France. With the signing of the treaty, Franklin, then 72 years of age, became America's first official ambassador to France; and Alexandre Gerard was appointed to represent France in the United States.

Benjamin Franklin in Paris[47]

France's recognition of the Independent United States of America was largely the work of Benjamin Franklin. With the treaties, Franklin and Silas Deane reaped the rewards of many months of quiet efforts to obtain the support of France, long an adversary of Britain. The Continental Congress had sent Silas Deane, a Yale graduate, merchant and delegate to the Congress from Groton, Connecticut, to France in March of 1776.[48] **In** reality, he was a special ambassador on a secret mission. In spite of

[47] Picture-Ridpath's History, Vol. XIV – The Age of Revolution – The French Revolution- page 631

[48] Silas Dean, Biography - http://members.tripod.com/~ntgen/bw/part_deane.html#bio1

his inability to speak French, he was able to negotiate large loans from French capitalists, and convince military officers of the French army to offer their service to George Washington.

In September of 1776, the Congress appointed its elder statesman, Benjamin Franklin, as a Commissioner to attempt to negotiate a treaty with the French government. He was already known to the French people and was warmly received.

In elegant and fashion-conscious Paris, the plainly dressed, but engaging and interesting inventor and stateman was a bit of an oddity. As Franklin himself put it in a letter to a friend,

> "Figure me in your mind, as jolly as formerly, and as strong and hearty, only a few years older; very plainly dressed, wearing my thin, gray, straight hair that peeps out under my only coiffure, a fine fur cap, which comes down my forehead almost to my spectacles. Think how this must appear among the powdered heads of Paris!"[49]

Although the amiable Franklin had great faith in the American cause, and confidence in their eventual victory, the British invasion of Philadelphia and the British troops' occupation of his own home which caused his daughter to flee, greatly concerned him.

Two months after the news of General Burgoyne's defeat at Saratoga reached Paris, the French became more interested in a treaty with the new nation, because they could see the possibility of an embarrassing defeat for their old enemy, Britain.

Secret emissaries from Britain began approaching Franklin in Paris with "conciliation" recommendations. As Ambassador to France, Benjamin Franklin was invited to be received in Versailles by the King of France, Louis XVI and his beautiful wife, Marie Antoinette, the archduchess of Austria, who at age 16 had married the heir to the throne of France.

The formal presentation of Franklin, as the representative of the free and independent United States of America, in the lavish court of the King and Queen was described by historian Benson Lossing in his *Household History for All Readers,* published in 1877, as follows:

[49] To Mrs. Thompson , Feb. 8 1777 – National Center for Constitutional Studies The Real Benjamin Franklin, A History of His Life - page 211

"Franklin and his colleagues were presented to the King and queen at Versailles, on the 20th of March. Willing to comply with the court etiquette on such occasions, the republican ambassador sent for a wig, and contemplated ordering a suit of blue velvet and lace.

"No wig in Paris would fit his capacious (very large) head; so he resolved to appear in his baldness, with his thin gray hair hanging down upon his shoulders. So he did appear in defiance of the chamberlain and fashion. Clad in an elegant suit of black velvet made as plain as one he would have worn at an evening party in Philadelphia, with white cambric ruffles in his bosom and at his wrists, white silk stockings and silver shoe-buckles, he won the admiration of all beholders in that brilliant assembly.

Queen Marie Antoinette of France[50] and King Louis XVI of France [51]

"The beautiful young queen bestowed her sweetest smiles upon him, and kept him near her person as much as possible during the audience. In one of the saloons of Paris a few evenings afterward, he was the center of attraction. His defiance of etiquette charmed the Parisians. The ladies pressed

[50] Picture- Queen Marie Antoinette, from Ridpath's History, Vol XIV page 645

[51] Picture – King Louis XVI of France, from Ridpath's History, Vol. XIV, page 627

around the Philosopher, and more enthusiastic ones saluted him with kisses on his forehead."[52]

Wig and Dress Styles in the Court of Louis XVI[53]

[52] By Benson J. Lossing, - A Household History for All Readers 1877- http://www.publicbookshelf.com/public_html/Our_Country_vol_2/resultsAm_bba.html

[53] Fashions for men, women and children –Reign Louis XVI of France - http://englishcountrydancing.org/frenchfashion.html

Chapter Five
A General's Treachery and a Girl's Heroism

There were times during the American Revolution that the new nation came very close to anarchy. The dedicated and patient George Washington said was it was "one of the most important periods" the Americans would ever face. Without unity and good government, Washington knew the nation could not succeed.

However, the suffering during the winter at Valley Forge, along with the military training of von Steuben, had brought the men of the various states together in a way nothing else could. George Washington took charge of a motley group of state militiamen who often refused to take orders from anyone they didn't choose or like, while ridiculing or arguing with one another, and transformed them into an army. After the winter at Valley Forge, when many of his men died or went home, Washington wrote a letter to his brother Augustine on June 10, 1778, describing his army:

> "The extreme fatigue and hardship which the soldiers underwent in the course of the Winter, added to the want of cloath, (clothes) and, I may add, provisions, (food) have rendered them very sickly, especially in the brigade you have mentioned (of No. Carolina); many deaths have happened in consequence, and yet the Army is in exceeding good Spirits."[54]

In the same letter to Augustine, General Washington told his brother what appeared to be holding up the British from leaving Philadelphia:

> "We have been kept in anxious expectation of the Enemy's evacuating Philadelphia for upwards of fourteen days; and I was at a loss, as they had Embarked all their Baggage, Stores, etc. on Board Transports, and had passed all those Transports (a few only excepted) below the Cheveaux de Frieze, to account for their delay; when behold on Friday last the additional Commissioners, to wit, Lord Carlisle, Govr.

---

[54] George Washington's letter to his brother Augustine, June 10, 1778 - http://etext.lib.virginia.edu/etcbin/toccer-new2?id=WasFi12.xml&images=images/modeng&data=/texts/english/modeng/parsed&tag=public&part=50&division=div1

Johnson, and Mr. Willem. Eden arrived at the City; whether this, heretofore, has been the cause of the delay I shall not undertake to say, but, more than probably, it will detain them for some days to come."

The Commissioners had been chosen to be peace emissaries to the Americans and to give the president of the Congress the "Conciliatory Acts, where Parliament repealed its oppressive measures, gave up the right to tax the colonies, and was ready to promise them representation in the British Parliament. The Commissioners arrived on June 6, totally unaware that three weeks before their departure from England, orders had been sent to Sir Henry Clinton, General Howe's replacement as commander of the British troops, to evacuate Philadelphia and concentrate his forces in New York.

As their letter was read to members of the Congress in session, it was almost indignantly rejected without completing the reading. Coming on the heels of the Treaty with France, the intent of the letter was to accuse France of signing the treaty "to prevent reconciliation and (to) prolong this destructive war." On June 17, the Commissioners were sent Congress' reply. They would be happy to cooperate as soon as the King of Great Britain demonstrated "a sincere disposition for peace, either by an explicit acknowledgment of the independence of the States or by withdrawal of his fleets and armies."

While waiting for Congress to respond, the Commissioners tried some other tactics. They attempted to bribe General Joseph Reed, who had been Washington's aide, with 10,000 pounds sterling and any office in the colonies he wanted, in exchange for his efforts to bring the colonies back to their dependent state on the King. Reed responded, "I am not worth purchasing; but such as I am, the King of Great Britain is not rich enough to do it."[55]

While the commissioners were in Philadelphia, General Washington waited. In the meanwhile, Howe had detached 5000 men to build up a planned British attack on French possessions in the West Indies in retaliation for France's recognition of the United States' independence. Three thousand of the British troops were sent to Florida, but the cavalry, in addition to other troops, had

---

[55] Quoted in Washington Irving's "*Life of Washington,* Vol. III, page 474

been sent to New York, along with provisions and baggage. General Clinton had only about 9000-10,000 men, while Washington's army had grown to more than 12,000, plus 1,300 militia, all much more proficient in arms after training under Baron von Stueben.

General Charles Lee[56]

During this time period, in early May of 1778, General Charles Lee, who had been captured in December of 1776, was traded for five Hessian officers in a prisoner-of-war exchange. He joined Washington's army at Valley Forge on May 20. In spite of his behavior in undermining Washington before being captured, Washington restored him to his previous place in the line of authority, giving him command of a division. Lee, who still had a circle of influential friends in Congress, then resumed his former role as a critic of the Commander in Chief.

As General Clinton prepared to evacuate Philadelphia, Washington called a council of war to discuss what kind of attack on the British the army would make. Lee spoke eloquently in opposition to any attack, and many of the other members of the council supported him, believing his military knowledge and experience to be superior to Washington's.

Before the council made a decision, word came that Sir Henry Clinton had already quietly left Philadelphia at 3:00 a.m. on June 18, and most of his troops, along with about 3000 civilian

[56] Picture and Biography of General Charles Lee - http://famousamericans.net/charleslee/

Tory supporters, had already crossed the Delaware River and by 10:00 a.m. were in New Jersey. Washington immediately broke camp at Valley Forge and pursued the British troops.

General Lee commanded the advance troops, but Lafayette, knowing that Lee opposed any attack on Clinton's troops, asked Washington to allow him to lead the attack. Washington agreed, providing Lee approved, and when asked, Lee "ceded the command without hesitation, observing to the marquis that he was well pleased to be freed from all responsibility for executing plans which he was sure would fail."

However, Lee then promptly changed his mind. He sent a note to Washington saying that by leading the advance, Lafayette, the younger and less experienced man, would in effect be at the "head of all six thousand men," a position that belonged rightfully to himself. On the evening of June 27, the British troops were camped on high ground near the city of Monmouth's Courthouse; Lee was camped about five miles away at Englishtown.

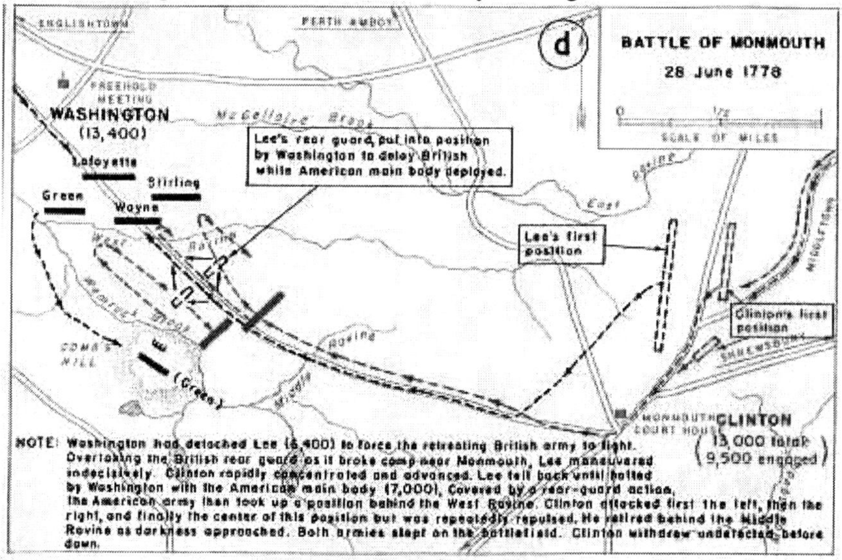

Battle of Monmouth Map[57]

[57] University of Virginia – Papers of George Washington - http://gwpapers.virginia.edu/revolution/monmouth/map1.html

Washington had ordered Lee to attack the retreating British troops at Monmouth before they got to the heights of Middletown, where the position would be less favorable. However, instead of attacking, Lee ordered a retreat without warning. Washington had just dismounted from his horse when a Patriot who lived in the area rode up to tell him his troops were retreating. At first Washington didn't believe him, and the man pointed to a frightened young fifer coming back from the front lines.

As Washington Irving described the scene, in the *Life of Washington:*

> "Springing on his horse, Washington had moved forward but a short distance when he met other fugitives, one in the garb of a soldier, who all concurred in the report. He now sent forward Colonels Fitzgerald and Harrison, to learn the truth, while he himself spurred past Freehold Meeting-house. Between that edifice and the morass beyond it, he met Grayson's and Patton's regiments in most disorderly retreat, jaded with heat and fatigue. Riding up to the officer at their head, Washington demanded whether the whole advanced corps were retreating. The officers believed they were.
>
> "It seemed incredible. There had been scarce any firing – Washington had received no notice of the retreat from Lee. He was still almost inclined to doubt when the heads of several columns of the advance began to appear. It was too evident – the whole advance was falling back on the main body, and no notice had been given to him. One of the first officers that came up was Colonel Shreve, at the head of his regiment; Washington, greatly surprised and alarmed, asked the meaning of this retreat. The colonel smiled significantly – he did not know – he had retreated by order. There had been no fighting excepting a slight skirmish with the enemy's cavalry, which had been repulsed.
>
> "A suspicion flashed across Washington's mind, of wrong-headed conduct on the part of Lee, to mar the plan of attack adopted contrary to his counsels. Ordering Colonel Shreve to march his men over the morass, halt them on the hill beyond and refresh them, he galloped forward to stop the retreat of the rest of the advance, his indignation kindling as he rode. At the rear of the regiment he met Major Howard; he too, could

give no reason for the retreat, but seemed provoked at it – declaring that he had never seen the like. Another officer exclaimed with an oath that they were flying from a shadow.

"Arriving at a rising ground, Washington beheld Lee approaching with the residue of his command in full retreat. By this time he was thoroughly exasperated.

"'What is the meaning of all this, sir?' demanded he, in the sternest and even fiercest tone, as Lee rode up to him.

"Lee for a moment was disconcerted and hesitated in making a reply, for Washington's aspect, according to Lafayette, was terrible.

"'I desire to know the meaning of this disorder and confusion,' was again demanded still more vehemently.

"Lee, stung by the manner more than the words of the demand, made an angry reply, and provoked still sharper expressions, which have been variously reported. He attempted a hurried explanation. His troops had been thrown into confusion by contradictory intelligence; by disobedience of order; by the meddling and blundering of individuals; and he had not felt disposed, he said, to beard the whole British army with troops in such a situation.

"'I have certain information,' rejoined Washington, 'that it was merely a strong covering party.'

"'That may be, but it was stronger than mine, and I did not think proper to run such a risk.'

"'I am very sorry,' replied Washington, 'that you undertook the command, unless you meant to fight the enemy.'

"'I did not think it prudent to bring on a general engagement.'

"'Whatever your opinion may have been,' replied Washington, disdainfully, 'I expected my orders would have been obeyed.'"[58]

The British were advancing on the troops and were minutes away. Washington quickly organized the troops to make a stand where they were and rode back to bring forward into the battle the rest of the troops. A hard battle was fought until nightfall. The conversation around the campfire among the exhausted troops was

---

[58] *Life of Washington* by Washington Irving, Monmouth, Vol. III, page 488

the strange behavior of General Charles Lee. All were ordered to sleep where they could. Washington wrapped himself in his cloak, and slept at the foot of a tree, among his soldiers.

At daybreak the drums beat the reveille, and the troops roused themselves, only to find that in the night the enemy had disappeared, leaving only four officers and 40 privates, too severely wounded to make the night march.

Molly Pitcher takes her fallen husband's Place in the Battle of Monmouth[59]

During the Battle of Monmouth, the heroism of the Commander in Chief was not the only heroism on the battlefield; the wife of an artilleryman, Mary Hays McCauly (better known as Molly Pitcher), had been with her husband, William Hays, during the harsh winter at Valley Forge and had marched with the American troops to Monmouth. The U.S. Army website tells the story:

"Her actions during the Battle of Monmouth on June 28, 1778, became legendary. That day at Monmouth was as hot as

[59] U.S. Army website – May Hays McCauly – takes her husbands place in battle - http://sill-www.army.mil/pao/pamolly.htm

Valley Forge was cold. Someone had to cool the hot guns and bathe parched throats with water.

"Across that bullet-swept ground, a striped skirt fluttered. Mary Hays McCauly was earning her nickname, "Molly Pitcher", by bringing pitcher after pitcher of cool spring water to the exhausted and thirsty men. She also tended to the wounded and once, heaving a crippled Continental soldier up on her strong young back, carried him out of reach of hard-charging Britishers. On her next trip with water, she found her artilleryman husband back with the guns again, replacing a casualty. While she watched, Hays fell wounded. The piece, its crew too depleted to serve it, was about to be withdrawn. Without hesitation, Molly stepped forward and took the rammer staff from her fallen husband's hands.

"For her heroic role, General Washington himself issued her a warrant as a noncommissioned officer. Thereafter, she was widely hailed as 'Sergeant Molly.' A flagstaff and cannon stand at her gravesite at Carlisle, Pennsylvania. A sculpture on the battle monument commemorates her courageous deed."

As for General Charles Lee, on the day following his treachery, he wrote a letter to General Washington complaining about the "cruel injustice" of Washington reprimanding him on the battlefield in front of the soldiers. Washington, ever patient, responded that he would have "an opportunity of justifying yourself to the army, to Congress, to America and to the world in general." Lee demanded a court-martial, and Washington promptly accommodated him. He was charged with disobedience of orders, misbehavior before the enemy and disrespect to the Commander in Chief in two letters.

He was convicted and relieved of command for a year. However, his anger and hatred for Washington got him into more trouble. He was eventually dismissed from the army and died in poverty and disgrace.

George Washington, after Lee's death, never made any negative remarks about him, only saying, "he possessed many great qualities."

Chapter Six
The War At Sea and Britain's Southern Strategy

After the June, 1778, Battle of Monmouth, the two armies, in effect, were stalemated, and a quick end to the Revolutionary War appeared out of reach. Both armies were approximately where they had been in 1776. General George Washington's headquarters was again at White Plains on the Hudson; and General Clinton and the British army were back in New York. Neither felt strong enough to attack the other.

The British plan originally had been to divide and conquer the American colonies by first seizing New England. That had not worked; however, intelligence coming out of the Southern Colonies convinced the British ministers in London that they would achieve total victory if they could first control the Southern Colonies, bring many Tory Loyalists into the British forces, and then sweep north.

The plan called for coordination between the powerful British fleet and its land forces. The Americans did not have a navy worthy to be called a navy; however, only two months after being chosen by the Continental Congress as Commander in Chief, George Washington had taken the first steps to develop an American navy to battle the British off the New England coast and to prey on British supply ships.

John Paul Jones[60]

In December of 1775, John Paul Jones, a young Scotsman, who would become the father of the American navy, received his lieutenant's commission from the Continental Congress for its

---

[60] World's Finest Navy - http://www.worldsfinestnavy.com/JPJ.html

navy. On 3 December, 1775, as first lieutenant of *Alfred*,[61] the first warship to be commissioned by the Continental Congress, he was the first to hoist the Grand Union Flag on an American navy ship.

The Grand Union Flag displayed the British Union Jack in the upper left corner, and 13 red and white stripes representing the united resistance by the colonies to tyranny,[62] but loyalty to the King. In February, 1776, John Paul Jones participated in the attack on Nassau, New Providence Island. He was appointed commander of the *Providence* on May 10, 1776.

Continental Sloop *Providence*[63]

In August, the 12-gun sloop departed for the Delaware Capes, and within a week John Paul Jones captured the whaling brigantine, *Britannia*. Shortly thereafter he saved *Providence* in a ten-hour chase with a much larger warship due to his superior

[61] The *Alfred*, - http://www.history.navy.mil/danfs/a/alfred.htm

[62] 250th Anniversary –John Paul Jones – US Navy - http://www.history.navy.mil/faqs/faq58-1.htm

[63] *The Continental Sloop Providence* - http://www.providenceri.com/sloop-providence.html

seamanship. He also captured three British merchant vessels. Jones would later declare that his best crew had been on board *Providence*.

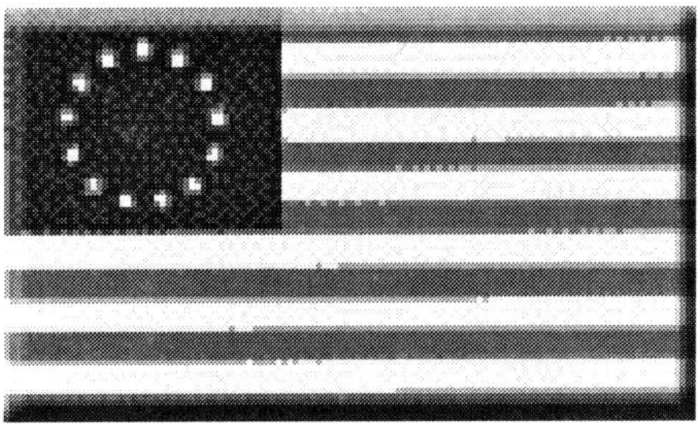

The Stars and Stripes, approved by Congress June 14, 1777

In November, 1777, John Paul Jones sailed for France in *Ranger*,[64] carrying word of Burgoyne's surrender at Saratoga. Admiral La Motte-Picquet returned Jones' salute at Quiberon Bay, on 14 February, 1778, as Jones approached France. This was the first time the Stars and Stripes, the flag adopted on June 14, 1777 by Congress to represent the united colonies, was recognized by a foreign power. .

Charles Hector Comte d'Estaing, French Admiral[65]

On July 11, 1778, one day after France declared war on Britain, a French fleet of 17 ships under the command of Charles Hector Comte d'Estaing arrived off New York Harbor with a twofold mission:

> "one of immediate service to their ally along the Atlantic coast; another of indirect service by making the English ports in

---

[64] *Ranger* Foundation - http://www.rangerfoundation.org/history2.htm

[65] Picture, Count D'Estaing – from An Outline History of the United States, page 196

the West Indies untenable. D'Estaing was imbued with the same ideas of liberalism that inspired the mind of Lafayette. Just before reaching the capes of Delaware, he wrote Washington that his talents and great actions 'have insured him, in the eyes of all Europe, the title, truly sublime, of Deliverer of America.'"[66]

Sea battle at St. Lucia, 1778[67] - Admiral Comte d'Estaing and Admiral Barrington,

The French ships, however, were too large to get across the sand bar into New York Harbor. He moved against a British garrison at Newport, Rhode Island, but Admiral Howe moved the British fleet down to meet him. The two fleets were about to engage in battle on August 11, when a fierce storm arose, scattering both fleets; d'Estaing limped to Boston Harbor for repairs and then sailed for the West Indies on November 4, after exchanging several letters with George Washington.

On October 2, 1778, George Washington wrote before d'Estaing sailed to the West Indies:

"Your observation on the inability of England to spare a sufficiency of Ships, men and money to continue hostilities in

---

[66] U.S. Army -d'Estaing- http://www.army.mil/cmh-pg/books/RevWar/Yorktown/AWC-Ytn-05.htm

[67] British National Maritime Museum -Admirals d'Estaing & Barrington, St. Lucia, West Indies, - http://www.nmm.ac.uk/mag/pages/mnuExplore/ViewLargeImage.cfm?ID=BHC0422&letter=b

America at the same time that she is engaged in a war with the United powers of France and Spain, appears to me conclusive; ... The concurring sentiment of the citizens of New York is that an evacuation will take place, and repeated intelligence indicates a part of the enemy's force destined for the West Indies."[68]

Count d'Estaing's failed efforts to defeat the British fleet angered many Americans and some of its generals. However, Washington knew that the 5,000 British soldiers in Philadelphia that were reassigned in 1778 to fight the French in the West Indies reduced the fighting forces he and his troops had to face. Britain's clear superiority was at sea, and, taking advantage of that superiority, General Clinton used that sea power to make pirate-style attacks on American Southern ports. Beginning in 1777, the British had developed their contacts with Native American tribes to attack the colonists. British intelligence indicated that Loyalist Tory support was concentrated in the South, and American Loyalists could be effectively used to fight the American rebels.

While General Howe had been reluctant to use Indians, because of their fierce tactics in war, General Clinton paid the chiefs and supplied them with guns for use in their raids on the colonies. Less than a week after the battle of Monmouth, a force of 800 Tories and Indians under Colonel John Butler swooped down from New York on a settlement of New Englanders in the Wyoming Valley on the Susquehanna River. Most of the men in the settlements, consisting of about 5000 people, were gone. Many were in the Continental Army. In the massacre hundreds of unarmed settlers were killed and scalped. Survivors fled. The British commander afterward reported the taking of "227 scalps," and blamed the massacre on the Mohawk chieftain, Joseph Brant. Brant, however, known to his people as Thayendanegea, was a well-educated, good-natured Episcopalian, who had translated the prayer book into his native tongue. He was not even in Wyoming Valley at the time.

---

[68] Washington's Letter to d'Estaing, October 2, 1778 - http://etext.lib.virginia.edu/etcbin/toccer-new2?id=WasFi13.xml&images=images/modeng&data=/texts/english/modeng/parsed&tag=public&part=12&division=div1

James Oglethorpe, founder of Savannah, Georgia [69]

On December 29, 1778, a British force of about 3,500 men seized control of Savannah, Georgia. At the time, the population of the youngest of the 13 colonies had only about 50,000 people, half of them slaves. Savannah was only 45 years old, having been founded in 1733, by James Oglethorpe, an anti-slavery English philanthropist who wanted to provide a new life for Protestant debtors from English prisons in a slave-free city.

For most of 1779 the two commanding generals watched each other with little real action, except for pirate-style raids from British ships along the coastline. Then, early in 1779, King Louis XVI gave John Paul Jones a merchant ship named *Duc de Duras*, which Jones refitted, repaired, and renamed *Bon Homme Richard* in honor of the man who made the gift possible, Benjamin Franklin who wrote "*Poor Richard's Almanac.*" [70]

On 23 September, 1779, John Paul Jones engaged *HMS Serapis*[71] in the North Sea off the coast of England. The *Bon Homme Richard* was blasted in the initial broadside which the two ships exchanged, losing much of her firepower and many of her gunners. Captain Richard Pearson, commanding *Serapis*, called out to Jones, asking if he surrendered. Jones replied: "I have not yet begun to fight!"

---

[69] Our Georgia History - http://ourgeorgiahistory.com/people/oglethorpe.html

[70] 20 Years Poor Richard's Almanac – by Benjamin Franklin - http://www.sage-advice.com/Poor_Richard_1755.htm

[71] U.S. Navy website – John Paul Jones – A Founder of the U.S. Navy - http://www.chinfo.navy.mil/navpalib/traditions/html/jpjones.html

John Paul Jones' *Bon Homme Richard* vs *Serapis* [72]

It was a bloody battle with the two ships[73] literally locked in combat. Sharpshooting marines and seamen in *Richard's* topsails raked *Serapis* with gunfire. Jones and his crew fought on, even while their ship was sinking beneath them. Finally, Captain Pearson tore down his colors and *Serapis* surrendered.

[72] John Paul Jones - Bon Homme Richard vs Serapis - http://www.multied.com/Revolt/BonneHome.html -
[73] John Paul Jones battle with Serapis - http://www.worldsfinestnavy.com/JPJ.html

Chapter 7
Washington's Concerns as the War Winds Down

1789 Portrait of George Washington by Edward Savage[74]

On December 18, 1778, Washington began a letter to his friend, Colonel Benjamin Harrison, who had been elected as Speaker of Virginia's House of Burgess, and he continued to add to the letter until December 30. Washington appears to be responding to the question: Now that the French are helping us, how soon will the war end?

George Washington was a prolific letter writer, but usually his letters were short. This letter is unique, not only in it warnings, but in its depth and its length. It is clear that he had given the comments in this letter considerable thought and felt that there was a serious threat to the very existence of America, not because of the British Army, but because of threats from within. He said the "great business of the Nation" was being ignored. Unity among the people was being lost in "party disputes and personal quarrels."

---

[74] 1789 Portrait of George Washington by Edward Savage - http://www.npg.si.edu/exh/gw/savage.htm

The economy was floundering, inflation was rampant, and Washington wrote:[75]

> "I can assign but two causes for the enemy's continuance among us and these balance so equally in my Mind, that I scarce know which of the two preponderates. The one is, that they are waiting the ultimate determination of Parliament; the other, that of our distresses; by which I know the commissioners went home not a little buoyed up; and sorry I am to add, not without cause.
>
> "What may be the effect of such large and frequent emissions, of the dissensions, parties, extravagance, and a general lax of public virtue Heaven alone can tell! I am afraid even to think of it; but it appears as dear to me as ever the Sun did in its meridian brightness, that America never stood in more eminent need of the wise, Patriotic, and Spirited exertions of her Sons than at this period.
>
> "And if it is not a sufficient cause for general lamentation, my misconception of the matter impresses it too strongly upon me, that the States separately are too much engaged in their local concerns, and have too many of their ablest men withdrawn from the general Council for the good of the common weal. In a word, I think our political system may be compared to the mechanism of a Clock; and that our conduct should derive a lesson from it for it answers no good purpose to keep the smaller wheels in order if the greater one which is the support and prime mover of the whole is neglected."
>
> In Washington's analogy of a clock, he compares the political system in 1778 to the intricate mechanism of a clock such as the one pictured, which has a complex system of wheels of various sizes, all of which must work in unison for the clock to tell the correct time.

---

[75] Washington's Letter to Benjamin Harrison, December 18&30 1778 - http://etext.lib.virginia.edu/etcbin/toccer-ew2?id=WasFi13.xml&images=images/modeng&data=/texts/english/modeng/parsed&tag=public&part=408&division=div1

Workings of a Town Clock [76]

In his analogy the smaller wheels may be compared to the 13 individual States; and the greater wheel, to the United States as a whole. He is saying that the people are so involved in their state governments that the central government, which is trying to fight a war, is being neglected. The conclusion, of course, is that if the central government and the Army failed to win the war, none of the states would survive.

The comparative powers and sovereignty of the state governments to the federal government, which Washington addresses in this analogy, became a hotly debated issue when the Constitution of the United States was being written nine years later in the 1787 Constitutional Convention in Philadelphia. In fact, it is still an issue debated today. How much authority should the states have, and how much authority should the federal government have to pass laws and enforce them, raise taxes, fight wars or build roads, government buildings and schools?

Washington went on to say:

> "How far the latter (keeping the smaller wheels in order) is the case does not become me to pronounce, but as there can

---

[76] Workings of a Town Clock - http://www.barnsley.co.uk/virtual/www.barnsley.co.uk/lis/41.html

be no harm in a pious wish for the good of one's Country I shall offer it as (my wish) that each State would not only choose, but absolutely compel their ablest men to attend Congress; that they would instruct them to go into a thorough investigation of the causes that have produced so many disagreeable effects in the Army and Country; in a word that public abuses should be corrected, and an entire reformation worked; without these it does not, in my judgment, require the spirit of divination to foretell the consequences of the present administration, nor to how little purpose the States, individually, are framing constitutions, providing laws, and filling offices with the abilities of their ablest men."

General Washington had seen great suffering in his army for years. He could have won the war decisively on several occasions if he had only had more, better trained and equipped soldiers. The best people, he felt, should be sent to Congress.

"These, if the great whole is mismanaged must sink in the general wreck and will carry with it the remorse of thinking that we are lost by our own folly and negligence, or the desire perhaps of living in ease and tranquility during the expected accomplishment of so great a revolution in the effecting of which the greatest abilities and the (most) honest men our (i.e. the American) world affords ought to be employed.

"It is much to be feared, my dear Sir, that the States in their separate capacities have very inadequate ideas of the present danger. Removed (some of them) far distant from the scene of action and seeing, and hearing such publications only as flatter their wishes they conceive that the contest is at an end, and that to regulate the government and police of their own State is all that remains to be done; but it is devoutly to be wished that a sad reverse of this may not fall upon them like a thunder clap that is little expected."

"It had been 13 years since the Stamp Act had prompted the colonies to meet in the Stamp Act Congress to address the problems all of them faced. It had been three and a half years since the first shots were fired at Lexington and Concord. Still, because the battles were scattered and communication was slow and imperfect, the lives of most people went on as usual "far distant" from the battlefield. The "publications," news reports, often told them only what they wanted to hear.

"I do not mean to designate particular States. I wish to cast no reflections upon any one. The Public believes (and if they do believe it, the fact might almost as well be so) that the States at this time are badly represented, and that the great, and important concerns of the nation are horribly conducted, for want either of abilities or application in the Members, or through discord and party views of some individuals; that they should be so, is to be lamented more at this time, than formerly, as we are far advanced in the dispute and in the opinion of many drawing to a happy period; have the eyes of Europe upon us, and I am persuaded many political Spies to watch, discover our situation, and give information of our weaknesses [77]and wants."

The General wanted to make it clear that his complaints were not personal attacks on those of any "particular" state. He just wanted his friend to understand that the public had a low opinion of their representatives in the Congress and felt that they either didn't know what they were doing or didn't care. He points out that now, with France as an ally, all of Europe had its eyes on America. They were wondering if it was possible for a group of people to run a country without a King.

"The story you have related of a proposal to redeem the paper money at its present depreciated value has also come to my ears, but I cannot vouch for the authenticity of it. I am very happy to hear that the Assembly of Virginia have put the completion of their Regiment upon a footing so apparently certain, but as one great defect of your past Laws for this purpose, has lain in the mode of getting the Men to the Army, I shall hope that effectual measures are pointed out in the present, to remedy the evil and bring forward all that shall be raised. The embargo upon provisions is a most salutary measure as I am afraid a sufficiency of flour will not easily be obtained even with money of higher estimation than ours.

---

[77] Washington's Letter to Benjamin Harrison-Dec. 18, 1778 - http://etext.lib.virginia.edu/etcbin/toccer-new2?id=WasFi13.xml&images=images/modeng&data=/texts/english/modeng/parsed&tag=public&part=408&division=div1

"I have seen nothing since I came here (on the 22d. Instant) to change my opinion of men or measures but abundant reason to be convinced, that our affairs are in a more distressed, ruinous, and deplorable condition than they have been in since the commencement of the War."

The reference Washington makes to paper money refers to the Congress having printed money, with nothing to back it up. The economy of the country was in a shambles with runaway inflation. Yet, still, many members of Congress would not even show up in Philadelphia to address the new nation's problems. In the next few sentences, Washington describes himself and his years of devoting his time and energies to helping the new nation survive, at great cost to his own personal financial situation:

"By a faithful laborer then in the cause. By a man who is daily injuring his private Estate without even the smallest earthly advantage not common to all in case of a favorable Issue to the dispute. By one who wishes the prosperity of America most devoutly and sees or thinks he sees it, on the brink of ruin, you are beseeched most earnestly my dear Colonel Harrison, to exert yourself in endeavoring to rescue your Country, by, (let me add) sending your ablest and best Men to Congress.

"These characters must not slumber, nor sleep at home, in such times of pressing danger; they must not content themselves in the enjoyment of places of honor or profit in their own Country, while the common interests of America are moldering and sinking into irretrievable (if a remedy is not soon applied) ruin, in which theirs also must ultimately be involved."

The common interests of America, were "moldering," that is, rotting away and would soon be beyond remedy. Why was that happening? Washington went on to explain:

"If I was to be called upon to draw a picture of the times, and of men; from what I have seen, heard, and in part know I should in one word say that idleness, dissipation and extravagance seem to have laid fast hold of most of them. That speculation, peculation, (dishonesty, stealing public funds) and an insatiable thirst for riches seems to have got the better of every other consideration and almost of every order of men.

"That party disputes and personal quarrels are the great business of the day whilst the momentous concerns of an empire, a great and accumulated debt; ruined finances, depreciated money, and want of credit (which in their consequences is the want of every thing) are but secondary considerations and postponed from day to day, from week to week as if our affairs wore the most promising aspect; after drawing this picture, which from my Soul I believe to be a true one I need not repeat to you that I am alarmed and wish to see my countrymen roused."

George Washington was a man of principle and patience. But, he clearly felt that the country was collapsing from within, not from the result of the war. To build a great nation, its people would have to live by the principles that would make it possible:

1. **a strong and effective military;**
2. **unity, not contention, among the people;**
3. **a strong and free economy;**
4. **and virtue and morality among the people.**

He stated:

"I have no resentments, nor do I mean to point at any particular characters; this I can declare upon my honor for I have every attention paid me by Congress than I can possibly expect and have reason to think that I stand well in their estimation but in the present situation of things I cannot help asking: Where is Mason, Wythe, Jefferson, Nicholas, Pendleton, Nelson, and another I could name; and why, if you are sufficiently impressed with your danger, do you not (as New York has done in the case of Mr. Jay) send an extra Member or two for at least a certain limited time till the great business of the Nation is put upon a more respectable and happy establishment.

"Your money is now sinking 5 per cent a day in this City; and I shall not be surprised if in the course of a few months a total stop is put to the currency of it. And yet an assembly, a concert, a dinner, or supper (that will cost three or four hundred pounds) will not only take men from acting in but even from thinking of this business while a great part of the officers of your Army from absolute necessity are quitting the Service and the more virtuous few rather than do this are sinking by sure degrees into beggary and want."

Washington was saying that, in spite of the threat to the nation, members of Congress were spending "three or four hundreds" pounds for entertainment to get their minds off their work when they needed to do be concentrating on saving the nation and keeping the army from disintegrating.

> "I again repeat to you that this is not an exaggerated account; that it is an alarming one I do not deny, and confess to you that I feel more real distress on account of the present appearances of things than I have done at any one time since the commencement of the dispute; but it is time to bid you once more adieu.
>
> "Providence has heretofore taken us up when all other means and hope seemed to be departing from us, in this I will confide."

This letter appears to indicate that Washington was feeling very discouraged at the time. He faced the year ahead trying to fight a war in a time of raging inflation that was making money worthless; party politics; apathy; contention; greed and immorality among many people, even in Congress; petty jealousies and even treason in top officers that threatened the country's very existence.

However, he never gave up. He believed that the cause of liberty was "upheld by the powers of heaven," when good citizens worked hard and were united in their efforts.

Chapter 8
Lack of Support Threatens the Army's Existence

The next two and a half years after Washington's letter of concern to Benjamin Harrison seemed to validate his worries. The British capture of Savannah[78] on December 29, 1778, was followed by their capture of Augusta, Georgia a month later. The British withdrew from Augusta two weeks later; however, by July 22, 1779, the State of Georgia was no longer functioning as a free and independent state as James Wright, the British Royal Governor, again returned to Savannah to direct the affairs of the city.[79]

Yet, by April 3, 1780, conditions for the army were so bad, and the discontent and lack of support for the army so intense that Washington wrote the following warning to Congress:

> "I think it my duty to touch upon the general situation of the Army at this juncture. It is absolutely necessary Congress should be apprised of it, for it is difficult to foresee what may be the result, and as very serious consequences are to be apprehended I should not be justified in preserving silence. There never has been a stage of the War in which the dissatisfaction has been so general or alarming. It has lately in particular instances worn features of a very dangerous complexion.
>
> "A variety of causes have contributed to this. The diversity in the terms of enlistments, the inequality of the rewards given for entering into the service; but still more the disparity in the provision made by the several States for their respective Troops. The system of State supplies, however, in the commencement, dictated by necessity, has proved in its operation pernicious beyond description. An Army must be raised, paid, subsisted and regulated upon an equal and uniform principle, or the confusions and discontents are endless. Little less than the dissolution of the Army would have been long since the consequence of a different plan, had it not been for a

---

78 North Georgia website- Savannah, Georgia, falls under British control http://ngeorgia.com/revolution/amrev13.html

79 North Georgia website- Lincoln & d'Estaing's siege of Savannah http://ngeorgia.com/revolution/amrev15.html

spirit of Patriotic virtue both in officers and men of which there are few examples; seconded by the unremitting pains that have been taken to compose and reconcile them to their situation.

"But these will not be able to hold out much longer against the influence of causes constantly operating and every day with some new aggravation.." [80]

General Henry Clinton[81]

In early March 1780, General Henry Clinton landed British forces near Charleston, South Carolina. They slowly closed in on the city trapping its defenders.

General Benjamin Lincoln[82]

In December 1778, the Continental Congress had replaced native North Carolinian Major General Robert Howe with Bostonian Major General Benjamin Lincoln as Southern

[80] Washington's letter to Congress – April 3, 1780 - http://etext.lib.virginia.edu/etcbin/toccer-new2?id=WasFi18.xml&images=images/modeng&data=/texts/english/modeng/parsed&tag=public&part=215&division=div1

[81] Patriot Source – General Henry Clinton http://www.patriotresource.com/people/clinton.html

[82] Patriot Resource – General Benjamin Lincoln, Bio- http://www.patriotresource.com/people/lincoln.html

Department Commander, with instructions to enlist 5000 men to retake Georgia. General Lincoln, however, faced the British forces with approximately 14,000 troops and on May 12, 1780 he was forced to surrender.

This was a severe blow to the colonies. Lincoln surrendered his entire force of 5,466 men. Meanwhile, Colonel Abraham Buford with 350 Virginians was moving south to reinforce the garrison. Lt. Col. Banastre Tarleton with a force of British cavalry took Buford by surprise at the Waxhaws, a district near the North Carolina border, and slaughtered most of his men, refusing to honor the white flag Buford displayed. It was the greatest loss of American manpower and equipment of the war and gave the British nearly complete control of the Southern Colonies. [83]

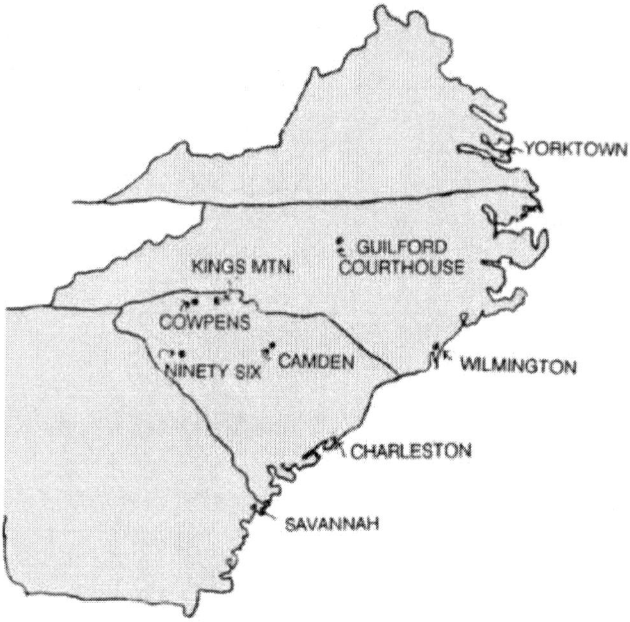

Southern Strategy map[84]

General Clinton took immediate steps to extend and secure British conquests and to re-establish royal authority in the South.

[83] American Revolution – Battle of Charleston - http://theamericanrevolution.org/battles/bat_char.asp

[84] National Park Service – Southern Campaign http://www.cr.nps.gov/seac/socamp.htm

After the capture of Charleston, Clinton returned to New York with about a third of his force, leaving General Charles Cornwallis with 8,000 men to follow up the victory.[85] Cornwallis established his main seaboard bases at Savannah, Beaufort, Charleston, and Georgetown. In the interior he extended his line of control along the Savannah River westward to Ninety-Six and northward to Camden and Rocky Mount.

General Johann de Kalb[86]

The defeat left General Johann de Kalb in command of the Southern Army. De Kalb, who was from Bavaria but served with the French Army, was left with literally no support and no food for his troops, and the country wide open for British taking. In July the Continental Congress, without consulting George Washington, Major General Horatio Gates, who commanded the troops at Saratoga, to replace General de Kalb and counter Britain's General Henry Clinton. General de Kalb was ordered by Congress to meet with Gates in South Carolina.

The First Maryland Brigade, led by Col. Smallwood, the Second Maryland Brigade, led by Col. William Gist, and the Delaware Regiment, led by a new commander, Lt. Col. Vaughan, consisting of about 1400 men marched South, and were joined at Camden with 2,000 militia from North Carolina and 700 militia from Virginia.

---

[85] American Revolution British Successes in the South - http://www.americanrevolution.com/BritishSuccess.htm

[86] Ridpath History, Vol XIV, Pg 630 – General Johann DeKalb

General Horatio Gates[87]

Gates then had approximately 4100 men, although the Delaware Regiment, which suffered heavy losses at the battle of Germantown, went south with about 280 men rather than its normal compliment of 500.

Lord Cornwallis, hearing of Gates' movements left Charleston, arrived in Camden on the same day that Gates did with about 2200 men. By moonlight, both armies moved out, meeting in the early morning hours in Gum swamp in the vicinity of Sanders Creek. Skirmishing broke out, but the actual attack took place at daylight. At about 10 AM, both armies advanced. The Virginia militia, who had never before been in battle, faced experienced British troops. When the British charged, the militia panicked and fled through the woods. Most of the North Carolina militia also broke and ran through the First Maryland Brigade, pursued by the British cavalry.

The Delaware and Maryland regiments held, led by De Kalb, whose horse had been shot from under him, and the British concentrated their attack against the Delaware and Maryland regiments as the militias fled, followed by General Horatio Gates who fled with his troops, trying to get them to return and fight. General DeKalb, fell with eleven wounds, dying in Camden three days later. The British buried him with full military honors.

Gates was never to live down the disgrace of his flight. The analysis of the shameful event was blamed on lack of military training in the militia on a U.S. Army website:[88]

---

[87]Patriot Source – General Horatio Gates
http://www.patriotresource.com/people/gates.html

The First Battle of Camden SC, Aug 16, 1780

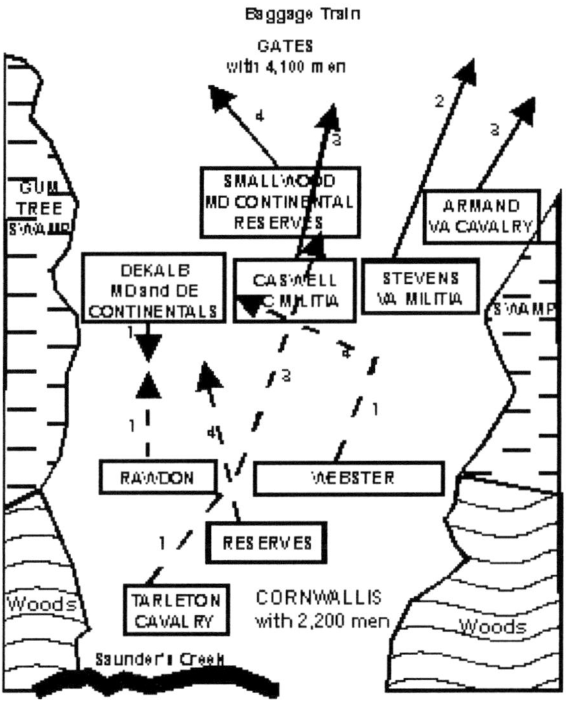

"The Battle of Camden presents a picture unique in the history of our country. The mention of it calls to mind the havoc wrought by untrained troops fleeing from a battle field, pursued by the phantoms of terror; troops that were fully expected by their leaders to fight, constituting two-thirds of the Army, terrifiedly rushing from the battle field without firing a shot, before scarcely any of their number were wounded; deserting the regular forces whom they might have protected and from whom protection would have been received.

"The cowardice of the militia, induced as it was by mob fear, was followed by no miraculous intervention whereby those who held their ground and bravely fought might be saved. The latter, in turn, were also overcome by the enemy. Their gallantry

---

[88]British Plans to Subjugate the Southern Provinces – Battle of Camden, S.C. August 16, 1780 -Paragraph 58 - http://www.army.mil/cmh-pg/books/RevWar/Camden/AWC-CAM2.htm

alone could not win victory from a more numerous foe of equal military merit." [89]

Death of Baron de Kalb in Battle of Camden[90]

What added to the distressing effect of the battle was the death of a gallant leader, well beloved by his adopted country, and the cruel and unjustifiable contumely heaped upon the Army, whose only mistake in this campaign was to have faith in the fighting spirit of his army, a confidence which was betrayed by all but the Maryland division, the Delaware regiment, the one regiment of North Carolinians, and the Artillery."

In the most disastrous battle of the Revolution for the Americans, 1000 men were killed and another 1000 captured; huge quantities of scarce ammunitions were confiscated; wagons and other transportation vehicles were lost.

While this military debacle was taking place, during the month of August, 1780, George Washington was also in motion

---

[89] Delaware Society, Sons of the American Revolution, -First Battle of Camden Battle Map - http://www.sar.org/dessar/camden96.htm

[90] Battle of Camden Death of Baron de Kalb –Copy of engraving by Alonzo Chappel – National Archives and Records

-

headed south towards the scene of the action. The lack of a central government for the United States, however, threatened the very existence of the Continental Army, and opponents of Washington in Congress made decisions that affected the war without even telling him. Impassable roads; shortages of food, clothing, tents and ammunition; combined with slow communications; untrained militia, who often thought they were better than the regular soldiers; and the loss of thousands of men and key officers in three months time in the Siege of Charleston and the Battle of Camden clearly threatened the fight for freedom.

On August 27, 1780, Washington wrote a circular letter to all the state governors[91] in which he stated:

> "It has been no inconsiderable support of our cause, to have had it in our power to contrast the conduct of our Army with that of the enemy, and to convince the inhabitants that while their rights were wantonly violated by the British Troops, by ours they were respected. This distinction must unhappily now cease, and we must assume the odious character of the plunderers instead of the protectors of the people, the direct consequence of which must be to alienate their minds from the Army and insensibly from the cause."

The problem was not really a lack of available food. It was the inability of the federal government to enforce decisions made by Congress, which was composed of representatives of all the states. Some states were not sending the food, clothing and other materials that Congress had requested. America's own people were literally starving the Army:

> "This army cannot possibly remain much longer together, unless very vigorous and immediate measures are taken by the States to comply with the requisitions made upon them," Washington warned. "The Commissary General has neither the means nor the power of procuring supplies; he is only to receive them from the several Agents."

---

[91] Washington's Letter to governors of all States on lack of food for army – August 27, 1780 http://etext.lib.virginia.edu/etcbin/toccer-new2?id=WasFi19.xml&images=images/modeng&data=/texts/english/modeng/parsed&tag=public&part=445&division=div1

Chapter 9
A Spy and a Traitor Plot to End American Freedom

[92]

There was an even more serious problem secretly brewing during the summer of 1780 that would surface in September. , About the same time Congress chose General Gates to be the Southern commander, h General Benedict Arnold had asked to be appointed commander of West Point, the fort on the Hudson that stopped the British from using the river to transport troops and materials to and from Canada.

In September of 1780, General Washington was conferring in Hartford, Connecticut with French officers in an effort to plan an ambitious coordinated attack on the British forces using the French Navy to block the British Navy and a combined force of French and American ground troops. At the same time Major General Benedict Arnold, the American Commander of West Point, was secretly meeting with Major John André, Adjutant General of the British Army, plotting to turn West Point over to the British in exchange for £10,000 sterling.

The plot was discovered, according to an account in Washington Irving's *Life of Washington*, by three young men that Irving referred to as "youngsters," (probably teen-agers,) as André crossed an area we would call a "no-man's land" in modern jargon.

---

[92] Benedict Arnold Biography – The hero traitor - http://www.benedictarnold.org/

It separated the British and Americans in New York but was controlled by neither. Irving described the scene as follows:

"He had not proceeded far, when coming to a place where a small stream crossed the road and ran into a woody dell, a man stepped out from the trees, leveled a musket, and brought him to a stand, while two other men, similarly armed, showed themselves prepared to second their comrade."

Capture of Major John Andre by Patriot youth[93]

"The man who had first stepped out wore a refugee uniform. At the sight of it, André's heart leapt, and he felt himself secure. Losing all caution, he exclaimed eagerly: 'Gentlemen, I hope you belong to our party?"

"'What party?' was asked.

" 'The lower party,' said André.

"'We do,' was the reply.

"All reserve was not at an end. André declared himself to be a British officer; that he had been up the country on particular business, and must not be detained a single moment. He drew out his watch as he spoke. It was a gold one, and served to prove to them that he was what he represented himself, gold watches being seldom worn in those days excepting by persons of consequence.

---

[93] Young Folks History of United States, by Thomas Wentworth Higginson, 1888, Pg. 210

"To his consternation, the supposed refugee now avowed himself and his companions to be Americans, and told André that he was their prisoner!"[94]

Only four days before André's capture, John Paulding, one of the three young Americans confronting Andre, had been imprisoned by the British and was wearing the coat given to him by one of his captors in exchange of a "good yeoman garment of which they stripped him." The young men, who had been patrolling their neighborhood to stop attacks on their home, stripped André and found concealed in his boots the plans in General Arnold's own handwriting of the plan to turn West Point over to the British Army.

André offered the young men "any sum of money" if they would let him go. He would give his horse, saddle, bridle and one hundred guineas, which was a considerable amount of money in 1780, and would send them to any place they wished. One young man, David Williams, asked André if he would give more, and the prisoner said he would give them any reward they named in goods or money and would stay with two of them while the third went to New York to get it.

At that point Paulding, according to testimony given by the other two young men, broke in and announced that if André gave ten thousand guineas, he would not go free. Paulding, Williams and Isaac Van Wart, the third young man, brought André to Lieutenant-colonel Jameson who, didn't seem to realize the import of the letter in André's boot and wrote a letter to Arnold, as his commanding general, telling him of the papers and that they had been dispatched by express to General Washington.

Washington was returning to his headquarters accompanied by Count Mathew Dumas, aide-de-camp to Rochambeau, who was an admirer of the Commander in Chief of the Americans. Washington Irving related the story of the turn-out in one of the towns as word was spread that General Washington was riding through, as told by the Count:

"We arrived there at night; the whole population had sallied forth beyond the suburbs. We were surrounded by a crowd of children carrying torches and reiterating the

---

[94] Life of Washington by Washington Irving, Volume IV, page 151

acclamations of the citizens; all were eager to touch the person of him whom they hailed with loud cries as their father, and they thronged before us so as almost to prevent our moving onward. General Washington, much affected, paused a few moments, and pressing my hand said: 'We may be beaten by the English. It is the chance of war; but there is an army they will never conquer!'"

Irving noted,

"These few words speak that noble confidence in the enduring Patriotism of his countrymen, which sustained him throughout all the fluctuating fortunes of the Revolution; yet at this very moment it was about to receive one of the cruelest of wounds."

Washington would soon learn that one of his major generals was a traitor who was, at that very moment, offering to destroy America's dream of liberty by helping the British seize West Point, the only thing blocking their total control of the Hudson River.

Benedict Arnold, inadvertently given warning by Jameson's report that he would soon be captured by his own troops, slipped away from the dinner table, motioned his wife to follow him, and told her they must at that moment flee for their lives. Shocked, his wife fainted and, without reviving her, Arnold fled to board a British ship. From the ship Arnold wrote a letter to Washington that stated:

"I ask no favor for myself. I have too often experienced the ingratitude of my country to attempt it; but from the known humanity of your Excellency, I am induced to ask your protection for Mrs. Arnold."

Washington did protect Mrs. Arnold, who had a very young baby and was shocked and distraught by her husband's behavior.

For quite some time the fate of the charming Major John André was discussed by many people, some of whom, especially women, felt he should not be harshly punished. Not surprisingly, André himself at one point discussed his possible fate with Major Tallmadge, who was his guard. As Tallmadge and André were riding side by side one day, André asked his guard what would be the result of his capture and in what light he would be regarded by

General Washington and a military tribunal, should one be ordered.

Tallmadge evaded the question as long as possible, but being urged to a full and explicit reply, gave it in the following words:

> "I had a much-loved classmate in Yale College by the name of Nathan Hale[95], who entered the army in 1775. Immediately after the battle of Long Island, General Washington wanted information respecting the strength, position and probable movements of the enemy. Captain Hale tendered his services, went over to Brooklyn, and was taken, just as he was passing the outposts of the enemy on his return; said I with emphasis – 'Do you remember the sequel to the story?'

Nathan Hale

'Yes,' said André, 'he was hanged as a spy! But you surely do not consider his case and mine alike?' 'Yes, precisely similar; and similar will be your fate.'"[96]

Nathan Hale, who was a 21-year-old school teacher, had visited the British encampments unsuspected, made drawings of the enemy's fortifications and made notes in Latin of information he gathered, but was caught by the British before he could get back. He was taken to General Howe's headquarters, and after a brief summary trial, his execution was ordered for the following morning. His request for a Bible before being executed was

---

[95] Connecticut Society Sons of American Revolution -Nathan Hale- http://www.ctssar.org/Patriots/nathan_hale.htm

[96] The Life of Washington, by Washington Irving, Vol. IV, page 174-75.

denied, and they tore up his last letter to his mother, because, his executioner said, "that the rebels should never know they had a man who could die with such firmness." Nathan Hale's last words were,

> "I only regret that I have but one life to lose for my country."

The capture of André, according to the account written by Washington Irving, "caused a great sensation at New York." He was a favorite of the British general Sir Henry Clinton, who wrote a letter to General Washington, claiming that André should be released because he had visited Benedict Arnold under the "sanction of a flag of truce."

Washington sent a dispatch to Clinton offering to exchange André for the American traitor, Benedict Arnold. Clinton rejected the offer.

André not only was popular among the British troops, there also were many Americans who were reluctant to see him executed. Several women pleaded for his life and Colonel Beverly Robinson, an old friend of Washington's who was a British sympathizer wrote a letter to Washington asking that he be spared.

Benedict Arnold sent a letter in which he "reasserted the right he had possessed, as commanding officer of the department, to transact all matters with which André" was charged, and claimed André should not suffer as a result, threatening that "if this warning should be disregarded, and he suffer, I call Heaven and earth to witness that your Excellency will be justly answerable for the torrent of blood that may be spilt in consequence."

A self-portrait drawn by Major John Andre[97] the day before he was executed

André himself wrote a letter, not begging for his life, but asking Washington and "a military tribunal to adapt the mode of my death to the feelings of a man of honor." He did not want to be hanged, the fate of criminals.

In spite of the many emotional and even threatening letters received, Washington did not reverse the Military Tribunal's sentence of hanging. To do so would have trivialized the seriousness of André's crime. Even at the dedication of a memorial to Andre those gathered were reminded by Henry J. Raymond, that André had "been commissioned to buy with gold what steel could not conquer; to drive a bargain with one ready for a price to become a traitor; to count out the thirty pieces of silver by which British generals and British gentlemen were not ashamed to purchase the betrayal of a cause, whose shining virtue repelled their power and dimmed the glory of their arms."

Nathan Hale was hanged and on October 2, 1780 the charming Major John André was executed for spying, as Major Tallmadge predicted.

Five days later, on October 7, Benedict Arnold wrote a Letter To The Inhabitants of America[98] trying to justify his

---

[97] Life of Washington, by Washington Irving – Pen sketch of Major Andre –Vol. IV, Page 199

[98] Benedict Arnold's Letter to the Inhabitants of America http://www.earlyamerica.com/earlyamerica/writings/arnold/index.html

betrayal and urge other Americans to do the same. It was published throughout the colonies and in London.

Arnold went on to command British forces against American troops in his native Connecticut. The dichotomy of feeling for Benedict Arnold, the hero and patriot and Benedict Arnold the traitor was best expressed by an American officer he captured there.[99]

"What would be my fate if I should be taken prisoner by the Americans?" the former patriot asked.

The officer replied:

> *"They will cut off that leg of yours wounded at Quebec and Saratoga and bury it with all the honors of war. Then they will hang the rest of you on a gallows!"*

Saratoga Battlefield Monument to Benedict Arnold's leg[100]

The Saratoga Battlefield today has a small statue of a leg, with no inscription at the place where Arnold was wounded.

---

[99] Benedict Arnold –The Traitor Who Saved America - http://www.magweb.com/sample/amr/ch28ben2.htm

[100] Ibid – Monument to Benedict Arnold's wounded leg

Chapter 10
A Trap Set for Cornwallis in Virginia

General Charles Cornwallis[101]

On the same day as André's execution, another battle was taking place in South Carolina. British General Cornwallis sent Major Patrick Ferguson to the foothills of the Alleghenies to arouse the Loyalist supporters of the Crown and put down the Patriot mountaineers. Ferguson sent a captured Patriot back into the hills with a message saying "that if they did not desist from their opposition to the British arms, and take protection under his standard, he would march his army over the mountains, hang their leaders, and lay their country waste with fire and sword." Instead of cowing the Patriots, Ferguson's warning incited them.

According to a report to General Gates written by Colonels William Campbell, Isaac Shelby and Benjamin Cleveland, without orders or formal military training, the mountaineers assembled about 900 men, all good marksmen, from the western counties of Virginia, North Carolina, (areas that later became Tennessee and South Carolina). On the top King's Mountain[102] the mountain men attacked Ferguson's forces, capturing, killing or wounding the

---

[101] General Charles Cornwallis – Portrait-
http://earlyamerica.com/portraits/cornwallis.html

[102] King's Mountain National Historical Park -
http://www.cr.nps.gov/history/online_books/glimpses3/glimpses2d.htm

entire force. A US Army War College analysis of the King's Mountain Battle written in 1928 [103] observed, "A defeat so overwhelming as that suffered by Ferguson's command is rare in warfare." King's Mountain was the turning point of the war in the South, stopping Cornwallis in his effort to subdue North Carolina.

After Benedict Arnold's desertion to the British, American's enemies now had access to many closely guarded secrets, including information about West Point's defenses. Washington took immediate steps to strengthen the fort. He ordered dependable Major-General Nathanael Greene to march with the Jersey, New York, New Hampshire and Stark's brigades to take temporary command of West Point.

On October 22, 1780, Washington put General Greene in charge of the Southern Army. He also detached Baron von Steuben to go with Greene to build up and train the Southern troops, and gave him the responsibility of conducting a Court-Martial of General Gates' behavior in the Battle of Camden with von Steuben presiding. Washington wrote.[104]

> "I wish this affair to be conducted with the greatest impartiality and with as much dispatch as circumstances will permit,"

On the same day Washington wrote to Baron von Steuben that in spite of the importance of his services to him, "yet as to the Southward, there is an army to be created, the mass of which is at present without any formation at all, your services there will be still more essential."[105]

Over the next few months, during the winter of 1780-1781, Washington prodded Congress and the States to provide the needed manpower and money, or to borrow the money needed to

---

[103] US Army War College 1928 – King's Mountain Battle http://www.tngenweb.org/revwar/Kingsmountain/warcollege2.html

[104] George Washington's Letter to Major-General Nathanael Greene – October 22, 1780 http://etext.lib.virginia.edu/etcbin/toccer-new2?id=WasFi20.xml&images=images/modeng&data=/texts/english/modeng/parsed&tag=public&part=218&division=div1

[105] George Washington's Letter to Baron von Steuben –October 22, 1780 - http://etext.lib.virginia.edu/etcbin/toccer-new2?id=WasFi20.xml&images=images/modeng&data=/texts/english/modeng/parsed&tag=public&part=220&division=div1

build up the American Army, as he worked to organize a combined force of American and French soldiers to attempt an attack on the British in New York.

In January of 1781, since his troops were too small to engage Cornwallis in a general battle, General Greene decided on a harassing action against British forts. He sent Brigadier General Daniel Morgan with 600 men towards Ninety-Six where there was a British Fort. Cornwallis sent Lieutenant Colonel Banastre Tarleton after Morgan, and the two forces met at Cowpens, South Carolina. Morgan won a decisive victory which helped set the stage for what happened later that year.

General Daniel Morgan[106]

On March 15, 1781, the Battle of Guilford, [107] North Carolina took place which, according to historian John Fiske, "though tactically a defeat for the Americans, was strategically a victory and the most important one since the capture of Burgoyne."

The numbers of General Greene's troops, which had numbered no more than about 1450, had more than tripled with Virginians by the time he reached tiny Guilford, North Carolina, a hamlet of less than 100 people. Though they were not experienced soldiers, there were enough to risk a battle, Greene thought, against

---

[106]National Park Service Brigadier General Daniel Morgan at Cowpens - http://www.nps.gov/cowp/dmorgan.htm

[107] National Park Service – Battle of Guilford, N.C. - http://www.cr.nps.gov/history/online_books/glimpses3/glimpses2f.htm

Cornwallis' 2200 experienced, battle hardened redcoats. At Guilford[108] General Green and the Americans retreated, leaving Cornwallis in possession of Guilford, but nearly 30% of his men had been lost. Greene's sharpshooters had killed 93, wounded 413 and there were 26 missing.

Cornwallis had failed to destroy the Americans, was far from his base in unfamiliar territory and retreated. He marched through Wilmington, North Carolina and on into Virginia toward the British base at Yorktown.

During the same time period, on January 2, 1781, the State of Virginia ceded a portion of its land west of the Appalachian Mountains to Congress. This paved the way for the ratification of the Articles of Confederation. It had been almost two years since the 12th State, Delaware, had ratified the Articles, however, until all 13 states ratified them, they were not in force.

Maryland refused to ratify them. As the price for its ratification, Maryland demanded that states with claims to the vast unsettled regions of the West transfer jurisdiction of these lands to the national government. Finally, two weeks before the Battle of Guilford, Maryland had ratified them on March 1, 1781, formally establishing the first government of the United Sates.

The adoption of the Articles of Confederation provided formal notice to the world that the Americans had become one nation, even if its structure was flawed "with no executive, no judiciary, no taxing power and no enforcement power," as Constitutional scholar Cleon Skousen put it.[109]

However, as a nation, finally, with some kind of real government, foreign nations could feel more confident in being repaid for loans and alliances they might make to the financially strapped and struggling United States of America.

As the commander in chief of a recognized new nation, in May, 1781, General Washington met with Count Jean Baptiste de

---

[108] National Park Service - The Battle of Guilford Courthouse http://www.cr.nps.gov/nr/twhp/wwwlps/lessons/32guilford/32facts1.htm

[109] The Five Thousand Year Leap – Structuring a New Government - by Cleon Skousen, page 20

Rochambeau and the Chevalier de Chastellux[110] to attempt the coordination of the ground and sea forces of the United States and France, not an easy task with primitive communication and transportation networks.

Rochambeau was the commander of the French forces, which King Louis XVI at Rochambeau's request had been increased to 6000 men.

Count de Rochambeau[111]

During the summer of 1781, General Cornwallis had fortified Yorktown, Virginia[112] at the mouth of the Chesapeake bay about 33 miles North of today's Norfolk, Virginia Naval Base. The British planned to use the Yorktown naval station for the British fleet in Southern waters and as a military base for further operations in the interior.

Slowly the forces came together. Washington brought his troops south. The French fleet sailed into the Chesapeake Bay, under Count de Grasse, who blocked the York River prevented the British fleet that sailed out of New York Harbor from assisting General Cornwallis from the sea bringing together the French and

---

110 Washington's Conference with Count de Rochambeau – May 21, 1781 - http://etext.lib.virginia.edu/etcbin/toccer-new2?id=WasFi22.xml&images=images/modeng&data=/texts/english/modeng/parsed&tag=public&part=118&division=div1

111 Count de Rochambeau Biography and Picture - http://www.richardferrie.com/roch.htm

112 National Park Service -Siege of Yorktown, Virginia - http://www.cr.nps.gov/history/online_books/glimpses3/glimpses2g.htm

American ground troops required planning and coordination. The patience and the tactical plans laid by Washington involved bringing the French and American ground troops together as the French fleet blocked the British ships Cornwallis relied on for supplies. On the night of September 28, 1781 the combined American and French forces began the Siege of Yorktown.[113]

Washington Irving described the closing hours of the Siege of Yorktown[114] when Cornwallis secretly prepared 16 large boats to enable his troops to escape across the York River as follows:

> "A large part of the troops were transported to the Gloucester side of the river before midnight, and the second division had actually embarked, when a violent storm of wind and rain scattered the boats, and drove them a considerable distance down the river. They were collected with difficulty. It was not too late to effect the passage of the second division before daybreak and an effort was made to get back the division which had already crossed. It was not done until morning was far advanced, and the troops in recrossing were exposed to the fire of the American batteries."

"The hopes of Lord Cornwallis were now at an end. His works were tumbling in ruins about him, under an incessant cannonade;(directed by Baron von Stueben) his garrison was reduced in number by sickness and death, and exhausted by constant watching and severe duty. Unwilling to expose the residue of the brave troops which had stood by him so faithfully, to the dangers and horrors of an assault, which could not fail to be successful, he ordered a parley to be beaten about ten o'clock on the morning of the 17th, and dispatched a flag with a letter to Washington proposing a cessation of hostilities."

---

113 National Park Service – The Siege of Yorktown Begins - http://www.cr.nps.gov/history/online_books/source/sb1/sb1f.htm

114 The Life of Washington, Vol. IV, Pg. 435 by Washington Irving

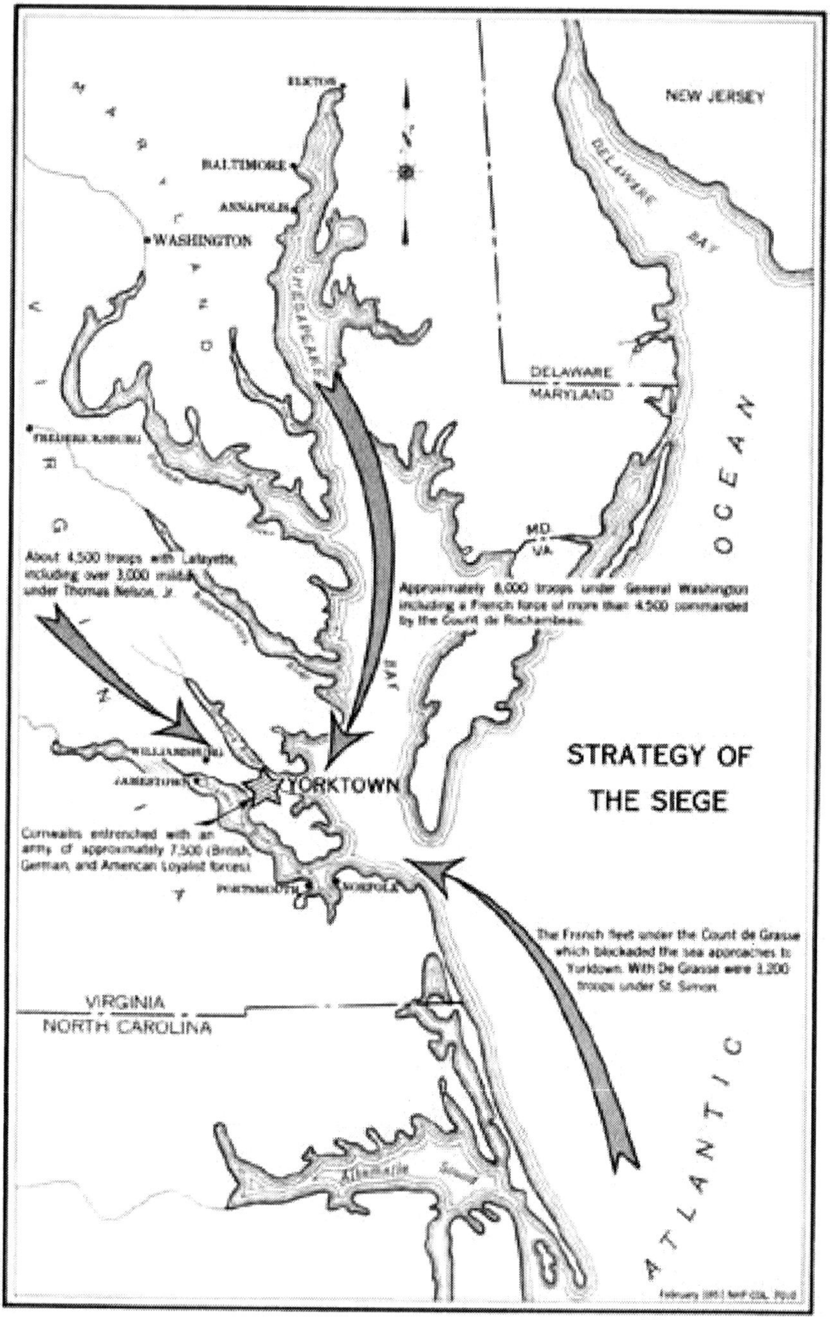

National Park Service -Map of Yorktown Siefe [115]

[115] National Park Service – Map – Yorktown 1781 - http://www.cr.nps.gov/history/online_books/hh/14/hh14b.htm

On October 19, 1781, in a report to Congress beginning,[116] Washington announced his victory:

"I have the honor to inform Congress, that a reduction of the British Army under the command of Lord Cornwallis, is most happily effected,"

On October 20, 1781, General Charles Cornwallis announced his defeat to his commanding officer, Sir Henry Clinton:[117]

"I have the mortification to inform your Excellency that I have been forced to give up the posts of York and Gloucester, and to surrender the troops under my commands by capitulation, on the 19th instant, as prisoners of war to the combined forces of America and France."

---

[116] Washington's letter to Congress – Surrender of Cornwallis - October 19, 1781 - http://etext.lib.virginia.edu/etcbin/toccer-new2?id=WasFi23.xml&images=images/modeng&data=/texts/english/modeng/parsed&tag=public&part=246&division=div1

[117] General Charles Cornwallis describes his defeat to General Henry Clinton - http://www.shsu.edu/~his_ncp/Yorktown.html

Chapter 11
Two Years Waiting For A Peace Treaty

It would be another two years before the peace treaty ending the American Revolution would be signed, on September 3, 1783.[118]

In the intervening two years, a period in which there was neither war nor peace, the incredible strain of ineffective government that had caused such suffering and the lengthening of the war began to come to a head. The soldiers, who had suffered and finally won the war, had not been paid for many months. Washington's pleadings to Congress on their behalf seemed to fall on deaf ears, but, in fact, there was little that Congress could do. It actually was nothing more than a debating society that could suggest actions to the States but had no enforcing powers.

Some of the men in Washington's army threatened to march on Congress while they were all still together and armed, to demand payment so they could feed their families.

One officer, Colonel Lewis Nicola, wrote a seven page letter to his Commander in Chief on May 22, 1782, which outlined the plight of the army, its hardships, lack of pay, suffering, etc., discussed the various forms of government and the inefficiency of Congress, and then proposed a 'scheme' for obtaining the just dues of the army:

> "This war must have shown to all, but to military men in particular, the weakness of republics, and the exertions the army has been able to make by being under a proper head."

Nicola had lost faith in the ability of a republic to govern fairly. It believed that the army, under Washington's leadership, had succeeded in spite of the incompetence of the Congress:

> "It will, I believe, be uncontroverted that the same abilities which have led us, through difficulties apparently unsurmountable by human power, to victory and glory, those qualities that have merited and obtained the universal esteem and veneration of an army, would be most likely to conduct and direct us in the smoother paths of peace."

---

118 Treaty of Paris, ending the American Revolution September 3, 1783 - http://theamericanrevolution.org/hdocs/paristreaty.asp

Nicola was urging Washington to take control of the government.

"Some people have so connected the ideas of tyranny and monarchy as to find it very difficult to separate them, it may therefore be requisite to give the head of such a constitution as I propose, some title apparently more moderate, but if all other things are once adjusted I believe strong arguments might he produced for admitting the title of King, which I conceive would be attended with some material advantage."

Nicola was prepared to choose a king for America, and proposed that that king be George Washington.

"Republican bigots will certainly consider my opinions as heterodox, (not in accord with established doctrine) and the maintainer thereof as meriting fire and fagots, I have therefore hitherto kept them within my own breast. By freely communicating them to your Excellency I am persuaded I run no risk, and that, tho disapproved of, I need not apprehend their ever being disclosed to my prejudice."

Washington responded to Nicola's offer to lead a campaign to make him King as follows:[119]

"Sir:

"With a mixture of great surprise and astonishment I have read with attention the Sentiments you have submitted to my perusal. Be assured Sir, no occurrence in the course of the War, has given me more painful sensations than your information of there being such ideas existing in the Army as you have expressed, and I must view with abhorrence, and reprehend with severity. For the present, the communication of them will rest in my own bosom, unless some further' agitation of the matter, shall make a disclosure necessary."

Washington promised to keep Nicola's proposal a secret, unless something happened to force him to reveal it. Then, instead of attacking Nicola for his suggestion that he turn against the

[119] Washington's Letter to Col. Lewis Nicola - http://etext.lib.virginia.edu/etcbin/toccer-new2?id=WasFi24.xml&images=images/modeng&data=/texts/english/modeng/parsed&tag=public&part=282&division=div1

Congress, he modestly suggests that he, Washington, might have somehow encouraged such a reprehensible suggestion:

> "I am much at a loss to conceive what part of my conduct could have given encouragement to an address which to me seems big with the greatest mischief that can befall my Country. If I am not deceived in the knowledge of myself, you could not have found a person to whom your schemes are more disagreeable;"

Then Washington points out that he, more than any man alive, was concerned for the soldiers and wanted justice done for their sacrifices for the country:

> "at the same time in justice to my own feelings I must add, that no Man possesses a more sincere wish to see ample justice done to the Army than I do, and as far as my powers and influence, in a constitutional way extend, they shall be employed to the utmost of my abilities to effect it, should there be any occasion. Let me conjure you then, if you have any regard for your Country, concern for yourself or posterity, or respect for me, to banish these thoughts from your Mind, and never communicate, as from yourself, or any one else, a sentiment of the like Nature."

Meanwhile, in London, Cornwallis' defeat at Yorktown and defeats at sea at the hands of the French led to the downfall of Lord North's ministry. On February 27, 1782, the House of Commons voted against further prosecuting the war in America and passed a bill authorizing the Crown to make peace with the former colonies.

Peace talks began in Paris on April 12, with Benjamin Franklin as the only commissioner representing the United States but with John Jay, John Adams and Henry Laurens arriving later. A preliminary Peace Treaty was signed on November 30, 1782, which recognized the independence of the United States, set the boundaries of the country, guaranteed fishing rights, validated debts due creditors of either country, and promised that the States would fully restore the rights and property of the Loyalists.

[120]

Unfinished portrait – John Jay, John Adams, Benjamin Franklin, Henry Laurens and Franklin's grandson, William Temple Franklin, secretary to the US delegation

With the signing of the final peace treaty on 3 September 1783, Britain marked her first major loss of colonial possession as she recognized America's independence. The treaty also made navigation of the Mississippi River open to all signatories, which included France, Spain and Holland, returned Florida to Spain and Senegal to France. The United States also gain fishing rights off Newfoundland. [121]

[120] Benjamin West Portrait of Treaty of Paris signing http://www.americanrevwar.homestead.com/files/TREATY.HTM

[121] Ibid -American Revolution – Treaty of Paris

Chapter 12
Angry Patriots Threaten a Military Coup

During this period in which there had been no peace treaty but no military battles, the discontent continued to smolder. Washington expressed concern over a measure proposed by Congress to reduce the size of his army scheduled for January 1, 1783.

He knew that the men would have no money even to return to their homes "after having spent the flower of their days and many of them their patrimonies, in establishing the freedom and independence of their country, and suffered everything that human nature is capable of enduring this side of death" only to be rewarded with the "ingratitude of the public" while drowning in debt.

Washington's Headquarters at Newburgh, N.Y.[122]

On the 10th of March, 1783, while in Winter Quarters in Newburgh, N.Y., twelve miles north of West Point, an anonymous paper was circulated through the camp. It called for a meeting at eleven o'clock the next day of general and field officers, of an officer from each company, and a delegate from the medical staff to consider a letter from their representatives in Philadelphia that had just been received. The meeting was for the army officers to adopt measures to "redress the grievances" they had with Congress.

[122] NY State Parks - Washington's Headquarters, Newburgh, New York-April 1782-Aug. 1793- http://nysparks.state.ny.us/cgi-bin/cgiwrap/nysparks/historic.cgi?p+29

Another anonymous letter circulated in the camp the following day which claimed to be from a "fellow-soldier" who had "shared in their toils and mingled in their dangers, and who till very lately had believed in the justice of his country."[123]

The letter was designed to incite the soldiers to anger and action:

> "Can you consent to wade through the vile mire of dependency, and owe the miserable remnant of that life to charity, which has hitherto been spent in honor? If you can, go, and carry with you the jest of Tories, and the scorn of Whigs; the ridicule, and what is worse, the pity of the world!
>
> "Go, starve and be forgotten! But if your spirits should revolt at this; if you have sense enough to discover and spirit sufficient to oppose tyranny, under whatever garb it may assume, whether it be the plain coat of republicanism, or the splendid robe of royalty; if you have yet learned to discriminate between a people and a cause, between men and principles; awake, attend to your situation and redress yourselves! If the present moment be lost, every future effort is in vain; and your threats then will be as empty as your entreaties now."[124]

The following day Washington issued a General Order[125] squashing the ad hoc meeting, called by the unknown activist:

> "The Commander in Chief having heard that a General meeting of the officers of the Army was proposed to be held this day at the Newbuilding in an anonymous paper which was circulated yesterday by some unknown person conceives (altho he is fully persuaded that the good sense of the officers would induce them to pay very little attention to such an irregular invitation) his duty as well as the reputation and true interest of the Army requires his disapprobation of such disorderly proceedings, at the same time he requests the General and Field officers with one officer from each company and a proper

---

[123] Life of Washington, by Washington Irving, Vol. 4, page 466

[124] Life of Washington, by Washington Irving, Vol. 4, page 467

[125] Washington's Letters – March 11, 1783 – General Orders - http://etext.lib.virginia.edu/etcbin/toccer-new2?id=WasFi26.xml&images=images/modeng&data=/texts/english/modeng/parsed&tag=public&part=240&division=div1

representative of the staff of the Army will assemble at 12 o'clock on Saturday next at the Newbuilding to hear the report of the Committee of the Army to Congress.

"After mature deliberation they will devise what further measures ought to be adopted as most rational and best calculated to attain the just and important object in view. The senior officer in Rank present will be pleased to preside and report the result of the Deliberations to the Commander in Chief."

The next day, another anonymous letter was circulated, responding to the Commander in Chief's General Order, but giving it what would be called today a "spin" that attempted to put Washington on the side of the author of the anonymous letter while subtly accusing him of not actually doing anything for the soldiers:

"Till now the commander in chief has regarded the steps you have taken for redress with good wishes alone; his ostensible silence has authorized your meetings and his private opinion sanctified your claims. Had he disliked the object in view, would not the same sense of duty which forbade you from meeting on the third day of the week, have forbidden you from meeting on the seventh?"[126]

The "anonymous" letter writers were later identified as Colonel Walter Stewart, the original organizer of the attempted coup who had gotten the support of an old antagonist of Washington's, General Horatio Gates, and General Gates' Aide de Camp, Major John Armstrong, Jr., who penned the letters.

By the time the meeting was held on March 15, the officers were assembled. Washington had previously sent for the officers, one at a time, in private and talked to them about the "loss of character of the whole army" that would result from accusing and emotionally charged resolutions. He called General Gates to the chair and then rose and apologized for appearing at the meeting, which he had not intended to do when he issued the order changing the meeting date.

The statements made in the anonymous letters made it necessary for Washington to voice his views. He had, in fact,

---

[126] Life of Washington – by Washington Irving – Vol. 4, page 470

written down his views and hesitated as he prepared to read to the belligerent officers. He paused and fumbled for his glasses, which most of the officers had never seen him wear, and said, apologetically:

> "Gentlemen, you will permit me to put on my spectacles, for I have not only grown gray, but almost blind, in the service of my country."

One officer, Major Samuel Shaw of Massachusetts, wrote in his memoirs of Washington's opening comment:

> "There was something so natural, so unaffected in this appeal, as rendered it superior to the most studied oratory; it forced its way to the heart, and you might see sensibility moisten every eye.
>
> "Happy for America that she has a Patriot army, and equally so that Washington is its leader. I rejoice in the opportunity I have had of seeing this great man in a variety of situations – calm and intrepid when the battle raged; patient and persevering under the pressure of misfortune; moderate and possessing himself in the full career of victory. Great as these qualifications deservedly render him, he never appeared to me more truly so than at the assembly we have been speaking of. On other occasions he has been supported by the exertions of an army and the countenance of his friends; but on this he stood single and alone. There was no saying where the passions of the army which were not a little inflamed, might lead; but it was generally allowed that further forbearance was dangerous and moderation had ceased to be a virtue.
>
> "Under these circumstances he appeared, not at the head of his troops, but, as it were, in opposition to them; and for a dreadful moment the interests of the army and its general seemed to be in competition! He spoke – every doubt was dispelled, and the tide of Patriotism rolled again in its wonted course. Illustrious man! What he says of the army may with equal justice be applied to his own character: 'Had this day been wanting, the world had never seen the last stage of perfection to which human nature is capable of attaining.'"[127]

---

[127] The Life of Washington, by Washington Irving –Vol. 4, page 475 quoted from Quincy's *Memoir of Major Shaw*

The anger of the soldiers was understandable, but the cause of Congress' neglect was not willful. It was caused by defects in the Articles of Confederation which gave the Congress the responsibility for the army, but did not allow it to have the authority to tax anyone to pay for it. At the time of these events were taking place, (later called the "Newburgh Conspiracy" because Washington's headquarters were in Newburgh, New York) the new American nation was financially bankrupt. It owed $6 million and had only $125,000.

Standing among his officers, who were now ready to listen to what he had to say, Washington read his speech,[128] which said, in part:

> "By an anonymous summons, an attempt has been made to convene you together; how inconsistent with the rules of propriety! how unmilitary! and how subversive of all order and discipline, let the good sense of the Army decide.
>
> "In the moment of this Summons, another anonymous production was sent into circulation, addressed more to the feelings and passions, than to the reason and judgment of the Army.
>
> "The author of the piece, is entitled to much credit for the goodness of his Pen and I could wish he had as much credit for the rectitude of his heart, for, as men see thro' different optics, (eyes) and are induced by the reflecting faculties of the mind, to use different means, to attain the same end, the author of the Address, should have had more charity, than to mark for suspicion, the man who should recommend moderation and longer forbearance, or, in other words, who should not think as he thinks, and act as he advises.
>
> "But he had another plan in view, in which candor and liberality of sentiment, regard to justice, and love of Country, have no part; and he was right, to insinuate the darkest suspicion, to effect the blackest designs."

---

[128] Washington's Speech to his officers, March 15, 1783 - http://etext.lib.virginia.edu/etcbin/toccer-new2?id=WasFi26.xml&images=images/modeng&data=/texts/english/modeng/parsed&tag=public&part=252&division=div1

The author of the anonymous letter, Washington observed, intended to take advantage of the passions" of the officers without giving them "time for cool, deliberative thinking." He then explained "upon what principles" he had opposed the "irregular and hasty meeting" scheduled for March 11:

"'The way is plain,' says the anonymous addresser. 'If War continues, remove into the unsettled country; there establish yourselves, and leave an ungrateful Country to defend itself.' But who are they to defend? Our Wives, our Children, our Farms, and other property which we leave behind us? Or, in this state of hostile separation, are we to take the two first (the latter cannot be removed), to perish in a Wilderness, with hunger, cold and nakedness?

"'If Peace takes place, never sheath your Swords.' says he until you have obtained full and ample justice;' this dreadful alternative, of either deserting our Country in the extremest hour of her distress, or turning our Arms against it, (which is the apparent object, unless Congress can be compelled into instant compliance) has something so shocking in it, that humanity revolts at the idea.

"My God! What can this writer have in view, by recommending such measures? Can he be a friend to the Army? Can he be a friend to this Country? Rather, is he not an insidious Foe? Some Emissary, perhaps, from New York, plotting the ruin of both, by sowing the seeds of discord and separation between the Civil and Military powers of the Continent?"

Washington did not just scold. He held out hope for a solution, based on his "decided opinion" that the Congress did appreciate the "merits and sufferings" of the soldiers and would, eventually "do it complete justice" when they were able to "discover and establish funds for this purpose."

Like all other large bodies, he reminded his officers, in Congress there were:

"a variety of different Interests to reconcile, their deliberations are slow. Why then should we distrust them? and, in consequence of that distrust, adopt measures, which may cast a shade over that glory which, has been so justly acquired; and tarnish the reputation of an Army which is celebrated thro' all

Europe, for its fortitude and Patriotism? and for what is this done? to bring the object we seek nearer? No! most certainly, in my opinion, it will cast it at a greater distance.

"For myself (and I take no merit in giving the assurance, being induced to it from principles of gratitude, veracity and justice), a grateful sense of the confidence you have ever placed in me, a recollection of the chearful assistance, and prompt obedience I have experienced from you, under every vicissitude of Fortune, and the sincere affection I feel for an Army, I have so long had the honor to Command, will oblige me to declare, in this public and solemn manner, that, in the attainment of complete justice for all your toils and dangers, and in the gratification of every wish, so far as may be done consistently with the great duty I owe my Country, and those powers we are bound to respect, you may freely command my Services to the utmost of my abilities.

"While I give you these assurances, and pledge myself in the most unequivocal manner, to exert whatever ability I am possessed of, in your favor, let me entreat you, Gentlemen, on your part, not to take any measures, which, viewed in the calm light of reason, will lessen the dignity, and sully the glory you have hitherto maintained.

"Let me request you to rely on the plighted faith of your Country, and place a full confidence in the purity of the intentions of Congress; that, previous to your dissolution as an Army they will cause all your accounts to be fairly liquidated, as directed in their resolutions, which were published to you two days ago, and that they will adopt the most effectual measures in their power, to render ample justice to you, for your faithful and meritorious Services.

"And let me conjure you, in the name of our common Country, as you value your own sacred honor, as you respect the rights of humanity, and as you regard the Military and National character of America, to express your utmost horror and detestation of the man who wishes, under any specious pretences, to overturn the liberties of our Country, and who wickedly attempts to open the flood Gates of Civil discord, and deluge our rising Empire in Blood.

"By thus determining, and thus acting, you will pursue the plain and direct road to the attainment of your wishes. You will defeat the insidious designs of our Enemies, who are compelled to resort from open force to secret Artifice. You will give one more distinguished proof of unexampled Patriotism and patient virtue, rising superior to the pressure of the most complicated sufferings; And you will, by the dignity of your conduct, afford occasion for Posterity to say, when speaking of the glorious example you have exhibited to mankind, 'had this day been wanting, the World had never seen the last stage of perfection to which human nature is capable of attaining.'"

When Washington left the meeting to allow his officers to discuss the issue and make their decisions, "a resolution was moved by the warm-hearted (General) Knox and seconded by General Putnam and passed unanimously, assuring him that the officers "reciprocated his sincerity of which the human heart is capable."

Then followed resolutions declaring that "no circumstances of distress or danger should induce a conduct calculated to sully the reputation and glory acquired at the price of their blood and eight years' faithful services; that they continued to have an unshaken confidence in the Congress and their country; and that the commander in chief should be requested to write to the President of Congress, earnestly entreating a speedy decision on the late address forwarded by a committee of the army."[129]

Washington's private feelings of exasperation with Congress surfaced a few days later in a letter to his cousin Lund Washington, manager of Mt. Vernon. He wrote:[130]

"The good sense, the virtue, and patient forbearance of the army, on this, as upon every other trying occasion which has happened to call them into action, has again triumphed: and appear'd with more lustre than ever. But if the States will not

---

[129] Resolutions by Washington's officers -Life of Washington, by Washington Irving, Vol 4 Page 475-476

[130] George Washington's letter to Lund Washington- March 19, 1783 http://wyllie.lib.virginia.edu:8086/perl/toccer-new?id=WasFi26.xml&images=images/modeng&data=/texts/english/modeng/parsed&tag=public&part=270&division=div1

furnish the supplies required by Congress, thereby enabling the Superintendant of Finance to feed, clothe, and pay the army; if they suppose the war can be carried on without money, or that money can be borrowed without permanent funds to pay the interest of it; if they have no regard to justice, because it is attended with expence; if gratitude to men, who have rescued them from the jaws of danger and brought them to the haven of Independence and Peace, is to subside, as danger is removed; if the sufferings of the army, who have borne, and forborne more than any other class of men in the United States; expending their health; and many of them their all, in an unremitted service of near eight years in the field, encountering hunger, cold and nakedness, are to be forgotten; if it is presumed there is no bounds to the patience of the army; or that when peace takes place, their claims for pay due, and rewards promised may die with the military non-existence of its member.

"If such, I say, should be the sentiments of the States; and that their conduct, or the conduct of some, does but too well warrant the conclusion, well may another anonymous addresser step forward, and with more effect than the last did, say with him, 'You have arms in your hands, do justice to yourselves, and never sheath the sword, 'till you have obtained it.'

"How far men, who labour under the pressure of accumulated distress, and are irritated by a belief that they are treated with neglect, ingratitude, and injustice in the extreme, might be worked upon by designing men, is worthy of very serious consideration. But justice, policy, yea common Sense, must tell every man that the creditors of the continent, cannot receive payments unless funds are provided for it, and that our national character, if these are much longer neglected, must be stamped with indelible infamy in every Nation of the world where the fact is known.'"

In a letter sent to each of the State governors, on June 8, 1783 Washington shared concerns and his vision for the future, touching on his concern for the weakness of the central government that existed under the Articles of Confederation and urging just treatment of the veterans of the war:[131]

> "If the resources of the Continent could have been properly drawn forth, that the distresses and disappointments which have very often occurred, have in too many instances, resulted more from a want of energy, in the Continental Government, than a deficiency of means in the particular States."

For the first time, as the war wound down and the inaction on the part of the Congress seemed to increase, Washington put his finger on the problem. The existing form of government was ineffective because it lacked an effective executive with the power to enforce Congress' resolutions:

> "That the inefficiency of measures, arising from the want of an adequate authority in the Supreme Power, from a partial compliance with the Requisitions of Congress in some of the States, and from a failure of punctuality in others, while it tended to damp the zeal of those which were more willing to exert themselves; served also to accumulate the expenses of the War, and to frustrate the best concerted Plans."

While Congress had no money, it did have control over a large chunk of unsettled land west of the Allegheny Mountains. On June 11, 1783, Washington wrote to the president of the Congress forwarding a "Petition from a large number of Officers of the Army in behalf of themselves, and such other Officers and Soldiers of the Continental Army" to settle for land, rather than money. Settling the Western lands with army veterans, Washington wrote, [132] would "give security to our frontiers."

Shortly thereafter on June 24, about 80 soldiers marched on Philadelphia from Lancaster, Pennsylvania to "obtain justice" from Congress and the State. Congress quickly fled the city.

---

[131] Washington's Circular Letter to Governor of the States-June 8, 1783 - http://wyllie.lib.virginia.edu:8086/perl/toccer-new?id=WasFi26.xml&images=images/modeng&data=/texts/english/modeng/parsed&tag=public&part=511&division=div1

[132] Washington's letter to Congress – June 11, 1783 - http://wyllie.lib.virginia.edu:8086/perl/toccer-new?id=WasFi27.xml&images=images/modeng&data=/texts/english/modeng/parsed&tag=public&part=19&division=div1

A few months later, on September 3, 1783, the Treaty of Paris, written largely by Benjamin Franklin was finally signed[133] and the war was officially over. Franklin's successful diplomacy in obtaining Britain's signature on the treaty was a remarkable achievement. Britain not only agreed to American independence, but ceded considerable territory, access to international waterways and fisheries along the Atlantic seaboard.

Washington Resigns his Commission by John Trumbull [134]

On December 23, 1783, to the astonishment of all of Europe, Commander in chief George Washington, who could have easily led a military coup to seize dictatorial power over the people of the United States of America, resigned his commission with a brief statement which began: [135]

> "Mr. President: The great events on which my resignation depended having at length taken place; I have now

---

[133] The Treaty of Paris, signed September 3, 1783 - http://theamericanrevolution.org/hdocs/paristreaty.asp

[134] Picture – Washington Resigns his Commission – John Trumbull 1824 - http://xroads.virginia.edu/~CAP/ROTUNDA/george_1.html

[135] Text of George Washington's speech resigning his commission – December 23, 1780 - http://etext.lib.virginia.edu/etcbin/toccer-new2?id=WasFi27.xml&images=images/modeng&data=/texts/english/modeng/parsed&tag=public&part=320&division=div1

the honor of offering my sincere Congratulations to Congress and of presenting myself before them to surrender into their hands the trust committed to me, and to claim the indulgence of retiring from the Service of my Country.

"Happy in the confirmation of our Independence and Sovereignty, and pleased with the opportunity afforded the United States of becoming a respectable Nation, I resign with satisfaction the Appointment I accepted with diffidence. A diffidence in my abilities to accomplish so arduous a task, which however was superseded by a confidence in the rectitude of our Cause, the support of the Supreme Power of the Union, and the patronage of Heaven.

"The Successful termination of the War has verified the most sanguine expectations, and my gratitude for the interposition of Providence, and the assistance I have received from my Countrymen, increases with every review of the momentous Contest."

With that, Washington happily retired to Mount Vernon to the country life he loved, content in the thought that he would spend the rest of his life in the bosom of his family, doing the things he loved best, managing his lands and enjoying his friends and family.

That was not to be.

Chapter 13
"Critical Period" Prompts Move To "A More Perfect Union"

1783 Map –Conflicting Territorial Claims[136]

Many historians called the six years from the defeat of Cornwallis in 1781 to 1787, when the Convention was called to amend the Articles of Confederation, the "critical period."

The 13 colonies became independent states in a confederation of states with no executive authority, but they held title to a vast empire from the seaboard settlements to the Mississippi River. At primarily Maryland's insistence, the Articles of Confederation were not ratified until the larger states that had territory which extended from the Atlantic Ocean to the Mississippi River ceded their unsettled territories to the federation for future states.

[136] History of the United States- pub. 1913 –Bourne and Benton, page 232

The Revolution ended with a Congress which had no taxing power and no executive authority but had several major problems to solve: fair treatment of veterans, many of whom were wounded; trade with other nations; war loans from other nations to pay and almost no money in the treasury; governing the Western territories and what the policy on slavery would be in the Western Territories.

As soon as the treaty of peace was signed, the British Government closed American trade with the West Indies. Only ships built and owned by British subjects were allowed to buy or sell in the Caribbean Island settlements. That was a serious blow to the economy of the new United States of America. Efforts to make a new commercial trading treaty with Great Britain were denied on the ground that America's general government was powerless to force the individual states to observe the agreement. The Treaty of Paris required the United States to restore the rights and property of the Loyalists, which several states simply refused to do. As a result, Britain refused to withdraw troops from posts in the Northwest Territories until the states were forced to abide by the treaty requirements concerning Loyalists.

Spain, also, would make no treaty unless duties were paid to the Spanish Colony of Louisiana through which the Mississippi flowed for 100 miles, and the Tripoli pirates held American sailors in captivity for a ransom that Congress could not pay. As historian John Fisk put it in *The Critical Period of American History,* "Our diplomacy failed because our weakness had been proclaimed to the world."

In the year the *Declaration of Independence* was signed, 1776, a book was written in Britain by Adam Smith entitled *An Inquiry into the Nature and Causes of the Wealth of Nations* which explained the connection between a nation's empire-building and its economy:

> "In the system of laws which has been established for the management of our American and West Indian colonies, the interest of the home-consumer (in Britain) has been sacrificed to that of the producer with a more extravagant profusion than in all our other commercial regulations. A great empire has been established for the sole purpose of raising up a **nation of customers** who should be obliged to buy from the shops of our

different producers all the goods with which these could supply them." [137]

Britain's policies of imposing regulations and taxes on the colonies were designed to force them, for example, to purchase tea from England rather than from nations that grew the product, to provide taxes for the British Government and customers for British merchants and manufacturers, while maintaining low prices for the raw materials from the states. The goal of this kind of controlled trade was to increase the wealth of the mother country and force the colonies to remain dependent consumers of the mother country. With the Treaty of Paris, the war was over, but the aftermath of the war seemed to be destroying the nation's economy.

While independence led to freedom from the British Navigation Acts, new laws by the House of Commons also closed U.S. trade with the islands off the West Indies, once a major trading partner of the colonies. In 1781 the new nation owed $40 million and was near bankruptcy. Congress appointed Robert Morris, signer of the Declaration of Independence and the financier of the Revolution[138] who repeatedly furnished the funds or supplies to keep Washington's soldiers eating, to serve as Superintendent of Finance.

Because Congress had no power to tax, and the States were not honoring their commitments, the Congress printed paper money that was worthless, and there was runaway inflation. Every effort Morris made to pay the nation's debts and stop the printing of worthless money that was destroying the nation's credit was ignored. He proposed a land tax, a poll tax, an excise tax and a house tax to help generate revenue for paying debts, but the states wouldn't agree. On January 24, 1783, facing an impossible situation, Morris told Congress he was would resign.

It was at this critical point that George Washington, wrote a "Circular Letter," that is, a letter to the governors of each of the 13 States expressing both his vision for the new nation and his

---

[137] The Wealth of Nations – by Adam Smith –Book IV, Chapter 8-Conclusion of the Mercantile System - http://www.econlib.org/library/Smith/smWN.html

[138] The Liberty Story –Robert Morris- http://www.libertystory.net/LSACTIONROBERTMORRIS.htm

concerns for its survival.[139] He first assured the governors of the states that while he had the "honor" of serving as Commander in Chief during the war, he now looked forward to retirement from public service and putting its affairs "into the hands of Congress."

He planned,

> "to return to that domestic retirement, which, it is well known, I left with the greatest reluctance, a Retirement, for which I have never ceased to sigh through a long and painful absence, and in which (remote from the noise and trouble of the World) I meditate to pass the remainder of life in a state of undisturbed repose."

Then he described the great treasure and opportunities for the future that lay before the infant nation:

> "The Citizens of America, placed in the most enviable condition, as the sole Lords and Proprietors of a vast Tract of Continent, comprehending all the various soils and climates of the World, and abounding with all the necessaries and conveniences of life, are now by the late satisfactory pacification, acknowledged to be possessed of absolute freedom and Independency.
>
> "They are, from this period, to be considered as the Actors on a most conspicuous Theatre, which seems to be peculiarly designated by Providence for the display of human greatness and felicity; Here, they are not only surrounded with every thing which can contribute to the completion of private and domestic enjoyment, but Heaven has crowned all its other blessings, by giving a fairer opportunity for political happiness, than any other Nation has ever been favored with.
>
> "Nothing can illustrate these observations more forcibly, than a recollection of the happy conjuncture of times and circumstances, under which our Republic assumed its rank among the Nations.
>
> "The foundation of our Empire was not laid in the gloomy age of Ignorance and Superstition, but at an Epocha

---

[139] Washington's Circular letter to the States, June 8, 1783 - http://etext.lib.virginia.edu/etcbin/toccer-new2?id=WasFi26.xml&images=images/modeng&data=/texts/english/modeng/parsed&tag=public&part=511&division=div1

when the rights of mankind were better understood and more clearly defined, than at any former period."

Washington reminded the governors that "Treasures of knowledge" were available to them from "Philosophers, Sages and Legislatures, through a long succession of years" and:

"The free exchange of information through letters and the extension of commerce, the "progressive refinement of Manners, the growing liberality of sentiment, and above all, the pure and benign light of Revelation, have had ameliorating influence on mankind and increased the blessings of Society.

"At this auspicious period, the United States came into existence as a Nation, and if their Citizens should not be completely free and happy, the fault will be entirely their own.

"Such is our situation, and such are our prospects: but notwithstanding the cup of blessing is thus reached out to us, notwithstanding happiness is ours, if we have a disposition to seize the occasion and make it our own.

On the one hand, Washington could see a great future ahead for America. Yet, there was also a very great danger. Americans would have to choose whether they would be:

"respectable and prosperous, or contemptible and miserable as a Nation; This is the time of their political probation, this is the moment when the eyes of the whole World are turned upon them, this is the moment to establish or ruin their national Character forever, this is the favorable moment to give such a tone to our Federal Government, as will enable it to answer the ends of its institution, or this may be the ill-fated moment for relaxing the powers of the Union, annihilating the cement of the Confederation, and exposing us to become the sport of European politics, which may play one State against another to prevent their growing importance, and to serve their own interested purposes.

"For, according to the system of Policy the States shall adopt at this moment, they will stand or fall, and by their confirmation or lapse, it is yet to be decided, whether the Revolution must ultimately be considered as a blessing or a curse: a blessing or a curse, not to the present age alone, for with our fate will the destiny of unborn Millions be involved."

Washington was very well aware that the nation had entered into a very critical period. It could go either way. He felt compelled to speak out and warn the governors:

"With this conviction of the importance of the present Crisis, silence in me would be a crime; I will therefore speak to your Excellency, the language of freedom and of sincerity, without disguise; I am aware, however, that those who differ from me in political sentiment, may perhaps remark, I am stepping out of the proper line of my duty, and they may possibly ascribe to arrogance or ostentation, what I know is alone the result of the purest intention, but the rectitude of my own heart, which disdains such unworthy motives, the part I have hitherto acted in life, the determination I have formed, of not taking any share in public business hereafter, the ardent desire I feel, and shall continue to manifest, of quietly enjoying in private life, after all the toils of War, the benefits of a wise and liberal Government, will, I flatter myself, sooner or later convince my Countrymen, that I could have no sinister views in delivering with so little reserve, the opinions contained in this Address.

"There are four things, which I humbly conceive, are essential to the well being, I may even venture to say, to the existence of the United States as an Independent Power:

"1st. An indissoluble Union of the States under one Federal Head.

"2dly. A Sacred regard to Public Justice.

"3dly. The adoption of a proper Peace Establishment, and

"4thly. The prevalence of that pacific and friendly Disposition, among the People of the United States, which will induce them to forget their local prejudices and policies, to make those mutual concessions which are requisite to the general prosperity, and in some instances, to sacrifice their individual advantages to the interest of the Community.

"These are the pillars on which the glorious Fabrick of our Independency and National Character must be supported; Liberty is the Basis, and whoever would dare to sap the foundation, or overturn the Structure, under whatever specious pretexts he may attempt it, will merit the bitterest execration, and the severest punishment which can be inflicted by his injured Country.

"On the three first Articles I will make a few observations, leaving the last to the good sense and serious consideration of those immediately concerned."

Washington not only recognized the absolute necessity for unity of purpose among the citizens, but also knew that the nation's enemies would do everything in their power to foment distrust and contention among the various states:

"Under the first head, altho' it may not be necessary or proper for me in this place to enter into a particular disquisition of the principles of the Union, and to take up the great question which has been frequently agitated, whether it be expedient and requisite for the States to delegate a larger proportion of Power to Congress, or not, Yet it will be a part of my duty, and that of every true Patriot, to assert without reserve, and to insist upon the following positions, That unless the States will suffer Congress to exercise those prerogatives, they are undoubtedly invested with by the Constitution, every thing must very rapidly tend to Anarchy and confusion.

"It is indispensable to the happiness of the individual States, that there should be lodged somewhere, a Supreme Power to regulate and govern the general concerns of the Confederated Republic, without which the Union cannot be of long duration.

Washington had experienced personally during the long war the trials and dangers attending the lack of any real executive or taxing power under a confederation. He strongly recommended:

"That there must be a faithful and pointed compliance on the part of every State, with the late proposals and demands of Congress, or the most fatal consequences will ensue, That whatever measures have a tendency to dissolve the Union, or contribute to violate or lessen the Sovereign Authority, ought to be considered as hostile to the Liberty and Independency of America, and the Authors of them treated accordingly, and lastly, that unless we can be enabled by the concurrence of the States, to participate of the fruits of the Revolution, and enjoy the essential benefits of Civil Society, under a form of Government so free and uncorrupted, so happily guarded against the danger of oppression, as has been devised and adopted by the Articles of Confederation, it will be a subject of regret, that so much blood and treasure have been lavished for no purpose, that so many sufferings have been encountered without a compensation, and that so many sacrifices have been made in vain."

Without "the Spirit of the Union," Washington warned, "we cannot exist as an Independent Power." The very independence of the new nation depended upon that unity of purpose:

"It is only in our united Character as an Empire, that our Independence is acknowledged, that our power can be regarded, or our Credit supported among Foreign Nations. The Treaties of the European Powers with the United States of America, will have no validity on a dissolution of the Union. We shall be left nearly in a state of Nature, or we may find by our own unhappy experience, that there is a natural and necessary progression, from the extreme of anarchy to the extreme of Tyranny; and that arbitrary power is most easily established on the ruins of Liberty abused to licentiousness."

The breadth of Washington's vision for the new nation of liberty, unity, commerce, education and justice also included a warning that the current state of near anarchy would lead to tyranny if not addressed. Three years later leaders of the states would meet to write a new constitution designed to solve the problems with which the new nation was afflicted.

Washington ended his letter to the Governors with a prayer for the nation he risked everything he had - time, property, creature comforts, his very life -to help found. He had survived eight years of war, treason of generals, watched his personal fortune dwindle, stopped a military coup by his own soldiers – and, it appeared, it might all fail if the growing spirit of contention continued. He wrote:

"I now make it my earnest prayer, that God would have you, and the State over which you preside, in his holy protection, that he would incline the hearts of the Citizens to cultivate a spirit of subordination and obedience to Government, to entertain a brotherly affection and love for one another, for their fellow Citizens of the United States at large, and particularly for their brethren who have served in the Field;

"And finally, that he would most graciously be pleased to dispose us all, to do Justice, to love mercy, and to demean ourselves with that Charity, humility and pacific temper of mind, which were the Characteristicks of the Divine Author of our blessed Religion, and without an humble imitation of whose example in these things, we can never hope to be a happy Nation."

In an era in which often the only book in many American homes was the Bible, in this final paragraph Washington alluded to a passage in the Book of Micah, in the Old Testament. The governors would understand his meaning through the partial quote of the prophet Micah, who lived in the 8th century B.C. during a very similar time of violence, contention, rampant materialism and lying. Micah told the rebellious people, that their God had shown them what was good and asked, "and what doth the Lord require of thee, but to do justly and love mercy and walk humbly with thy God?"

The phrase to "do justice" or "do justly" is defined in dictionaries of that era as living "in a just manner; in conformity to law, justice or propriety; by right; honestly, fairly; accurately, exactly."

The early dictionaries defined the phrase to "love mercy" as "the disposition to overlook injuries, or to treat an offender better than he deserves, to forgive an obligation, out of compassion for the offender or debtor." To "do justice" is the opposite of "demanding justice," which usually leads to disunity and conflict. To love mercy, in a person's actions, is the opposite of condemning, ridiculing or being critical of others.

The nation would not succeed, nor would it even survive, Washington believed, without unity and honesty among a people who would "do justice" and be compassionate about the failures of their neighbors.

When the colonies declared their independence from England and formed one nation, that union was to be a perpetual union. That, Washington believed, could only happen if the people abandoned their petty jealousies and regional conflicts.

Chapter 14
Post-War Anarchy Looms

Seventy-eight years later, as the Southern States threatened to secede from the Union, the new Republican President Abraham Lincoln declared, as did George Washington, that the Union of the States was perpetual:[140]

President Abraham Lincoln[141]

> "In legal contemplation the Union is perpetual confirmed by the history of the Union itself. The Union is much older than the Constitution. It was formed, in fact, by the Articles of Association in 1774. It was matured and continued by the Declaration of Independence. It was further matured, and the faith of all the then thirteen States expressly plighted and engaged that it should be perpetual, by the Articles of Confederation in 1778. And finally, in 1787, one of the declared objects for ordaining and establishing the Constitution was 'to form a more perfect Union.'"

---

[140] Yale Avalon Project – Abraham Lincoln's First Inaugural address - http://www.yale.edu/lawweb/avalon/presiden/inaug/lincoln1.htm

[141] White House Biography–President Abraham Lincoln - http://www.whitehouse.gov/history/presidents/al16.html

Some, without fanfare, took action to open up trade, which was being strangled by the British. In 1784, Robert Morris sent his ship *The Empress of China* to Canton, China.[142] *The Empress* carried lead, 2,600 animal skins, fine camlet cloth, cotton, and a few barrels of pepper.[143] It also carried 30 tons of ginseng, a root that grew wild in North America. The Chinese valued ginseng for its healing powers.

Morris' agent, Samuel Shaw of Boston, traded those items for tea, nankeen (Chinese cotton), tableware, silk, and spice, all eagerly sought in America, and opened up trade with China.

Mt. Vernon[144]

As Washington watched the Potomac River flow past Mt. Vernon, and as he traveled on and near other rivers, he had a vision of using the Potomac River as a trade route to the interior of the nearly roadless continent. Upon returning to Mt. Vernon after resigning his commission, in March of 1785, he hosted the Mt. Vernon Conference in his home[145] where commissioners from

---

[142] Robert Morris' *Empress of China* - http://www.raken.com/american_wealth/shipping_merchants/china_traders1.asp
[143] Columbia University –Cargo of *Empress of China* - http://www.columbia.edu/itc/eacp/webcourse/chinaworkbook/for_pol/ch_trade.htm
[144] Mt. Vernon –Washington's Home for 45 years - http://www.mountvernon.org/mtour/one.asp
[145] National Park Service-Mt. Vernon Conference , March 1785 - http://www.nps.gov/thst/mtver.htm

Virginia and Maryland met to consider a combined effort to make the Potomac River navigable.

Eight years of war convinced George Washington that a good road and transportation network were important for the nation's defense system. This was the beginning of efforts to create a federal transportation network that eventually led to federally financed interstate highways in America.

An August 22, 1785, letter to James McHenry[146] clearly indicated that Washington felt a stronger central government was required to "establish a national character, or be considered as on a respectable footing by the powers of Europe." McHenry apparently objected to a stronger central government for fear it would enrich some of the states more than others.

"I am sorry I cannot agree with you," Washington wrote. "...We are either a united people under one head, and for federal purposes; or we are thirteen independent sovereignties, eternally counteracting each other."

George Washington, while enjoying his return to Mt. Vernon was getting more and more concerned about whether the nation he helped form would be able to survive. In a letter to James Warren, who had been President of the Massachusetts Provincial Congress, Washington wrote:[147]

> "The confederation appears to me to be little more than a shadow without the substance, and Congress a nugatory (worthless) body, their ordinances being little attended to. To me it is a solecism (contradiction) in politics; indeed it is one of the most extraordinary things in nature, that we should confederate as a nation, and yet be afraid to give the rulers of that nation (who are creatures of our own making, appointed for a limited and short duration, and who are amenable to every

[146] Washington's Letter to James McHenry, August 22, 1785 - http://etext.lib.virginia.edu/etcbin/toccer-new2?id=WasFi28.xml&images=images/modeng&data=/texts/english/modeng/parsed&tag=public&part=162&division=div1

[147] George Washington to James Warren, October 7, 1785 - http://etext.lib.virginia.edu/etcbin/toccer-new2?id=WasFi28.xml&images=images/modeng&data=/texts/english/modeng/parsed&tag=public&part=210&division=div1

action and may be recalled at any moment, and are subject to all the evils which they may be instrumental in producing) sufficient powers to order and direct the affairs of the same. By such policy as this the wheels of government are clogged."

In the summer of 1785, debt-ridden farmers rebelled when the Massachusetts legislature adjourned without heeding petitions to stop farm and home foreclosures

Daniel Shays and his men at Court House[148]

In an armed rebellion led by Daniel Shays a group of about 500 men, most of them war veterans, forced a court to adjourn. Although the rebellion was put down in a few months, it was of great concern to George Washington and other Patriot leaders.

On January 16, 1786, the State of Virginia passed the Virginia Statute for Religious Freedom, a document written by Thomas Jefferson that he considered equal to his accomplishment in writing the Declaration of Independence. The Virginia Statute,

---

[148] Shay's Rebellion - http://www.sjchs-history.org/Shays.html

which became the model later for the First Amendment to the U.S. Constitution, stated:

> "That no man shall be compelled to frequent or support any religious worship, place or ministry whatsoever, nor shall be enforced, restrained, molested or burdened, in his body or goods, nor shall otherwise suffer on account of his religious opinions or belief; but that all men shall be free to profess, and by argument to maintain, their opinions in matters of religion, and that the same shall in no wise diminish, enlarge or affect their civil capacities."[149]

The year 1786 was the low point of the economic depression caused primarily by a sharp drop in trade with Britain after the Paris Peace Treaty was signed. Farm wages dropped as much as 20% and the combination of money shortages, high taxes and insistent creditors brought financial ruin to many, and desperation to some.

On August 7, 1786, Charles Pinckney of South Carolina introduced a proposal to reorganize the government to address the weaknesses of the Articles of Confederation. In September the Annapolis Convention to discuss important commercial issues "to remedy the defects of the Federal Government"[150] was held in Annapolis, Maryland with representatives of only five of the 13 colonies represented: New York, New Jersey, Pennsylvania, Delaware and Virginia.

Among the commissioners signing the Annapolis Convention document were Alexander Hamilton, James Madison, John Dickinson and Edmond Randolph, who would meet the following year to help write and sign the Constitution of the United States of America.

In his introduction to the resolution passed at the Annapolis Convention, James Madison wrote:

> "Having witnessed, as a member of the Revolutionary Congress, the inadequacies of the powers conferred by the "Articles of Confederation," and having become, after the

---

[149] The Virginia Statute for Religious Freedom - http://www.religlaw.org/interdocs/docs/virreligfreedom1785.htm

[150] Annapolis Convention –Proceedings of Commissioners to Remedy Defects of the Federal Government – with an introduction by James Madison - http://www.jmu.edu/madison/annapoli.htm

expiration of my term of service there, a member of the Legislature of Virginia, I felt it to be my duty to spare no efforts to impress on that body the alarming condition of the United States proceeding from that cause, and the evils threatened by delay, in applying a remedy."

A total reorganization of the central government was the only hope for the nation's survival. In a letter to his friend Marquis Lafayette, who had returned to France, George Washington wrote[151] of the problems facing the young nation:

"You will long ere this have heard of the Insurrection in the State of Massachusetts; to trace the causes would be difficult, and to detail their progress would be unnecessary as the steps taken by that government and the proceedings generally are very minutely related in the public gazettes with which I am informed you are regularly supplied.

"I shall therefore proceed to the more pleasing part of the business and inform you that the tumults are at an end and the principals fled to Canada. It is apprehended however that an act of the Legislature disfranchising those who were aiding or abetting, is pregnant with as much evil as good, as the operation is too extensive.

"These disorders are evident marks of a defective government; indeed the thinking part of the people of this Country are now so well satisfied of this fact that most of the Legislatures have appointed, and the rest it is said will appoint, delegates to meet at Philadelphia on the second Monday in May next in a general Convention of the States to revise and correct the defects of the federal System.

"Congress have also recognized, and recommended the measure. What may be the result of this meeting is hardly within the scan of human wisdom to predict. It is considered however as the last essay to support the present form."

---

[151] Washington's Letter to Lafayette on correcting the "defects in the Articles of Confederation http://lcweb2.loc.gov/cgi-bin/query/r?ammem/mgw:@field(DOCID+@lit(gw290142))

Chapter 15
"Correcting the Defects" in the Articles of Confederation

James Madison was a key member of the Constitutional Convention which convened in Philadelphia in May 1787. On May 14, its opening day, delegates from only two states, Virginia and Pennsylvania had arrived. Eventually, all the states except Rhode Island sent delegates.

A total of 74 delegates were appointed to the convention. Only 55 actually attended sessions. Rhode Island refused to participate in what they saw as a conspiracy to overthrow the established government. The flamboyant Patrick Henry not only refused to attend, but campaigned against ratification of the Constitution after it was written. Henry and other state political leaders feared the strengthening of the central government, objected to the powers given to the president to call out the militia and allowing Congress the power to tax.

George Washington[152]

Eleven days later, enough delegates had shown up to have a quorum, and the first order of business was choosing a president for the Convention. Robert Morris of New Jersey arose and nominated George Washington. It was seconded by John Rutlidge of South Carolina who observed that he expected the vote to be

---

[152] National Archives– George Washington – http://www.archives.gov/national_archives_experience/constitution_founding_fathers_virginia.html#washington

unanimous and that the presence of General Washington would insure that "no improper speech" would take place.[153] Washington was unanimously elected.

George Wythe[154]

The only other action taken on May 25 was the appointment of a rules committee composed of George Wythe of Virginia, Alexander Hamilton of New York, and Charles Pinckney of South Carolina. Wythe, a dignified and learned man, was America's first professor of law. He taught Thomas Jefferson and James Monroe, who became Presidents, and other leaders, including John Marshall, who became Chief Justice of the Supreme Court, and Henry Clay, who was one of America's greatest orators.

Rufus King[155]

[153] Yale University –Avalon Project -Debates of 1787 Constitutional Convention as reported by James Madison
http://www.yale.edu/lawweb/avalon/debates/514525.htm

[154] National Archives-George Wythe -
http://www.archives.gov/national_archives_experience/constitution_founding_fathers_virginia.html#Wythe

On Monday, May 28, Wythe's Rules Committee reported. One of the rules authorized "any member to call for the yeas & nays and have them entered on the minutes." Rufus King of Massachusetts objected, and George Mason of Virginia seconded his motion to eliminate that rule, saying,[156] "it was unnecessary to exhibit this evidence of the votes; and improper as changes of opinion would be frequent in the course of the business & would fill the minutes with contradictions."

Edmund Randolph[157]

On May 29, 1787, Edmund Randolph of Virginia "opened the main business" of the Convention by first listing the defects of the Articles of Confederation and then "Resolved that the Articles of Confederation[158] ought to be so corrected & enlarged as to accomplish the objects proposed by their institution; namely, "common defence, security of liberty and general welfare."[159]

According to notes taken by Robert Yates, a delegate from New York, Randolph defined five defects of the Confederation:

1. "that the confederation produced no security against foreign invasion; congress not being permitted to prevent a war nor to support it by their own authority-Of this he cited many

---

[155] Library of Congress- Rufus King - http://memory.loc.gov/ammem/bdsds/king.html

[156] Avalon Project – Debates of 1787 Constitutional Convention –May 28, 1787 - http://www.yale.edu/lawweb/avalon/debates/528.htm

[157] Library of Congress – Edmund Randolph - http://memory.loc.gov/ammem/bdsds/randolph.html

[158] Avalon Project – Articles of Confederation – http://www.yale.edu/lawweb/avalon/artconf.htm

[159] Avalon Project – Debates of 787 Constitutional Convention – May 29,1787 - http://www.yale.edu/lawweb/avalon/debates/529.htm

examples; most of which tended to shew, that they could not cause infractions of treaties or of the law of nations, to be punished: that particular states might by their conduct provoke war without control; and that neither militia nor draughts being fit for defence on such occasions, enlistments only could be successful, and these could not be executed without money.

2. "that the federal government could not check the quarrels between states, nor a rebellion in any, not having constitutional power nor means to interpose according to the exigency:

3. "that there were many advantages, which the U. S. might acquire, which were not attainable under the confederation-such as a productive impost-counteraction of the commercial regulations of other nations-pushing of commerce ad libitum-&c &c.

4. "that the federal government could not defend itself against the encroachments from the states.

5. "that it was not even paramount to the state constitutions, ratified, as it was in many of the states."

Yates then notes that Randolph "next reviewed the danger of our situation, appealed to the sense of the best friends of the U. S. -- the prospect of anarchy from the laxity of government everywhere; and to other considerations." Randolph then proposed fifteen resolutions "which he explained one by one:"

"1. Resolved that the Articles of Confederation ought to be so corrected & enlarged as to accomplish the objects proposed by their institution; namely, "common defence, security of liberty and general welfare."

"2. Resolved therefore that the rights of suffrage in the National Legislature ought to be proportioned to the Quotas of contribution, or to the number of free inhabitants, as the one or the other rule may seem best in different cases.

"3. Resolved that the National Legislature ought to consist of two branches.

"4. Resolved that the members of the first branch of the National Legislature (the House of Representatives) ought to be elected by the people of the several States every _____ for the term of ____; to be of the age of ____ years at least, to receive liberal stipends by with they may be compensated for the devotion of their time to public service; to be ineligible to any office established by a particular State, or under the authority of the United States, except those peculiarly belonging to the functions of the first branch, during the term of service, and for the space of ____ after its expiration; to be incapable of reelection for the space of ____ after the expiration of their term of service, and to be subject to recall.

"5. Resolved that the members of the second branch of the National Legislature ought to be elected by those of the first, out of a proper number of persons nominated by the individual Legislatures, to be of the age of ----- years at least; to hold their offices for a term sufficient to ensure their independency; to receive liberal stipends, by which they may be compensated for the devotion of their time to public service; and to be ineligible to any office established by a particular State, or under the authority of the United States, except those peculiarly belonging to the functions of the second branch, during the term of service, and for the space of ----- after the expiration thereof.

"6. Resolved that each branch ought to possess the right of originating Acts; that the National Legislature ought to be impowered to enjoy the Legislative Rights vested in Congress by the Confederation & moreover to legislate in all cases to which the separate States are incompetent, or in which the harmony of the United States may be interrupted by the exercise of individual Legislation; to negative all laws passed by the several States, contravening in the opinion of the National Legislature the articles of Union; and to call forth the force of the Union agst. any member of the Union failing to fulfill its duty under the articles thereof.

"7. Resolved. that a National Executive be instituted; to be chosen by the National Legislature for the term of ----- years, to receive punctually at stated times, a fixed compensation for the services rendered, in which no increase or diminution shall be made so as to affect the Magistracy, existing at the time of increase or diminution, and to be ineligible a second time; and that besides a general authority to execute the National laws, it ought to enjoy the Executive rights vested in Congress by the Confederation.

"8. Resolved that the Executive and a convenient number of the National Judiciary, ought to compose a Council of revision with authority to examine every act of the National Legislature before it shall operate, & every act of a particular Legislature before a Negative thereon shall be final; and that the dissent of the said Council shall amount to a rejection, unless the Act of the National Legislature be again passed, or that of a particular Legislature be again negatived by ----- of the members of each branch.

"9. Resolved that a National Judiciary be established to consist of one or more supreme tribunals, and of inferior tribunals to be chosen by the National Legislature, to hold their offices during good behaviour; and to receive punctually at stated times fixed compensation for their services, in which no increase or diminution shall be made so as to affect the persons actually in office at the time of such increase or diminution. that the jurisdiction of the inferior tribunals shall be to hear & determine in the first instance, and of the supreme tribunal to hear and determine in the dernier resort, all piracies & felonies on the high seas, captures from an enemy; cases in which foreigners or citizens of other States applying to such jurisdictions may be interested, or which respect the collection of the National revenue; impeachments of any National officers, and questions which may involve the national peace and harmony.

"10. Resolved. that provision ought to be made for the admission of States lawfully arising within the limits of the United States, whether from a voluntary junction of Government & Territory or otherwise, with the consent of a number of voices in the National legislature less than the whole.

"11. Resolved that a Republican Government & the territory of each State, except in the instance of a voluntary junction of Government & territory, ought to be guarantied by the United States to each State

"12. Resolved that provision ought to be made for the continuance of Congress and their authorities and privileges, until a given day after the reform of the articles of Union shall be adopted, and for the completion of all their engagements.

"13. Resolved that provision ought to be made for the amendment of the Articles of Union whensoever it shall seem necessary, and that the assent of the National Legislature ought not to be required thereto.

"14. Resolved that the Legislative Executive & Judiciary powers within the several States ought to be bound by oath to support the articles of Union

"15. Resolved that the amendments which shall be offered to the Confederation, by the Convention ought at a proper time, or times, after the approbation of Congress to be submitted to an assembly or assemblies of Representatives, recommended by the several Legislatures to be expressly chosen by the people, to consider & decide thereon"

Edmund Randolph's 15 resolutions were later called "The Virginia Plan" during debates in the Convention.

On May 29, Charles Pinckney[160] of South Carolina, also introduced a "draught of a federal Government" which he had prepared "to be agreed upon between the free and independent States of America. Pinckney asked that "his plan be referred to the Committee of the Whole appointed to consider the state of the American Union." It was never debated, but some of his ideas did become part of the Constitution.

Charles Pinckney - South Carolina

The following day, May 30, Charles Pinckney of South Carolina asked Randolph if he intended to "abolish the State Governments altogether." Randolph explained his resolutions were general and meant only to "introduce the outlines of the system he had in view."[161] Randolph and James Madison moved "that the rights of suffrage in the national Legislature ought to be

[160] Library of Congress – Charles Pinckney - http://www.law.umkc.edu/faculty/projects/ftrials/conlaw/marrysouthcar.html

[161] Avalon Project –1787 Federal Convention –May 30- Will Randolph's Plan Abolish State Govt. - http://www.yale.edu/lawweb/avalon/debates/530.htm

proportioned." That altered the method of voting authorized by the Articles of Confederation – which gave each colony an equal vote regardless of its population.

General Charles Cotesworth Pinckney[162]-

Several delegates, including Charles Pinckney's second cousin, General Charles Cotesworth Pinckney, also of South Carolina, expressed doubt the Convention had the authority "to authorize a discussion of a system founded on different principles from the federal Constitution."

Gouverneur Morris[163] - Pennsylvania

Gouverneur Morris of Pennsylvania, who supported the move towards a stronger central government, explained the

---

[162] National Archives –Charles Cotesworth Pinckey- http://www.law.umkc.edu/faculty/projects/ftrials/conlaw/marrysouthcar.html

[163] National Archives and Records- Gouverneur Morris http://www.law.umkc.edu/faculty/projects/ftrials/conlaw/marrypenn.html

difference between a "national" and a "federal" system of government:

"The distinction between a federal and national, supreme government," he said, is that a federal government is "a mere compact resting on the good faith of the parties" while a national government is "a compleat and compulsive operation."[164] He contended that in all communities there "must be one supreme power, and one only."

Roger Sherman[165] - Connecticut

On Monday, May 31, 1787, the Convention postponed discussion on the first three of Randolph's resolutions and began debate on the fourth, which called for the people to elect the members of the "first branch," or House of Representatives. That, some delegates maintained, would be democracy which was considered by many to be comparable to anarchy. Roger Sherman of Connecticut said the people should have "as little to do" as may be possible about the government because "they lack information and are constantly liable to be misled."

---

[164] Avalon Project-May 30, 1787-Difference between National and Federal governments http://www.yale.edu/lawweb/avalon/debates/530.htm

[165] National Archives and Records Connecticut - Roger Sherman- http://www.law.umkc.edu/faculty/projects/ftrials/conlaw/marryconnect.html

Elbridge Gerry[166] - Massachusetts

Elbridge Gerry of Massachusetts said,

"The evils we experience flow from the excess of democracy. The people do not want virtue, but are the dupes of pretended patriots. In Massachusetts it had been fully confirmed by experience that they are daily misled into the most baneful measures and opinions by the false reports circulated by designing men, and which no one on the spot can refute."

George Mason[167] - Virginia

George Mason of Virginia rose to vigorously refute the arguments of Sherman and Gerry. According to the notes of Rufus

---

[166] National Archives – Gerry Elbridge - http://www.law.umkc.edu/faculty/projects/ftrials/conlaw/marrymass.html

[167] National Archives and Records – George Mason http://www.law.umkc.edu/faculty/projects/ftrials/conlaw/marryvirginia.html

King on May 31, 17887, Mason argued strongly for an election of the larger branch by the people. Mason said: [168]

> "It was to be the grand depository of the democratic principle of the Government. It was, so to speak, to be our House of Commons. It ought to know and sympathise with every part of the community; and ought therefore to be taken not only from different parts of the whole republic, but also from different districts of the larger members of it, which had in several instances particularly in Virginia, different interests and views arising from difference of produce, of habits &c &c. We ought to attend to the rights of every class of the people."

Mason also

> "often wondered at the indifference of the superior classes of society to this dictate of humanity & policy; considering that however affluent their circumstances, or elevated their situations, might be, the course of a few years, not only might but certainly would, distribute their posterity throughout the lowest classes of Society. Every selfish motive therefore, every family attachment, ought to recommend such a system of policy as would provide no less carefully for the rights and happiness of the lowest than of the highest orders of citizens."

James Wilson[169] - Pennsylvania

Then James Wilson of Pennsylvania rose to speak. Wilson was known in Philadelphia as an opponent to the Republican

[168] Avalon Project – Federal Convention of 1787 –May 31, 1787
http://www.yale.edu/lawweb/avalon/debates/531.htm

[169] National Archives – James Wilson, Pennsylvania
http://www.law.umkc.edu/faculty/projects/ftrials/conlaw/marrypenn.html

Constitution of his state and, although he signed the Declaration of Independence, he had joined the moderates in voting for the three week postponement of the vote. Wilson was second only to James Madison during that four months of debate in shaping the language that would eventually become the Constitution of the United States.

Wilson opposed senators being selected by either the State Legislatures, or by the "first branch of the national Legislature," (the House of Representatives," because he believed the second branch of the legislature (the Senate) ought to be independent of both the House of Representatives and the State Legislatures.

According to Rufus King's notes,[170] Wilson

> "contended strenuously for drawing the most numerous branch of the Legislature immediately from the people. He was for raising the federal pyramid to a considerable altitude, and for that reason wished to give it as broad a basis as possible. No government could long subsist without the confidence of the people. In a republican Government this confidence was peculiarly essential...On examination it would be found that the opposition of States to federal measures had proceeded much more from the officers of the States, than from the people at large."

James Madison[171] - Virginia

[170] Avalon Project–May 31, 1787 –Rufus King Notes – House Representation http://www.yale.edu/lawweb/avalon/debates/531.htm

James Madison's view concerning the issue,[172] was that:

"the popular election of one branch of the National Legislature (is) essential to every plan of free Government." He also observed that in some of the states "one branch of the legislature was composed of men already removed from the people by an intervening body of electors. That if the first branch of the general legislature should be elected by the State Legislatures, the second branch elected by the first - the Executive by the second together with the first; and other appointments again made for subordinate purposes by the Executive, the people would be lost sight of altogether; and the necessary sympathy between them and their rulers and officers, too little felt."

Madison advocated that the:

"second branch of the Legislature, and in the Executive & judiciary branches of the Government" be selected through "refining the popular appointments by successive filtrations." However, he believed the federal government they were creating "would be more stable and durable, if it should rest on the solid foundation of the people themselves, than if it should stand merely on the pillars of the Legislatures."

On June 1, the Convention took up Randolph's 7th resolution, the creation of a national executive. Should that be one president, or several? How long a term should the executive serve? After a period of debate, James Madison moved[173] that "before a choice should be made between a unity and a plurality in the Executive" the Convention should "fix the extent of the Executive authority."

On June 4, by a vote of seven to three the Convention voted for a single executive to head the nation.[174] They also voted ten to

---

[171] White House – Biography of James Madison - http://www.whitehouse.gov/history/presidents/jm4.html

[172] Avalon Project–May 31, 1787 –James Madison-Popular Election of the House - http://www.yale.edu/lawweb/avalon/debates/531.htm

[173] Avalon Project-1787 Federal Convention-June 1, 1787 –James Madison-Executive Authority http://www.yale.edu/lawweb/avalon/debates/601.htm

[174] Avalon Project –1787 Federal Convention-June 4, 1787 http://www.yale.edu/lawweb/avalon/debates/604.htm

zero on giving the president the authority to veto legislation at will. The delegates then voted unanimously against a motion to allow the president to veto legislation without any check, but agreed to Eldridge Gerry's motion giving Congress the authority, by a two-thirds vote of each body, " to overrule the revisionary check" (veto.)

Chapter 16
Madison Warns About Danger of Activist Judges

The convention next considered Randolph's 9th resolution to establish a National Judiciary. On an 8-2 vote, with Maryland and Connecticut opposing, the establishment of a court system was approved. The delegates added only that the judiciary would "consist of one supreme tribunal, and of one or more inferior tribunals."

The following day, June 5, there was considerable debate on how judges would be appointed. Should it be by the president alone? Or should it be by the Congress? James Madison opposed the appointment of judges by the legislature "or any numerous body. Besides, the danger of intrigue and partiality, many of the members were not judges of the requisite qualifications. The Legislative talents which Resolution 11 required "for guaranteeing to States Republican Government and territory" were very different from those of a Judge, commonly recommended men to the favor of Legislative Assemblies."[175] Madison moved to strike out "appointment by the Legislature" and come back at a later time to consider it again. The motion was seconded by James Wilson and passed with a 7-2 vote.

James Madison objected to any of the three branches of government having power over any other branch. He was especially concerned about the Judiciary having control. He believed the ultimate responsibility lay with the people themselves. Years later he said on the judgeship issue:[176]

> "In a government whose vital principle is responsibility, it never will be allowed that the Legislative and Executive Departments should be compleatly subjected to the Judiciary, in which that characteristic feature is so faintly seen."

Resolution 10, which called for making a provision for the admission of new states to the Union, passed on a voice vote."

---

[175] Avalon Project–1787 Federal Convention-June 5, 1787 - http://www.yale.edu/lawweb/avalon/debates/605.htm

[176] James Madison University- Judiciary Power
http://www.jmu.edu/madison/quotepeople.htm

William Paterson[177] - New Jersey

Resolution 11, “for guarantying to States Republican Government and territory” was postponed, on the objection of William Paterson of New Jersey until the “point of representation could be decided.” This would become the major stumbling block for the delegates. Under the Articles of Confederation, each state, regardless of population, had one vote. The Virginia Plan called for representation based on population, which would give states with larger populations more power than small states such as New Jersey. On June 15, 1787 William Paterson would introduce his own plan that would challenge Edmund Randolph’s plan.

Resolution 12, "for continuing Congress till a given day and for fulfilling their engagements," produced no debate and passed quickly 9-2.

Resolution 13, that provision “ought to be made for hereafter amending the system now to be established, without requiring the assent of the Natl. Legislature," was opposed by Charles Pinckney of South Carolina and supported by Eldridge Gerry of Massachusetts. It was also postponed.

Resolution 14 "requiring oaths from the State officers to support National Government,” according to the notes of James Madison, “was postponed after a short uninteresting conversation.”

Resolution 15 "recommending Conventions under appointment of the people to ratify the new Constitution" produced a lively debate. Roger Sherman of Connecticut thought popular approval unnecessary, and James Madison of Virginia

---

[177] National Archives –William Paterson Bio - http://www.law.umkc.edu/faculty/projects/ftrials/conlaw/marrynewjers.html

thought it essential. Others had other ideas. Resolution 15 also was postponed for a future debate.

On June 6 the delegates began discussing how the two houses of congress would be chosen.[178] Should it be by the people, or by the state legislatures? Charles Pinckney of South Carolina introduced a motion "that the first branch of the national Legislature be elected by the State Legislatures, and not by the people." It was seconded by John Rutledge of South Carolina.

Elbridge Gerry of Massachusetts argued[179] that in his state where the people elected the state assembly "the worst men get into the Legislature. Several members of that Body have lately been convicted of infamous crimes." He proposed that, "It was necessary on the one hand that the people should appoint one branch of the Govt. in order to inspire them with the necessary confidence. But he wished the election on the other to be so modified as to secure more effectually a just preference of merit."

James Wilson of Virginia "wished for vigor in the government, but he wished that vigorous authority to flow immediately from the legitimate source of all authority. The Govt. ought to possess not only 1st. the force, but 2dly. the mind or sense of the people at large. The Legislature ought to be the most exact transcript of the whole Society."

Roger Sherman of Connecticut believed,[180] "The right of participating in the National Government would be sufficiently secured to the people by their election of the State Legislatures." They would not need to directly elect members of the national Congress.

George Mason of Virginia pointed out,[181] "Under the existing Confederacy, Congress represents the States not the people of the States: their acts operate on the States, not on the individuals. The case will be changed in the new plan of Govt. The people will be represented; they ought therefore to choose the Representatives."

---

[178]Avalon Project–1787 Federal Convention -June 6, 1787- Debate of choosing members House & Senate http://www.yale.edu/lawweb/avalon/debates/606.htm

[179] Ibid - Elbridge Gerry (MA)-popular election

[180] Ibid - Roger Sherman (CT)-State Legislatures elect

[181] Ibid – George Mason (VA)-Under Articles of Confederation, States, not people are represented in Congress

James Madison of Virginia[182] "considered an election of one branch at least of the Legislature by the people immediately, as a clear principle of free Govt. and that this mode under proper regulations had the additional advantage of securing better representatives, as well as of avoiding too great an agency of the State Governments in the General one."

However, he also asked,

> "Was it to be supposed that republican liberty could long exist under the abuses of it practised in some of the States?"

Madison pointed out,

> "All civilized Societies would be divided into different Sects, Factions, & interests, as they happened to consist of rich & poor, debtors & creditors, the landed, the manufacturing, the commercial interests, the inhabitants of this district or that district, the followers of this political leader or that political leader, the disciples of this religious Sect or that religious Sect. In all cases where a majority are united by a common interest or passion, the rights of the minority are in danger. What motives are to restrain them?... The lesson we are to draw from the whole is that where a majority are united by a common sentiment, and have an opportunity, the rights of the minor party become insecure."

The solution, Madison believed, was

> "to enlarge the sphere, & thereby divide the community into so great a number of interests & parties, that in the 1st. place a majority will not be likely at the same moment to have a common interest separate from that of the whole or of the minority; and in the 2d. place, that in case they should have such an interest, they may not be apt to unite in the pursuit of it."

---

[182] Ibid –James Madison –(VA) popular Election

John Dickinson of Delaware[183]

John Dickinson of Delaware observed it was

> "essential that one branch of the Legislature should be drawn immediately from the people; and as expedient that the other should be chosen by the Legislatures of the States."

George Read[184] **- Delaware**

However, George Read of Delaware thought the delegates were worrying too much about the state governments, since, he observed,

> "A national Govt. must soon of necessity swallow all of them up. They will soon be reduced to the mere office of electing the National Senate."

William Pierce of Georgia favored[185] "an election by the people as to the 1st. branch & by the States as to the 2d. branch; by

---

[183] National Archives – John Dickinson (Del) Biography - http://www.law.umkc.edu/faculty/projects/ftrials/conlaw/marrydelaware.html

[184] National Archive – George Read –Bio - Ibid

which means the Citizens of the States would be represented both individually & collectively."

General Charles Cotesworth Pinckney of South Carolina, "wished to have a good National Govt. & at the same time to leave a considerable share of power in the States."

James Wilson of Pennsylvania, disturbed by Read's apparent dismissal of State governments, rose to say,[186] He saw:

> "no incompatibility between the National & State Govts. provided the latter were restrained to certain local purposes; nor any probability of their being devoured by the former. In all confederated Systems ancient & modern the reverse had happened."

Wilson then moved for a vote on the motion to have the House of Representatives selected by the state legislatures. It was defeated 8-3 with New York, Connecticut and Georgia voting "Aye."

David Brearly [187] **- New Jersey**

From June 7 to June 13 the delegates wrangled over how members of the two houses of congress and the president would be chosen. The smaller states wanted representation equal to the larger states. Some wanted the congress to choose the president.

---

[185] National Archive – William Pierce Bio - http://www.law.umkc.edu/faculty/projects/ftrials/conlaw/marrygeorgia.html

[186] Avalon Project–1787 Federal Convention -June 6, 1787 http://www.yale.edu/lawweb/avalon/debates/606.htm

[187] National Archives-David Brearley- http://www.law.umkc.edu/faculty/projects/ftrials/conlaw/marrynewjers.html

States with larger populations challenged the smaller states to agree to pay the same amount of taxes towards maintenance of the national government.

On Saturday, June 9, Paterson of New Jersey brought up Resolution 4 again, which dealt with voting rules for the "First House" of the national legislature, or the House of Representatives Paterson's motion was seconded by David Brearly, also from New Jersey. Brearly argued that the states with the larger populations, Massachusetts, Pennsylvania and Virginia, would dominate the other ten states.

Paterson objected to the notion that the national government

> "is to be formed so as to operate on the people and not on the States" and concluded that he would "had rather submit to a monarch, to a despot, than to such a fate. He would not only oppose the plan here but on his return home do every thing in his power to defeat it there."[188]

On Monday morning, June 11, Roger Sherman of Connecticut made a suggestion that was little noted at the time,[189] but which would eventually be seriously considered and end up saving the Convention.

James Madison stated that Sherman

> "proposed that the proportion of suffrage in the 1st. branch should be according to the respective numbers of free inhabitants; and that in the second branch or Senate, each State should have one vote and no more. He said as the States would remain possessed of certain individual rights, each State ought to be able to protect itself: otherwise a few large States will rule the rest. The House of Lords in England he observed had certain particular rights under the Constitution, and hence they have an equal vote with the House of Commons that they may be able to defend their rights."

Sherman's suggestion was the first in a day in which a variety of suggestions were made to equalize the states, including

---

[188] Avalon Project-1787 Federal Convention-June 9, 1787
http://www.yale.edu/lawweb/avalon/debates/609.htm

[189] Avalon Project-1787 Federal Convention-June 11,1787
http://www.yale.edu/lawweb/avalon/debates/611.htm

one from Benjamin Franklin that would have given part of Pennsylvania to New Jersey to enlarge its boundaries.

At that point, however, compromise was not in the air. Finally, on June 15, 1787, William Paterson of New Jersey laid before the Congress a plan[190] that he asked be substituted for Randolph's plan, which had been discussed and parts voted on for three weeks.

The Paterson Plan consisted of nine resolutions designed to revise, correct and enlarge the Articles of Confederation rather than write a new Constitution.

Resolved:

1. "that the Articles of Confederation ought to be so revised, corrected & enlarged..."
2. "that authorized Congress to pass tax laws..."
3. "that Congress be authorized to make 'requisitions in proportion to the whole number of white & other free citizens & inhabitants of every age sex and condition including those bound to servitude for a term of years & three fifths of all other persons...except Indians not paying taxes..."
4. "that Congress be authorized to choose the president or presidency..."
5. "that the president appoint judges for a federal Judiciary..."
6. "that all Acts passed by Congress and treaties ratified by the United States shall be the supreme law of the land..."
7. "that provision be made for the admission of new States into the Union..."
8. "that the rule for naturalization be the same in every State..."
9. "that a Citizen convicted of committing a crime in one state be considered guilty in all states..."

This new plan generated even more heated debate among the delegates. Randolph and his supporters viewed the Paterson Plan as a political power play. On June 16, according to the notes

---

[190] Avalon Project-1787 Federal Convention-Jun 15,1787 http://www.yale.edu/lawweb/avalon/debates/615.htm

of Alexander Hamilton, Charles Pinckney of South Carolina charged,[191]

> "Give New Jersey an equal vote, and she will dismiss her scruples, and concur in the National. system. He (Paterson) thought the Convention authorized to go any length in recommending, which they found necessary to remedy the evils which produced this Convention."

Edmund Randolph, according to Hamilton,[192]

> "was not scrupulous on the point of power. When the salvation of the Republic was at stake, it would be treason to our trust, not to propose what we found necessary. He painted in strong colours, the imbecility of the existing Confederacy, & the danger of delaying a substantial reform."

On June 18, Alexander Hamilton rose to speak for the first time[193] and outlined his objections to both plans.

> "Two Sovereignties can not co-exist within the same limits. Giving powers to Congresss must eventuate in a bad Government or in no Government, he said. The plan of N. Jersey therefore will not do. What then is to be done?"

On the third day of debate on the New Jersey Plan, James Madison[194] challenged Paterson directly on his claim that the Articles of Confederation, "having been formed by unanimous consent, could be dissolved by unanimous Consent only." During the Revolution, he charged, "violations of the federal articles had been numerous & notorious. Among the most notorious was an act of New Jersey herself; by which she expressly refused to comply with a constitutional requisition of Congress." Under contract law, that would be grounds for nullifying the Confederation compact.

The delegates voted 8-2 to postpone discussion on Resolution 1 of the Paterson Plan, with New Jersey and New York opposing. A motion by Rufus King for a vote on the preference of the delegates for the Randolph or the Paterson Plan was seven for

---

[191] Avalon Project- Federal Constitution-Jun 16, 1787 http://www.yale.edu/lawweb/avalon/debates/616.htm

[192] Ibid

[193] Avalon Project-Federal Constitution-Jun 18, 1787 http://www.yale.edu/lawweb/avalon/debates/618.htm

[194] Avalon Project-Federal Constitution-Jun 19, 1787 http://www.yale.edu/lawweb/avalon/debates/619.htm

the Randolph Plan, and three opposed, (New York, New Jersey and Delaware) with Maryland divided.

Chapter 17
Erecting a "Kingdom At War With Itself"

Oliver Ellsworth[195] - Connecticut

On June 20, 1787, Oliver Ellsworth of Connecticut moved that Resolution 1 of the Randolph plan should read,[196] "that the Government of the United States ought to consist of a supreme legislative, Executive and Judiciary."

He also said that change "would drop the word national, and retain the proper title 'the United States.'" He recommended the "plan of the Convention to go forth as an amendment to the Articles of Confederation, since under this idea the authority of the Legislatures could ratify it."

Edmund Randolph agreed to the change, and the Convention moved to consider Resolution 2 of the Randolph Plan, "that the national Legislature ought to consist of two branches." National was changed to "the United States."

John Lansing, who with his fellow delegate from New York, Robert Yates, soon left the convention because they opposed any system that would consolidate the United States into one government," gave a long speech in opposition to the Randolph Plan.

In order to have a national government, the states would have to give up their sovereignty, Lansing stated. He declared:

---

[195] National Archives – Daniel Ellsworth, CT
http://www.law.umkc.edu/faculty/projects/ftrials/conlaw/marryconnect.html

[196] Avalon Project-1787 Federal Convention-Jun 20, 1787 Res. 1-Va. Plan
http://www.yale.edu/lawweb/avalon/debates/620.htm

John Lansing[197] - New York

"It could not be expected that those possessing Sovereignty could ever voluntarily part with it. It was not to be expected from any one State, much less from thirteen.".

George Mason rose to refute Lansing's arguments. Mason identified the two main points of the opposition to the Randolph plan as the lack of power in the Convention to consider the plan and its lack "of practicability." The power rested with the people, not with the delegates, Mason explained, which was why the people needed to vote to ratify the new plan.

According to Alexander Hamilton's notes, Mason said,

"Is it to be thought that the people of America, so watchful over their interests; so jealous of their liberties, will give up their all, will surrender both the sword and the purse, to the same body, and that too not chosen immediately by themselves? They never will. They never ought. Will they trust such a body, with the regulation of their trade, with the regulation of their taxes; with all the other great powers, which are in contemplation?"

And, as for its practicality, Mason argued, he believed the mind of the people of America was settled on two points:

1. in an attachment to Republican Government.

2. in an attachment to more than one branch in the Legislature.

---

[197] National Archives-John Lansing, NY
http://www.law.umkc.edu/faculty/projects/ftrials/conlaw/marrynewyork.html

Luther Martin[198] - Maryland

Luther Martin of Maryland spoke, supporting "the importance of State Governments" but insisting,

> "Congress represented the (State) Legislatures; and it was the Legislatures not the people who refused to enlarge their powers."

Roger Sherman of Connecticut also supported Lansing's position, seeing no need for two branches of congress since, he believed, the delegates to congress represented the state, not the people.

A vote taken on "the question for postponing in order to take up Mr. Lansings proposition" was defeated 6 to 4 with Maryland divided.

On June 21, the debate on the Randolph's Virginia Plan and Paterson's New Jersey plan, was defined by James Wilson as

> "how the general government and individuality of the particular States could be reconciled to each other; and how the latter could be secured against the former?"

While Alexander Hamilton seemed alone in contending "for an abolition of the State governments," most of the delegates expressed concern over the balance of power between the two extremes.

---

[198] National Archives-Luther Martin, Md
http://www.law.umkc.edu/faculty/projects/ftrials/conlaw/marrymaryland.html

William Samuel Johnson[199] - Connecticut

William Samuel Johnson of Connecticut, who is called "Doctor Johnson" in the minutes of the Continental Congress, observed the New Jersey Plan was

"calculated to preserve the individuality of the States," and the Virginia Plan "did not profess to destroy this individuality altogether, but was charged with such a tendency."[200]

James Wilson felt that

> "the general Government would be in perpetual danger of encroachments from the State Governments."

James Madison believed there

> "was less danger of encroachment from the General Government than from the State Governments"

Madison reminded the delegates that history indicated Confederacies were more apt to end in "anarchy than in tyranny." The experience of the 13 colonies, he said, "had fully illustrated this tendency."

A motion "that the Legislature ought to consist of two Branches" passed on a 7-3 vote, with New York, New Jersey and Delaware voting "no" and Maryland divided.

The remainder of the day's debate was on who should pay the salaries for the members of the national legislature. Should it be the states or the national government?

---

[199] National Archives –William Samuel Johnson, CT. http://www.law.umkc.edu/faculty/projects/ftrials/conlaw/marryconnect.html

[200] Avalon Project —Wm. Johnson – State or National Government –Jun 21, 1797- http://www.yale.edu/lawweb/avalon/debates/621.htm

Hugh Williamson[201] - North Carolina

Hugh Williamson of North Carolina reminded fellow delegates that there would be new western states with different interests join the union, and they would be poor states with little money to pay for their representatives. The old states, he thought, should not have to "pay the expenses of men who would be employed in thwarting their measures & interests."[202]

James Wilson's motion to fix the minimum age of a member of the House at 25 was passed on a vote of seven ayes, with Massachusetts, Pennsylvania and Georgia voting "no," and New York divided.

On June 23, again the Convention took up the issue of payment[203] for the members of the National Legislature. A motion to "an adequate compensation to be paid out of the Treasury of the United States" was defeated in a vote 5-5, with Georgia divided.

This prompted General Pinckney of South Carolina to move to strike out a provision that would prohibit members of the national legislature from holding office in the state. He said:

> "It would seem from the ideas of some that we are erecting a Kingdom to be divided against itself."

Roger Sherman agreed, adding, "It would seem that we are erecting a Kingdom at war with itself. The Legislature ought not to fettered in such a case on the question."

---

[201] National Archives-Hugh Williamson- North Carolina http://www.law.umkc.edu/faculty/projects/ftrials/conlaw/marrynorthcar.html

[202] Avalon Project-1787 Federal Convention-June 22, 1787 http://www.yale.edu/lawweb/avalon/debates/622.htm

[203] Avalon Project-1787 Federal Convention -June 23, 1787- On payment for Members of Legislature- http://www.yale.edu/lawweb/avalon/debates/623.htm

General Pinckney moved that the 1st Branch of Government (House of Representatives) be appointed by the state legislatures instead of elected by the people. That motion was defeated 6-4 with Delaware, New Jersey, Connecticut and South Carolina voting "aye," and Maryland divided.

Then General Pinckney moved that the people elect the 1st Branch of Government. That motion passed 9-1 with New Jersey voting "no" and Maryland divided.

A final action voted down a three year term for the 1st Branch, and a two year term was approved.

For the next two days the Convention delegates debated payment for members of the national legislature and how corruption might be prevented. Should the states, or the national government pay the salaries of the representatives?

James Madison expressed his opinion that the "compensation for the National government" should be "independent of the State governments."

He also said members of the legislature were "too much interested to ascertain their own compensation. It would be indecent to put their hands into the public purse for the sake of their own pockets."

Alexander Hamilton strongly felt that the state governments should not be the "paymasters of the national government."

On June 22 James Wilson moved that salaries of the 1st. branch "be ascertained by the National Legislature," and be paid out of the national treasury. The motion was rejected in a vote of 7-2, with New Jersey and Pennsylvania voting "aye" with Massachusetts and Georgia divided.

General Pinckney's motion was approved 8-3 with Massachusetts, Pennsylvania and Delaware voting "no."

The issue involved in this heated debate was members of state legislatures creating what James Madison called the "evil" of "unnecessary offices" in the states to be held by their friends and relatives at the expense of the public treasury.

On June 25, the Convention again took up Resolution 4 of the Virginia Plan which would determine how members of the "lst Branch" would be chosen and paid. Charles Pinckney said:

"The efficacy of the System will depend on this article."

It was the article causing the greatest amount of contention in the Convention because it would determine the relative power of each state. If the people voted directly for the members of the lst Branch, and the number of representatives was determined by population in the states, then smaller, less populated states would lose power.

The inability of the delegates to agree on this issue was illustrated by a rapid series of nine votes during the day. Not being able to agree on the composition of the House of Representatives, the delegates took up the composition of the Senate. About all they agreed on that day was that the minimum age of senators would be age 30.

On June 26 the delegates further debated the formation and terms of the Senate. Nathaniel Gorham of Massachusetts moved the term of a senator be six years, and his motion was seconded by James Wilson. George Read of Delaware moved the term of a senator be nine years, and he was seconded by Jacob Broom of Delaware.

At that point James Madison observed[204] that, to decide the term of service, the Convention needed to first determine why a second branch of the legislature was needed. Members of a second branch "were first to protect the people against. their rulers: secondly to protect the people against the transient impressions into which they themselves might be led."

Since those "charged with the public happiness, might betray" the trust of the people, it was necessary "to divide the trust

---

[204] The Avalon Project-1787 Federal Convention-June 26- Composition of Senate - http://www.yale.edu/lawweb/avalon/debates/626.htm

between different bodies of men, who might watch & check each other."

Madison explained,

"In framing a system which we wish to last for ages, we should not lose sight of the changes which ages will produce. An increase of population will of necessity increase the proportion of those who will labour under all the hardships of life, & secretly sigh for a more equal distribution of its blessings. These may in time outnumber those who are placed above the feelings of indigence. According to the equal laws of suffrage, the power will slide into the hands of the former. No agrarian[g] attempts have yet been made in this Country, but symptoms, of a leveling spirit, as we have understood, have sufficiently appeared in a certain quarters to give notice of the future danger.

"How is this danger to be guarded against on republican principles? How is the danger in all cases of interested coalitions to oppress the minority to be guarded against? Among other means by the establishment of a body in the Govt. sufficiently respectable for its wisdom & virtue, to aid on such emergences, the preponderance of justice by throwing its weight into that scale."

With those objectives in mind, the second branch should, Madison thought, have a longer term of office than the first branch. He believed they would "decide forever the fate of Republican Government" and warned, "We ought not only to provide every guard to liberty that its preservation could require, but be equally careful to supply the (corrections for) defects which our own experience had particularly pointed out."

James Wilson of Pennsylvania brought up a point that had not yet been discussed, concerning the Senate – foreign relations:

"Every nation may be regarded in two relations

1. to its own citizens.
2. to foreign nations.

"It is therefore not only liable to anarchy & tyranny within, but has wars to avoid & treaties to obtain from abroad. The Senate will probably be the depositary of the powers

---

[g] Agrarian-an equal division of lands among all citizens

concerning the latter objects. It ought therefore to be made respectable in the eyes of foreign Nations. The true reason why G. Britain has not yet listened to a commercial treaty with us has been, because she had no confidence in the stability or efficacy of our Government."

George Mason of Virginia did not make a motion, but reminded the delegates "One important object in constituting the Senate was to secure the rights of property." He suggested, in fact, that only men with property be allowed to serve in the Senate.

A motion to pay Senators out of the public treasury for their services was opposed by many delegates because it was assumed they would all be men of property and wealth. Oliver Ellsworth's motion that the Senators "not be paid by the national treasury" but be paid by their states failed on a 6-5 vote.

A motion by Hugh Williamson of North Carolina that Senators be "ineligible to & incapable of holding offices under the United States" passed 8-3, with Massachusetts, New York and New Jersey voting against it.

Chapter 18
Franklin Warns of being Divided by Local Interests

On June 27 the Convention again considered the issue that seemed to engender the most heated and divisive debate, "the rules of suffrage in the 2 branches." The question was, should the number of votes allowed the House of Representatives be according to the population of the individual state or should each state have only one vote, as in the Articles of Confederation?

Alexander Martin[205] - North Carolina

Alexander Martin of North Carolina spoke for most of the day in opposition to representation in the House based on population. Rufus King, who took notes for the 27th, wrote that Martin "contended at great length and with great eagerness that the General Government was meant merely to preserve the State Governments, not to govern individuals: that its powers ought to be kept within narrow limits; that if too little power was given to it, more might be added; but that if too much, it could never be resumed."

On the following day, Alexander Martin resumed his speech which was recorded by Rufus King as, "contending that the General Government ought to be formed for the States, not for individuals: that if the States were to have votes in proportion to their numbers of people, it would be the same thing whether their representatives were chosen by the Legislatures or the people; the smaller States would be equally enslaved..."

Rufus King observed at the end of Martin's speech that it

---

[205] National Archives -Alexander Martin, North Carolina http://www.law.umkc.edu/faculty/projects/ftrials/conlaw/marrynorthcar.html

"was delivered with much diffuseness & considerable vehemence."

James Madison of Virginia rose to declare he "could neither be convinced that the rule contended for, equal representation for the states without regard to population, was just, nor (was it) necessary for the safety of the small States."

Roger Sherman of Connecticut observed, "The question is not what rights naturally belong to men; but how they may be most equally & effectually guarded in Society."

Benjamin Franklin - [206]

On June 28, 1787 the acrimonious debate on representation had been raging in the Philadelphia State House for more than a month, when the aged and infirm Benjamin Franklin made what was probably his longest speech of the entire session:[207]

> "The small progress we have made after 4 or five weeks close attendance & continual reasonings with each other, our different sentiments on almost every question, several of the last producing as many noes as ayes, is methinks a melancholy proof of the imperfection of the Human Understanding. We indeed seem to feel our own want of political wisdom, since we have been running about in search of it. We have gone back to ancient history for models of Government, and examined the different forms of those Republics which having been formed with the seeds of their own dissolution now no longer exist.

[206] Benjamin Franklin – 1786 - 1790 http://www.english.udel.edu/lemay/franklin/statesman.html

[207] Avalon Project –1787 Federal Convention-Jun 28-Benjmin Franklin's speech on prayer- http://www.yale.edu/lawweb/avalon/debates/628.htm

And we have viewed Modern States all round Europe, but find none of their Constitutions suitable to our circumstances.

"In this situation of this Assembly, groping as it were in the dark to find political truth, and scarce able to distinguish it when presented to us, how has it happened, Sir, that we have not hitherto once thought of humbly applying to the Father of lights to illuminate our understandings? In the beginning of the Contest with Great Britain, when we were sensible of danger we had daily prayer in this room for the divine protection.-

"Our prayers, Sir, were heard, & they were graciously answered. All of us who were engaged in the struggle must have observed frequent instances of a superintending providence in our favor. To that kind providence we owe this happy opportunity of consulting in peace on the means of establishing our future national felicity. And have we now forgotten that powerful friend? or do we imagine that we no longer need his assistance?

"I have lived, Sir, a long time, and the longer I live, the more convincing proofs I see of this truth - that God Governs in the affairs of men. And if a sparrow cannot fall to the ground without his notice, is it probable that an empire can rise without his aid?

"We have been assured, Sir, in the sacred writings, that 'except the Lord build the House they labour in vain that build it.' I firmly believe this; and I also believe that without his concurring aid we shall succeed in this political building no better, than the Builders of Babel: We shall be divided by our little partial local interests; our projects will be confounded, and we ourselves shall become a reproach and bye word down to future ages. And what is worse, mankind may hereafter from this unfortunate instance, despair of establishing Governments by Human wisdom and leave it to chance, war and conquest.

"I therefore beg leave to move that henceforth prayers imploring the assistance of Heaven, and its blessings on our deliberations, be held in this Assembly every morning before we proceed to business, and that one or more of the Clergy of this City be requested to officiate in that Service."

Roger Sherman Connecticut, treating Franklin's statement as a motion, seconded it.

Alexander Hamilton of New York argued that prayer at this point in the proceedings would "lead the public to believe that the embarrassments and dissensions within the Convention, had suggested this measure."

Franklin and Sherman replied that "omission of a duty could not justify a further omission-that the rejection of such a proposition would expose the Convention to more unpleasant animadversions than the adoption of it: and that the alarm out of doors that might be excited for the state of things within, would at least be as likely to do good as ill."

Hugh Williamson of North Carolina observed that the real reason there had been no prayer was because "the Convention had no funds" to pay the preacher.

The matter was resolved when Edmund Randolph of Virginia proposed "that a sermon be preached at the request of the convention on 4th of July, the anniversary of Independence; & thenceforward prayers be used in ye Convention every morning."

Benjamin Franklin seconded the motion, and every session of Congress since that date to the present has opened with prayer.

On the morning of June 29, the notes of Rufus King indicate that a new feeling pervaded the debate. William Samuel Johnson of Connecticut began the meeting by observing,

> "The controversy must be endless whilst Gentlemen differ in the grounds of their arguments; Those on one side considering the States as districts of people composing one political Society; those on the other considering them as so many political societies.
>
> "The fact is that the States do exist as political Societies, and a Govt. is to be formed for them in their political capacity, as well as for the individuals composing them. Does it not seem to follow, that if the States as such are to exist they must be armed with some power of self-defence. This is the idea of [Col. Mason] who appears to have looked to the bottom of this matter.
>
> "Besides the Aristocratic and other interests, which ought to have the means of defending themselves, the States have their interests as such, and are equally entitled to like means. On the whole he thought that as in some respects the States are to be considered in their political capacity, and in

others as districts of individual citizens, the two ideas embraced on different sides, instead of being opposed to each other, ought to be combined; that in one branch the people, ought to be represented; in the other the States."

Nathaniel Gorham of Massachusetts bluntly observed that whether the small states were in or out of the Union they would have the same problem. The large states would at least be able to defend themselves. But, "What would be the situation of Delaware in case of a separation of the States? Would she not lie at the mercy of Pennsylvania? Would not her true interest lie in being consolidated with her, and ought she not now to wish for such a union with Pa. under one Government as will put it out of the power of Pennsylvania to oppress her?"

James Madison of Virginia "entreated the gentlemen representing the small States to renounce a principle which was confessedly unjust, which could never be admitted, & if admitted must infuse mortality into a Constitution which we wished to last forever. He prayed them to ponder well the consequences of suffering the Confederacy to go to pieces."

Alexander Hamilton of New York noted,

"The truth is it is a contest for power, not for liberty. Will the men composing the small States be less free than those composing the larger. The State of Delaware having 40,000 souls will lose power, if she has 1/10 only of the votes allowed to Pa. having 400,000."

Eldridge Gerry of Massachusetts, who had helped write the Articles of Confederation, warned that the "present Confederation was dissolving" and noted "we never were independent States, were not such now, & never could be even on the principles of the Confederation. The States & the advocates for them were intoxicated with the idea of their sovereignty."

He lamented, "Instead of coming here like a band of brothers, belonging to the same family, we seemed to have brought with us the spirit of political negotiators."

A motion by John Lansing of New York for each state, regardless of population, to have the same number of votes in the House was defeated 6-4. Those voting to retain the power they had under the Articles of Confederation were New York, (which would one day become the most populous state in the Union,) Connecticut, New Jersey and Delaware. Maryland was divided.

With the House of Representatives vote settled as based on population, the Convention next considered the vote in the Senate. On Saturday, June 30, 1787, James Wilson who was against equal votes of states in the Senate argued "Such an equality will enable the minority to control in all cases whatsoever, the sentiments and interests of the majority. Seven States will control six."[208]

Oliver Ellsworth of Connecticut argued:

> "'that the minority will rule the majority' is not true. The power is given to the few to save them from being destroyed by the many. If an equality of votes had been given to them in both branches, the objection might have had weight. Is it a novel thing that the few should have a check on the many? Is it not the case in the British Constitution the wisdom of which so many gentlemen have united in applauding? Have not the House of Lords, who form so small a proportion of the nation a negative on the laws, as a necessary defence of their peculiar rights against the encroachments of the Commons.?"

James Madison replied that with equal representation the small states:

> "1. could obstruct the wishes and interests of the majority, 2, could extort measures repugnant to the wishes and interest of the Majority and 3. could impose measures adverse thereto; as the 2d. branch will probably exercise some great powers, in which the 1st. will not participate."

On Monday, July 2, 1787, Oliver Ellsworth moved for a vote that would give each state one vote in the Senate.[209] His motion failed with Massachusetts, Pennsyvlania, Maryland, North Carolina, and South Carolina voting "no." New York, New Jersey, Connecticut, Delaware, Maryland voted "aye." George was divided. The vote was another tie.

---

[208] Avalon Project-1787 Federal Constitution-Jun 30th -Vote in the Senate - http://www.yale.edu/lawweb/avalon/debates/630.htm

[209] Avalon Project-1787 Federal Constitution-July 2nd-Committee Chosen to Consider Senate vote http://www.yale.edu/lawweb/avalon/debates/702.htm

Roger Sherman of Connecticut spoke:[210] "We are now at a full stop," and nobody he supposed meant that we should break up without doing something. A committee he thought most likely to hit on some expedient."

There was debate for and against the motion for a committee, but when the vote was taken, it passed with 10-1 with only Pennsylvania in opposition to a committee which was chosen by ballot.

Gunning Bedford, Jr. - Delaware[211]

The members chosen for the committee were, Elbridge Gerry of Massachusetts, Oliver Ellsworth of Connecticut, Robert Yates[212] of New York, William Paterson of New Jersey, Dr. Benjamin Franklin of Pennsylvania, Gunning Bedford, Jr. of Delaware, Alexander Martin of North Carolina, James Mason of Virginia, William Davy of North Carolina, John Rutlidge of South Carolina, and Alexander Baldwin of Georgia.

The Convention was adjourned until after the 4th of July holiday.

On July 5, 1787 the committee reported. Its recommendations, as reported by Elbridge Gerry were:

> "1. That in the 1st. branch of the Legislature each of the States now in the Union shall be allowed 1 member for every 40,000 inhabitants of the description reported in the 7th

---

[210] Avalon Project-1787 Federal Constitution-July 5th- Report of Committee on Senate suffrage- http://www.yale.edu/lawweb/avalon/debates/705.htm

[211] National Archives – Gunning Bedford, Jr. – Delaware http://www.law.umkc.edu/faculty/projects/ftrials/conlaw/marrydelaware.html

[212] National Archives – Robert Yates, New York Bio http://www.law.umkc.edu/faculty/projects/ftrials/conlaw/marrynewyork.html

Resolution of the Comittee of the whole House: that each State not containing that number shall be allowed 1 member: that all bills for raising or appropriating money, and for fixing the Salaries of the officers of the Government of the U. States shall originate in the 1st branch of the Legislature, and shall not be altered or amended by the 2d branch: and that no money shall be drawn from the public Treasury but in pursuance of appropriations to be originated in the 1st Branch.

"That in the 2d branch each State shall have an equal vote."

John Rutlidge moved that the votes of members be weighted based on how much money each state contributed to the federal treasury. That motion was voted down 9-1 with Georgia not voting. Only South Carolina, John Rutlidge's state, voted in favor.

On July 6 Gouverneur Morris of Pennsylvania moved a vote to fix the representation for each state at the Committee's recommendation of 40,000 per representative.[213] It passed 8-3, with New York, New Jersey and Delaware opposed.

Gouverneur Morris also spoke in opposition to the Committee recommendation that only the House be allowed to introduce "money plans" (Appropriations bills.)

James Mason of Virginia, a member of the Committee, explained

"The consideration which weighed with the Committee was that the 1st. branch would be the immediate representatives of the people, the 2d. would not. Should the latter have the power of giving away the people's money, they might soon forget the source from whence they received it."

The vote on the Committee's report that allowed only the House (the lst Branch) to introduce money bills passed with 5 votes in favor, four opposed, and 3 states divided.

With these matters resolved, the remaining "critical question," Elbridge Gerry of Massachusetts said the following day, July 7, was:

---

[213] Avalon Project- -Jul.6, 1787-Gourverneur Morris Moves to Set House Representation - http://www.yale.edu/lawweb/avalon/debates/706.htm

"Shall the clause allowing each State one vote in the 2d. branch, stand as part of the Report"?

The debate centered on two points: The number of inhabitants of each state and the value of the property of each state. The wealthiest of the states, and the state with the largest population was Virginia and the Virginia delegates felt their states should have the largest number of representatives. That was opposed by states that wanted to limit the power of Virginia.

William Paterson of New Jersey stated,[214] "He could regard Negro slaves in no light but as property. They are no free agents, have no personal liberty, no faculty of acquiring property, but on the contrary are themselves property, & like other property entirely at the will of the Master.[215]

"Has a man in Virginia. a number of votes in proportion to the number of his slaves? And if Negroes are not represented in the States to which they belong, why should they be represented in the Genl. Govt. What is the true principle of Representation?"

Paterson reasoned that in setting the representation in Congress of the State of Virginia, the entire population of slaves should be totally eliminated. Since, at the time, 39% of Virginia's population and 43% of South Carolina's population were slaves, eliminating or reducing the count of slaves would give the non-slave states greater power in the national Congress.

James Madison of Virginia reminded Paterson, the man who introduced the plan that all states have equal representation,

"'that his doctrine of Representation which was in its principle the genuine one, must for ever silence the pretensions of the small States to an equality of votes with the large ones. They ought to vote in the same proportion in which their citizens would do, if the people of all the States were collectively met.' He suggested as a proper ground of compromise, 'that in the first branch the States should be represented according to their number of free inhabitants; and in

---

[214] Avalon Project-1787 Convention-July 7, 1787-Voting Rights of the U.S. Senate - http://www.yale.edu/lawweb/avalon/debates/707.htm

[215] Avalon Project-1787 Convention-July 9, 1787-Would slaves be counted as persons or property- http://www.yale.edu/lawweb/avalon/debates/709.htm

the 2d which had for one of its primary objects the guardianship of property, according to the whole number, including slaves.'"[216]

Rufus King responded that he:

"had always expected that as the Southern States are the richest, they would not league themselves with the Northern unless some respect were paid to their superior wealth. If the latter expect those preferential distinctions in Commerce & other advantages which they will derive from the connection they must not expect to receive them without allowing some advantages in return. Eleven out of 13 of the States had agreed to consider Slaves in the apportionment of taxation; and taxation and Representation ought to go together."[217]

The only state at the Convention of the 13 states that had no slaves was Rufus King's home state, Massachusetts, which had ended slavery in 1780.

The 1790 census, taken three years after the Convention, showed e there were 632,804 slaves[218] in the five Southern States of Virginia, Maryland, North Carolina, South Carolina and Georgia. The other seven slave-holding states of Connecticut, New York, New Jersey, New Hampshire, Delaware, Pennsylvania, and Rhode Island had 48,973. By insisting that five slaves be counted as only three persons the Northern states cut the representation in Congress of the South by six representatives, while the fewer number of slaves in the North did not affect any of the Northern States' representation.

By the following day, July 10, the delegates approved a compromise solution which, in effect, allowed the Northern States (called the Eastern States by delegates) control of the Congress. Rufus King reported for the committee chosen to allocate the number of delegates for each state that a total of 65 delegates would form the first House of Representatives.

---

[216] Ibid

[217] Ibid

[218] Virginia Western University – Slave Population 1790 http://www.vw.vccs.edu/vwhansd/HIS121/Census1790.html

The population of the United States, according to its first census 3 years later, was 3,648,213. The 13 states' population was:

New Hampshire 3. (1790 Pop. 141,899
Massachusetts 8. (1790 Pop. 378,556)
Rhode Island 1. (1790 Pop. 69,112)
Connecticut 5. (1790 Pop. 237,655)
New York 6. (1790 Pop. 340,241)
New Jersey 4. (1790 Pop. 184,139)
Pennsylvania 8. (1790 Pop. 433,611)
Delaware 1. (1790 Pop. 59,096)

The Southern States would have 29 delegates:

Maryland 6. (1790 Pop. 329,728)
Virginia 10. (1790 Pop. 747,550)
North Carolina 5. (1790 Pop. 395,005)
South Carolina 5. (1790 Pop. 249,073)
Georgia 3. (1790 Pop. 82,548)

The slave populations of the 5 Southern states in 1790 was 34.5% in Georgia, 32.2% in Maryland, 25.6% in North Carolina, 43% in South Carolina and 39.1% in Virginia.

By counting slaves as only 3/5th of a person, the 8 Northern states guaranteed their control of Congress. In the 1790 census[219], the 8 northern states had a total population of 1,844,309 and had 36 members of congress. The 5 Southern states, with a 1790 population of 1,803,904 had 49.4% of the population, and were allocated only 29 members of Congress. Instead of having 49.4% of the House of Representatives, they had 44.4%. The Northern states, with 50.6% of the actual population of the new nation, had 55.4% of the new House of Representatives. The South, with 49.4% of the population of the new nation had 44.6% of the representation in the House of Representatives.

This imbalance was not lost on the entire Southern delegation. On July 12, after continued debate on the subject of counting inhabitants of states, the delegates passed 8-2 a motion that a census be taken every ten years, with Connecticut and New Jersey opposed.

Charles Pinckney of South Carolina then moved to count "blacks equal to the whites in the ratio of representation." This he urged was nothing more than justice. "The blacks are the labourers, the peasants of the Southern States: they are as productive of pecuniary resources as those of the Northern States. They add equally to the wealth, and considering money as the sinew of war, to the strength of the nation. It will also be politic with regard to the Northern States, as taxation is to keep pace with Representation. The motion "for rating Blacks as equal to Whites instead of as 3/5"[220] was defeated on 8-2. Massachusetts, Connecticut, New Jersey, Delaware, Maryland, Virginia and North Carolina voted "no." Only South Carolina and Georgia voted in favor of "rating Blacks as equal to Whites" instead of counting them as 3/5th of a person.

A motion by Edmund Randolph of Virginia to eliminate the consideration of "wealth" in determining the number of representatives from each state passed 9-0, with Maryland divided.

Reflecting this vote, the Constitution, as originally written, stated in Article I, Section II:

> "Representatives and direct taxes shall be apportioned among the several states which may be included within this union, according to their respective numbers, which shall be determined by adding to the whole number of free persons, including those bound to service for a term of years, and excluding Indians not taxed, three fifths of all other Persons."

The imbalance in Congress naturally led to continued efforts on the part of Southerners to strengthen State Rights. By 1856, when the U.S. Supreme Court ruled in the Dred Scott case that any slave or even a free black whose ancestors were slaves (and therefore counted as only 3/5th of a person) were not, under the U.S. Constitution to be considered "persons" or citizens even when free. The decision became a major issue in the Lincoln-Douglas Debates in their race for the U.S. Senate in 1858.

It was even a greater issue by 1860 in the Presidential race, when angry pro-slavery advocates split and nominated two

---

[220] Avalon Project-1787 Federal Convention-Census and 3/5 rule for counting blacks - http://www.yale.edu/lawweb/avalon/debates/712.htm

candidates, Democrats Stephen A. Douglas of Illinois, supporter of the "Missouri Compromise" on slavery, and John C. Breckinridge of Kentucky, a pro-slavery candidate. The short-lived Constitutional Union party, running on a vague platform designed to sidestep the slavery issue and save the Union, nominated John Bell, of Tennessee. The voters cast 1,864,735 votes[221] for Abraham Lincoln, who had made his opposition to the institution of slavery a matter of principle, and 2,821,157 votes for the other three candidates. Only 33% of the voters cast a clear vote for Abraham Lincoln. 67%, a two-thirds majority, voted in for pro-slavery candidates or to evade the issue one way or the other through "compromise." With only 33% of the vote, Abraham Lincoln won. The issue, left unresolved by the Declaration of Independence and the Constitutional Convention, finally made War Between the States inevitable.

Following the Civil War, in 1868, the Fourteenth Amendment modified Article I, Section 2 to allow freed slaves the right to vote, but Indians who are not taxed are still excluded:

"Representatives shall be apportioned among the several States according to their respective numbers, counting the whole number of persons in each State, excluding Indians not taxed."

---

[221] Lincoln's Election – University of Virginia - http://valley.vcdh.virginia.edu/outlines/election.html

Chapter 19
The Constitution Begins to Come Together

In less than a month, the men gathered in Philadelphia would present to the new nation a Constitution with a preamble that read:

> "We the people of the United States, in order to form a more perfect union, establish justice, insure domestic tranquility, provide for the common defense, promote the general welfare, and secure the blessings of liberty to ourselves and our posterity, do ordain and establish this Constitution for the United States of America."

The Declaration of Independence, which some of the delegates had signed, declared,

> "WE hold these Truths to be self-evident, that all Men are created equal, that they are endowed by their Creator with certain unalienable Rights, that among these are Life, Liberty and the Pursuit of Happiness -- That to secure these Rights, Governments are instituted among Men, deriving their just Powers from the Consent of the Governed, that whenever any Form of Government becomes destructive of these Ends, it is the Right of the People to alter or to abolish it, and to institute new Government, laying its Foundation on such Principles, and organizing its Powers in such Form, as to them shall seem most likely to effect their Safety and Happiness."

However, in June 1787, as the eleventh anniversary of the signing of that document approached, many delegates at the Constitutional Convention were having difficulty trusting the people who had the unalienable rights to make correct decisions. A "union," according to the dictionary, is a "number of persons, societies, states or the like joined or associated together for some common purpose."

In 1776 thirteen individual colonies had joined together for a common purpose – to resist the policies and actions of the King of England and his ministers. On the same day Edmund Randolph proposed the Declaration of Independence, he also proposed the Articles of Confederation. The Articles were written, and debated then, on November 15, 1777, they were unanimously adopted. The Articles, which declared the new Confederation to be a "perpetual union" were in force after ratification by Maryland, 1 March 1781.

The states had succeeded in working together, although imperfectly, as long as a common purpose existed. When the war was won, and all the states were independent of Britain, conflicts arose. Without war, what "common purpose" existed between Virginia with a predominately Anglican population and Maryland with a predominately Catholic population?

Unity was one of the four legs George Washington believed were necessary to sustain a free and independent government, along with a strong military for a common defense, free trade for a strong economy, and a moral and virtuous people, that. Yet the colonies had been settled largely to accommodate one or another special interest group. Many of those special interests were religious in nature where one particular religion was encouraged to flourish, but not for all religions to flourish.

In Puritan Massachusetts in 1660, Mary Dyer,[222] a Quaker, was hung for her persistent support of Quaker beliefs.

---

[222] Mary Dyer, a Quaker, is hung in Puritan Massachusetts for preaching view contrary to Puritanism - http://www.loc.gov/exhibits/religion/rel01-2.html

Maryland's Toleration Act, for example, passed in the colony in 1649, said, in part, to "use or utter any reproachful Speeches, words or language concerning the said Holy Trinity, or any of the said three persons thereof, shall be punished with death and confiscation or forfeiture of all his or her lands and goods to the Lord Proprietary and his heirs." [223]

On the other hand, the adjoining colony, Virginia, passed a law in 1641 that stated "it should not be lawful under the penalty aforesaid for any popish priest that shall hereafter arrive to remain above five days after warning given for his departure by the Governor or commander of the place where he or they shall be, if wind and weather hinder not his departure...."[224]

In eight years of war, the state regiments had largely maintained their individual identities, led by officers from their own states. Once the war was over, the challenge facing the delegates at the Constitutional Convention was to find a common purpose around which to unite.

Alexander Hamilton – New York[225]

Soon Alexander Hamilton would tell the people of New York in *Federalist Paper* #1[226] as they considered whether or not to adopt the newly written Constitution of the United States:

[223] Maryland Toleration Act 1649 - http://odur.let.rug.nl/~usa/D/1601-1650/maryland/mta.htm

[224] Virginia's 1600s Religion Laws - http://www.iath.virginia.edu/vcdh/jamestown/rlaws.html#6

[225] National Archives – Alexander Hamilton – New York http://www.law.umkc.edu/faculty/projects/ftrials/conlaw/marrynewyork.html

"AFTER an unequivocal experience of the inefficiency of the subsisting federal government, you are called upon to deliberate on a new Constitution for the United States of America. The subject speaks its own importance; comprehending in its consequences nothing less than the existence of the UNION, the safety and welfare of the parts of which it is composed, the fate of an empire in many respects the most interesting in the world.

"It has been frequently remarked that it seems to have been reserved to the people of this country, by their conduct and example, to decide the important question, whether societies of men are really capable or not of establishing good government from reflection and choice, or whether they are forever destined to depend for their political constitutions on accident and force.

"If there be any truth in the remark, the crisis at which we are arrived may with propriety be regarded as the era in which that decision is to be made; and a wrong election of the part we shall act may, in this view, deserve to be considered as the general misfortune of mankind."

Failure to adopt the Constitution, Hamilton said, would be a misfortune for all of mankind.

John Jay – New York[227]

John Jay, also from New York who helped write the Treaty of Paris that ended the Revolution, wrote on the subject of unity, in *Federalist Paper* #2:[228]

---

[226] Federalist Papers - #1 – By Alexander Hamilton - http://www.yale.edu/lawweb/avalon/federal/fed01.htm

[227] Columbia University - John Jay – Biography - http://www.columbia.edu/cu/lweb/eresources/archives/jay/biography.html

"It has until lately been a received and uncontradicted opinion that the prosperity of the people of America depended on their continuing firmly united, and the wishes, prayers, and efforts of our best and wisest citizens have been constantly directed to that object. But politicians now appear, who insist that this opinion is erroneous, and that instead of looking for safety and happiness in union, we ought to seek it in a division of the States into distinct confederacies or sovereignties."

James Madison

James Madison, in *Federalist Paper* #10, wrote:[229]

"Among the numerous advantages promised by a well-constructed Union, none deserves to be more accurately developed than its tendency to break and control the violence of faction. By a faction, I understand a number of citizens, whether amounting to a majority or a minority of the whole, who are united and actuated by some common impulse of passion, or of interest, adverse to the rights of other citizens, or to the permanent and aggregate interests of the community."

In effect the delegates at the Constitutional Convention realized that a free and thriving nation needs union, or unity of purpose, that reaches beyond what today we would call "special interests." (A "special interest" group or "faction" seeks advantage

---

[228] John Jay – Federalist Paper #2 - http://lcweb2.loc.gov/const/fed/fed_02.html
[229] James Madison – Federalist Paper #10 - http://lcweb2.loc.gov/const/fed/fed_10.html

or support for their personal or group concerns, rather than that of the entire nation.)

Only a short time before, that unity was embodied in the King of England. A King, however was definitely something they did NOT want. Yet, experience was proving that a confederation with no national leader was not working. Anarchy threatened. Every effort to give the national government executive power, however, brought objections for fear that executive would one day become a king.

On July 17, after two months of proclaiming what they did not want, Gouverneur Morris of Pennsylvania suggested that the Convention decide what powers they DID want the federal government to have before deciding how its members were selected. Edmund Randolph called Morris' suggestions "a formidable idea indeed," and it was adopted.

Gunning Bedford of Delaware moved to alter the Virginia Plan's Resolution 6, to give Congress the power, "to legislate in all cases for the general interests of the Union, and also in those to which the States are separately incompetent."

It passed 6-4, with Connecticut, Virginia, South Carolina and Georgia voting no.

However, a motion to give the National Congress the right to veto "all laws passed by the several States contravening in the opinion of the Nat: Legislature the articles of Union, or any treaties subsisting under the authority of ye. Union" was rejected by a vote of 7-3 with only Virginia, Massachusetts and North Carolina voting "aye."

The next debate concerned how the President should be elected. Should the state legislatures choose the President or the people in the states? Allowing the direct election of the President by the Congress and his impeachment by the same body, Gouverneur Morris of Pennsylvania stated, would make the President "the mere creature of the Legislature." He moved to strike out "National Legislature" and insert "citizens of U.S."

Roger Sherman of Connecticut, Gouverneur Morris and James Wilson of Pennsylvania, and Charles Pinckney of South Carolina all spoke in opposition to the people directly electing the President. This caused George Mason of Virginia to observe,

"It is curious to remark the different language held at different times. At one moment we are told that the Legislature is entitled to thorough confidence, and to indefinite power. At another, that it will be governed by intrigue & corruption, and cannot be trusted at all."

He opposed direct election of the President by the people.

The delegates rejected a motion for the people to select the President and a motion for the state legislatures to select the President and postponed the issue to consider later.

On July 18, the delegates passed[230] with no debate motions giving the President the authority to veto bills passed by Congress, but allowed Congress to override his veto with a 2/3 majority.

The delegates also approved Resolution 11 to create a judiciary branch of government "to consist of one supreme tribunal" and discussed at length how the judges would be appointed. George Mason felt the same people who could impeach the President should not select him. Nathaniel Gorham of Massachusetts felt that allowing the Senate to choose the judges would lead "to intrigue & cabal."

James Madison of Virginia moved that the "Judges should be nominated by the Executive, and such nomination should become an appointment if not disagreed to within days by 2/3 of the 2d. branch."

Nathaniel Gorham of Massachusetts moved "that the Judges be nominated and appointed by the Executive, by and with the advice and consent of the 2d. branch (Senate) and every such nomination shall be made at least days prior to such appointment." Massachusetts had used that system for 140 years.

Presidential appointments, with the advice and consent of the Senate were eventually adopted.

The delegates then took up the questions of how long judges should serve and what their salaries should be, usually a difficult issue on which to find agreement. However, with little debate the delegates approved Resolution 12, empowering the

---

[230] Avalon Project – 1787 Federal Constitution –July 18, -Choosing the President and judges, putting down rebellion - http://www.yale.edu/lawweb/avalon/debates/718.htm

National Legislature to appoint "inferior tribunals" (state courts); Resolution 13 giving jurisdiction to the Supreme Court for "all cases arising under the National laws: And to such other questions as may involve the National peace and harmony;" Resolution 14 providing for the admission of new States; and Resolution 15 "that provision ought to be made for the continuance of Congress and for the completion of their engagements."

Resolution 16, which stated "that a Republican Constitution & its existing laws ought to be guarantied to each State by the U. States," created a lively discussion on rebellion and who would be responsible for putting down rebellion in the states.

After considerable discussion and several suggested changes in wording, James Wilson of Pennsylvania moved that the wording be "that a Republican form of Government shall be guarantied to each State and that each State shall be protected against foreign and domestic violence."

The wording was agreed to unanimously.

Chapter 20
Separation of Powers – "Freedom's Fundamental Principle"

On July 19, 1787, Governeur Morris of Pennsylvania told the delegates,

"It is necessary to take into one view all that relates to the establishment of the Executive; on the due formation of which must depend the efficacy & utility of the Union among the present and future States. It has been a maxim in Political Science that Republican Government is not adapted to a large extent of Country, because the energy of the Executive Magistracy can not reach the extreme parts of it.

"Our Country is an extensive one. We must either then renounce the blessings of the Union, or provide an Executive with sufficient vigor to pervade every part of it." He also pointed out that "one great object of the Executive is to controul the Legislature. The Legislature will continually seek to aggrandize & perpetuate themselves; and will seize those critical moments produced by war, invasion or convulsion for that purpose. It is necessary then that the Executive Magistrate should be the guardian of the people, even of the lower classes, against. Legislative tyranny, against the Great & the wealthy who in the course of things will necessarily compose the Legislative body. Wealth tends to corrupt the mind & to nourish its love of power, and to stimulate it to oppression...[231]

"The Executive therefore ought to be so constituted as to be the great protector of the Mass of the people. -It is the duty of the Executive to appoint the officers & to command the forces of the Republic: to appoint

1. ministerial officers for the administration of public affairs.

2. officers for the dispensation of Justice. Who will be the best Judges whether these appointments be well made? The people at large, who will know, will see, will feel the effects of them. Again who can judge so well of the discharge of military

[231] Avalon Project –1787 Federal Convention, July 19, 1787-Need for a strong executive - http://www.yale.edu/lawweb/avalon/debates/719.htm

duties for the protection & security of the people, as the people themselves who are to be protected & secured?"

James Madison of Virginia supported Morris' views, saying:

> "If it be a fundamental principle of free Government that the Legislative, Executive & Judiciary powers should be separately exercised, it is equally so that they be independently exercised.
>
> "There is the same & perhaps greater reason why the Executive should be independent of the Legislature, than why the Judiciary should: A coalition of the two former powers would be more immediately & certainly dangerous to public liberty. It is essential then that the appointment of the Executive should either be drawn from some source, or held by some tenure, that will give him a free agency with regard to the Legislature. This could not be if he was to be appointable from time to time by the Legislature."[232]

This led to vigorous debate on how the President would be elected, and how and by whom judges would be appointed and how the separation of powers could be maintained.

On July 21, James Madison again brought up his motion, which had been postponed "that the Judges should be nominated by the Executive & such nominations become appointments unless disagreed to by 2/3 of the 2d. branch of the Legislature."

Debate resumed on Madison's motion. When the vote was called, Madison's motion passed 6-3, with Massachusetts, Pennsylvania and Virginia voting "no."

On Monday, July 23, Resolution 17, for future amendments to the Constitution, was agreed to without debate. The provision there, "ought to be made for future amendments of the articles of Union."

After some debate, Resolution 18, based on Edmund Randolph's resolution "requiring the Legislative, Executive, and

---

[232] Ibid – Executive Powers, James Madison-July 19- http://www.yale.edu/lawweb/avalon/debates/719.htm

Judiciary of States to be bound by oath to support the articles of Union," was voted on and adopted.

The Convention then opened debate on Resolution 19, ""referring the new Constitution to Assemblies to be chosen by the people for the express purpose of ratifying it." How would these ratifying assemblies be chosen and who would choose them?

On July 24, again the delegates discussed how the executive would be appointed, repeating most of the previous statements on the subject and voting to approve that the National Legislature select the executive. This was followed by a discussion on how long he was to serve and whether or not he could run for re-election a second time. Terms of office suggested ranged from 8 years, to 10, 11, 12, 15 and 20 years. Each number was debated.

Finally, James Wilson of Pennsylvania said, The difficulties and perplexities into which the House is thrown proceed from the election by the Legislature which he was sorry had been reinstated. The inconveniency of this mode was such that he would agree to almost any length of time in order to get rid of the dependence which must result from it."

Governeur Morris of Pennsylvania observed, "Of all possible modes of appointment that by the Legislature is the worst. If the Legislature is to appoint, and to impeach or to influence the impeachment, the Executive will be the mere creature of it."

The delegates voted to postpone the question. It was taken up again on July 25, still without agreement.

On July 26, a motion to adopt an amended resolution on the National Executive was passed 6-3, with Virginia divided. Both George Washington and James Madison voted "no." The resolution said: "that a National Executive be instituted-to consist of a single person-to be chosen by the Natl. legislature-for the term of seven years-to be ineligible a 2d. time-with power to carry into execution the natl. laws-to appoint to offices in cases not otherwise provided for-to be removable on impeachment & conviction of malpractice or neglect of duty-to receive a fixed compensation for the devotion of his time to the public service, to be paid out of the Natl. treasury."

At the end of the day the Convention adjourned until August 6 to give the Committee of Detail time to write the

Constitution as agreed to through July 26 and report back to the Convention.

On August 6, 1787, the committee delivered to each delegate a copy of the first draft of the Constitution.[233] The preamble read:

> "We the people of the States of New Hampshire, Massachusetts, Rhode-Island and Providence Plantations, Connecticut, New-York, New-Jersey, Pennsylvania, Delaware, Maryland, Virginia, North-Carolina, South-Carolina, and Georgia, do ordain, declare, and establish the following Constitution for the Government of Ourselves and our Posterity."

They were not yet thinking of themselves as **"We the People of the United States of America."**

It would take another month to resolve all the "postponed" issues. Who should be able to vote? Should only property owners be allowed to vote? What is the definition of a "freeholder?"

Gouverneur Morris of Pennsylvania did not like the wording of Article IV Section 1 of the draft which read: "The members of the House of Representatives shall be chosen every second year, by the people of the several States comprehended within this Union. The qualifications of the electors shall be the same, from time to time, as those of the electors in the several States, of the most numerous branch of their own legislatures."

He moved that the wording be changed[234] "to restrain the right of suffrage to freeholders."

A freeholder was a property or estate owner. Only those who owned property would be able to vote. That brought up the question of what is "property?"

George Mason of Virginia said, "We all feel too strongly the remains of ancient prejudices, and view things too much through a British medium. A Freehold is the qualification in England, and hence it is imagined to be the only proper one. The true idea in his opinion was that every man having evidence of

---

[233] Avalon Project-1787 Federal Constitution-Aug. 6 –First Draft of new Federal Constitution printed - http://www.yale.edu/lawweb/avalon/debates/806.htm

[234] Avalon Project-1787 Federal Constitution-Aug. 8, -Should ordinary people have the right to vote? - http://www.yale.edu/lawweb/avalon/debates/808.htm

attachment to and permanent common interest with the Society ought to share in all its rights and privileges.

> "Was this qualification restrained to freeholders? Does no other kind of property but land evidence a common interest in the proprietor? Does nothing besides property mark a permanent attachment. Ought the merchant, the monied man, the parent of a number of children whose fortunes are to be pursued in his own Country, to be viewed as suspicious characters, and unworthy to be trusted with the common rights of their fellow Citizens."

James Madison of Virginia observed, "The right of suffrage is certainly one of the fundamental articles of republican Government, and ought not to be left to be regulated by the Legislature."

According to the notes taken at the Convention, Benjamin Franklin of Pennsylvania reminded the delegates "that we should not depress the virtue & public spirit of our common people; of which they displayed a great deal during the war, and which contributed principally to the favorable issue of it."

He related the honorable refusal of the American seamen who were carried in great numbers into the British Prisons during the war, to redeem themselves from misery or to seek their fortunes, by entering on board the Ships of the Enemies to their Country; contrasting their patriotism with a contemporary instance in which the British seamen made prisoners by the Americans, readily entered on the ships of the latter on being promised a share of the prizes that might be made out of their own Country.

This proceeded, he said, from the different manner in which the common people were treated in America & G. Britain. He did not think that the elected "had any right in any case to narrow the privileges of the electors."

Two articles in the resolution that had been the subject of considerable debate were still disliked by many delegates, especially those from the larger states:

Article 4 Section 5 of the draft: "All bills for raising or appropriating money, and for fixing the salaries of the officers of Government, shall originate in the House of Representatives, and shall not be altered or amended by the Senate. No money shall be drawn from the Public Treasury, but in pursuance of appropriations that shall originate in the House of Representatives."

And Article 5 Section 1. "The Senate of the United States shall be chosen by the Legislatures of the several States. Each Legislature shall chuse two members. Vacancies may be supplied by the Executive until the next meeting of the Legislature. Each member shall have one vote."

Benjamin Franklin of Pennsylvania, however, considered[235] the two clauses, the originating of money bills, and the equality of votes in the Senate, as essentially connected by the compromise which had been agreed to.

On August 9, 1787 the debate began to bog down over the admission of foreigners into the Country in debating the period of time Senators must live in the United States before being permitted to run for that office. Governeur Morris argued there was "the danger of admitting stranger into our public councils" Charles Pinkney warned that, since the Senate have the power to make treaties "there is a peculiar danger and impropriety in opening its door to those who have foreign attachments." .

Benjamin Franklin argued in favor of "foreigners" stating that while he was not against setting a reasonable time for residence in the country prior to being allowed to run for the Senate he would be "very sorry to see any thing like illiberality inserted in the Constitution. The people in Europe are friendly to this County. Even in the Country with which we have been lately at war, we have now and had during the war, a great many friends not only among the people at large but in both houses of Parliament.

> "In every other Country in Europe all the people are our friends. We found in the course of the Revolution that many strangers served us faithfully- and that many natives took part against their Country. When foreigners after looking about for some other Country in which they can obtain more happiness, give a preference to ours it is a proof of attachment which ought to excite our confidence and affection."

---

[235] Avalon Project-1787 Federal Constitution-Aug. 9-Two Sections trouble Large states - http://www.yale.edu/lawweb/avalon/debates/809.htm

The treatment of "foreigners" today, in the 21st Century, is as heated as it was during the Constitutional Convention of 1787. Should they be welcomed as assets to our nation or kept out as threats to our national security?

Chapter 21
Morris: Are Slaves "Men or Property?"

When Article IV Section 4 was discussed, the slavery issue again came up.

Rufus King of Massachusetts pinpointed a glaring contradiction in the evolving document which has troubled the people of the United States every since. He declared,[236] "In two great points the hands of the Legislature were absolutely tied. The importation of slaves could not be prohibited and exports could not be taxed. Is this reasonable? What are the great objects of the General System?

1. defense against foreign invasion.
2. against internal sedition.
3. Shall all the States then be bound to defend each; and shall each be at liberty to introduce a weakness which will render defense more difficult?

"Shall one part of the U. S. be bound to defend another part, and that other part be at liberty not only to increase its own danger, but to withhold the compensation for the burden? If slaves are to be imported shall not the exports produced by their labor, supply a revenue the better to enable the general government to defend their masters? - There was so much inequality & unreasonableness in all this, that the people of the Northern States could never be reconciled to it."

Gouverneur Morris of Pennsylvania moved to insert "free" before the word inhabitants. He said he "never would concur in upholding domestic slavery.[237] It was a nefarious institution. It was the curse of heaven on the States where it prevailed. Compare the free regions of the Middle States, where a rich & noble cultivation marks the prosperity & happiness of the people, with the misery & poverty which overspread the barren wastes of Virginia, Maryland & the other States having slaves."

When the Revolution began in 1775, slavery was legal in all 13 colonies. In 1780 Pennsylvania passed a gradual

---

[236] Avalon Project-1787 Federal Constitution-Aug. 8 – On Importation of Slaves- http://www.yale.edu/lawweb/avalon/debates/808.htm
[237] Ibid - http://www.yale.edu/lawweb/avalon/debates/808.htm

emancipation bill which freed slave children when they reached the age of 28. In Massachusetts, slavery was ended in 1783. Both Rhode Island and Connecticut passed gradual emancipation legislation in 1784.

Furthermore, the Continental Congress had passed the Northwest Ordinance in July of 1787 declaring that the lands ceded to the United States by the Treaty of Paris by Britain would allow "neither slavery nor involuntary servitude" in the territory.[238]

The Northwest Territory included all the land west of Pennsylvania and northwest of the Ohio River. The modern states of Ohio, Indiana, Illinois, Michigan and Wisconsin, and the eastern part of Minnesota, were once part of the Northwest Territory.

Gouverneur Morris asked:

> "Upon what principle is it that the slaves shall be computed in the representation? Are they men? Then make them Citizens and let them vote. Are they property? Why then is no other property included? The Houses in this city (Philadelphia) are worth more than all the wretched slaves which cover the rice swamps of South Carolina.
>
> "The admission of slaves into the Representation when fairly explained comes to this: that the inhabitant of Georgia and S. Carolina who goes to the Coast of Africa, and in defiance of the most sacred laws of humanity tears away his fellow creatures from their dearest connections and damns them to the most cruel bondages, shall have more votes in a government instituted for protection of the rights of mankind, than the Citizen of Pennsylvania or New Jersey who views with a laudable horror, so nefarious a practice."

At the time the Constitution was being debated in 1787, the only two states that still allowed importation of slaves were Georgia and South Carolina. Six weeks prior to Rufus King and Gouverneur Morris making their strong anti-slavery statements, both had voted, as had the rest of the Northern State delegations, plus Virginia and Maryland delegations to defeat a motion

---

[238] Northwest Ordinance – July 13, 1787 - http://www.yale.edu/lawweb/avalon/nworder.htm

introduced and supported by Georgia and South Carolina to give fully U.S. citizenship to slaves.

On August 22, 1787 the Convention again was confronted with the real meaning of slavery when they began to discuss Article VII, Sect. 4 of the draft of the Constitution which read:

> "No tax or duty shall be laid by the Legislature on articles exported from any State; nor on the migration or importation of such persons as the several States shall think proper to admit; nor shall such migration or importation be prohibited."

Again the debate centered on the evils of slavery, although the word "slavery" was never mentioned in the Constitution. Roger Sherman of Connecticut observed that "the abolition of Slavery seemed to be going on in the U. S. and that the good sense of the several States would probably by degrees compleat it."[239]

George Mason of Virginia charged:

> "This infernal traffic originated in the avarice of British Merchants. The British Government constantly checked the attempts of Virginia to put a stop to it. The present question concerns not the importing States alone but the whole Union."

Allowing slavery to continue, he said, created problems.

> "Maryland & Virginia ... had already prohibited the importation of slaves expressly. North Carolina had done the same in substance. All this would be in vain if South Carolina & Georgia be at liberty to import. The Western people are already calling out for slaves for their new lands, and will fill that Country with slaves if they can be got thro' South Carolina & Georgia. Slavery discourages arts & manufactures. The poor despise labor when performed by slaves."[240]

On August 25, General C. Cotesworth Pinckney of South Carolina moved to strike out the words "the year eighteen hundred" as the year limiting the importation of slaves, and to insert the words "the year eighteen hundred and eight." The motion was seconded by Nathanial Gorham of Massachusetts.

---

[239] Avalon Project-1787 Federal Constitution-Aug. 22 – Slavery Issue – Article VII, Sect. 4 - http://www.yale.edu/lawweb/avalon/debates/822.htm

[240] Ibid- http://www.yale.edu/lawweb/avalon/debates/822.htm

James Madison of Virginia observed that 20 years more of importing slaves, from 1787 to 1808 "will produce all the mischief that can be apprehended from the liberty to import slaves. So long a term will be more dishonorable to the National character than to say nothing about it in the Constitution."[241]

In the debate Madison said he:

> "thought it wrong to admit in the Constitution the idea that there could be property in men. The reason of duties did not hold, as slaves are not like merchandize, consumed,"

Pinckney's motion passed 7-4, with New Jersey, Pennsylvania, Delaware and Virginia voting "no." Twenty years later, on March 2, 1807 Thomas Jefferson, who was then President of the United States, signed into law and *An Act to Prohibit the Importation of Slaves."*[242] Any person, whether American or not, from owners, workmen loading or preparing a ship to be used in transporting slaves would be fined $20,000. Any ship used for the purpose of transporting slaves "shall be forfeited to the use of the United States" and those involved in transporting the slaves "may be seized, prosecuted and condemned in any court of the United States having jurisdiction thereof."

From August 25 to September 3, 1787 the delegates debated a of smaller issues at the Constitutional Convention. Changes were made on sections of the Constitution that involved trade, the creation of new states, ratification of the Constitution, members of Congress being ineligible to hold other offices, and wording changes on existing sections.

Still remaining, unresolved, however, was how the president would be chosen, by whom he would be chosen and what powers he would have under the new Constitution.

---

[241] The Avalon Project –1787 Federal Constitution–Aug. 25 – Ending Slave Trade in 1808 - http://www.yale.edu/lawweb/avalon/debates/825.htm

[242] Teaching American History – 1807 An Act to Prohibit the Importation of Slaves http://teachingamericanhistory.org/library/index.asp?document=179

Chapter 22
The Electoral College Compromise

Basically the issue that was still unresolved, the election of the President, involved a power struggle between the strength and sovereignty of the states and the strength and sovereignty of the people. Some delegates insisted the State Legislatures should choose the president. Others pointed out that the people themselves had the right to choose those who govern.

On September 4, 1787, a report from the 11 member committee chosen August 31st from each state to suggest "additions and alterations" on unresolved issues was made by David Brearley of New Jersey. The New York Delegates had left by then and Rhode Island had never sent delegates.

The committee proposed[243] in Article 10, Section 1 that the President "shall hold his office during the term of four years, and together with the vice-President, chosen for the same term, be elected in the following manner, viz. Each State shall appoint in such manner as its Legislature may direct, a number of electors equal to the whole number of Senators and members of the House of Representatives to which the State may be entitled in the Legislature.

> "The Electors shall meet in their respective States, and vote by ballot for two persons, of whom one at least shall not be an inhabitant of the same State with themselves; and they shall make a list of all the persons voted for, and of the number of votes for each, which list they shall sign and certify and transmit sealed to the Seat of the General Government, directed to the President of the Senate-The President of the Senate shall in that House open all the certificates; and the votes shall be then and there counted.
>
> "The Person having the greatest number of votes shall be the President, if such number be a majority of that of the electors; and if there be more than one who have such majority, and have an equal number of votes, then the Senate shall

[243] The Avalon Project – 1787 Federal Constitution –Sept 4 – Committee report on election of the President - http://www.yale.edu/lawweb/avalon/debates/904.htm

immediately choose by ballot one of them for President: but if no person have a majority, then from the five highest on the list, the Senate shall choose by ballot the President. And in every case after the choice of the President, the person having the greatest number of votes shall be vice- president: but if there should remain two or more who have equal votes, the Senate shall choose from them the vice-President.

"The Legislature may determine the time of choosing and assembling the Electors, and the manner of certifying and transmitting their votes."

On September 4, the delegates agreed on impeachments proceedings to remove the President but could not agree on what to do in case the election of the President ended in a tie. The delegates would not agree on giving the Senate the power to choose the President in case of a tie.

On September 5, a flurry of motions to reconsider parts of the Constitution already approved took up most of the day.[244]

On September 8, the delegates debated and voted on impeachment of the President and on the treaty-making powers of the Senate. They also selected five members, William Samuel Johnson of Connecticut, Alexander Hamilton of New York, Governeur Morris of Pennsylvania, James Madison of Virginia and Rufus King of Massachusetts, as the committee "to revise the stile of and arrange the articles which had been agreed to by the House."[245]

On September 10, as the Constitution was in the final stages of completion, Edmund Randolph of Virginia, who introduced the plan the delegates were about to adopt, rose to state his objections to the document.[246] According to the notes of James Madison, his objections were:

---

[244] The Avalon Project –1787 Federal Constitution – Sept. 5, 1787 – Motions to reconsider approved sections - http://www.yale.edu/lawweb/avalon/debates/905.htm

[245] Avalon Project – 1787 Federal Constitution-Sept. 8 –Style Committee selected to finalize Constitution - http://www.yale.edu/lawweb/avalon/debates/908.htm

[246] Avalon Project-1787 Federal Constitution-Sept 10-Randolph's Objections to Constitution- http://www.yale.edu/lawweb/avalon/debates/910.htm

- "the Senate's being made the Court of Impeachment for trying the Executive
- "on the necessity of 3/4 instead of 2/3 of each house to overrule the negative of the President
- "on the smallness of the number of the Representative branch,
- "on the want of limitation to a standing army-on the general clause concerning necessary and proper laws
- "on the want of some particular restraint on navigation acts
- "on the power to lay duties on exports
- "on the Authority of the General Legislature to interpose on the application of the Executives of the States
- "on the want of a more definite boundary between the General & State Legislatures-and between the General and State Judiciaries
- "on the unqualified power of the President to pardon treasons
- "on the want of some limit to the power of the Legislature in regulating their own compensations.

Randolph asked:

> "With these difficulties in his mind, what course was he to pursue? Was he to promote the establishment of a plan which he verily believed would end in tyranny? He was unwilling, he said, to impede the wishes and Judgment of the Convention, but he must keep himself free, in case he should be honored with a seat in the Convention of his State, to act according to the dictates of his judgment."

He proposed that the Constitution go from the Convention to the state legislatures, and from these to state conventions with the power to adopt, reject or amend. Key Virginia delegates, Edmund Randolph, George Mason, George Wythe and James McClurg, did not sign the Constitution. Virginians James Madison, George Washington and John Blair did sign it.

On September 12, 1787, the Constitution of the United States emerged from the style committee with printed copies for each delegate.

Hugh Williamson of North Carolina moved to change the 3/4 rule to overrule a Presidential veto, which he had requested changed to 2/3. His motion passed 6-4 with Massachusetts, Pennsylvania, Delaware and Virginia voting "no" and New Hampshire divided.

George Mason of Virginia expressed concern that a Bill of Rights had not prefaced the Constitution. Elbridge Gerry of Massachusetts moved that a Bill of Rights be written and added to the document. His motion was seconded by George Mason. The motion was defeated 10-0 with Massachusetts absent. [247]

A number of motions to make last minute changes in the Constitution were nearly all defeated, including a motion by James Mason to "insert something pointing out and guarding against the danger of" a standing army in time of peace.

On September 17, 1787, the Constitution was read to the delegates, and the first to rise was 81-year- old Dr. Benjamin Franklin, of Pennsylvania, with his written remarks in his hand. They were read to the Convention by George Mason.[248]

> "Mr. President
>
> "I confess that there are several parts of this constitution which I do not at present approve, but I am not sure I shall never approve them: For having lived long, I have experienced many instances of being obliged by better information, or fuller consideration, to change opinions even on important subjects, which I once thought right, but found to be otherwise. It is therefore that the older I grow, the more apt I am to doubt my own judgment, and to pay more respect to the judgment of others.
>
> "Most men indeed as well as most sects in Religion, think themselves in possession of all truth, and that wherever others differ from them it is so far error. Steele a Protestant in a Dedication tells the Pope, that the only difference between our Churches in their opinions of the certainty of their doctrines is,

---

[247] Avalon Project-1787 Federal Constitution, Sept 12 –Constitution presented by Style Committee - http://www.yale.edu/lawweb/avalon/debates/912.htm

[248] Avalon Project – 1787 Federal Constitution- Sept. 17, 1787 –Benjamin Franklin's speech on the Constitution- http://www.yale.edu/lawweb/avalon/debates/917.htm

the Church of Rome is infallible and the Church of England is never in the wrong. But though many private persons think almost as highly of their own infallibility as of that of their sect, few express it so naturally as a certain French lady, who in a dispute with her sister, said 'I don't know how it happens, Sister but I meet with no body but myself, that's always in the right-Il n'y a que moi qui a toujours raison.'

"In these sentiments, Sir, I agree to this Constitution with all its faults, if they are such; because I think a general Government necessary for us, and there is no form of Government but what may be a blessing to the people if well administered, and believe farther that this is likely to be well administered for a course of years, and can only end in Despotism, as other forms have done before it, when the people shall become so corrupted as to need despotic Government, being incapable of any other.

"I doubt too whether any other Convention we can obtain, may be able to make a better Constitution. For when you assemble a number of men to have the advantage of their joint wisdom, you inevitably assemble with those men, all their prejudices, their passions, their errors of opinion, their local interests, and their selfish views. From such an assembly can a perfect production be expected?

"It therefore astonishes me, Sir, to find this system approaching so near to perfection as it does; and I think it will astonish our enemies, who are waiting with confidence to hear that our councils are confounded like those of the Builders of Babel; and that our States are on the point of separation, only to meet hereafter for the purpose of cutting one another's throats.

"Thus I consent, Sir, to this Constitution because I expect no better, and because I am not sure, that it is not the best. The opinions I have had of its errors, I sacrifice to the public good. I have never whispered a syllable of them abroad. Within these walls they were born, and here they shall die. If every one of us in returning to our Constituents were to report the objections he has had to it, and endeavor to gain partisans in support of them, we might prevent its being generally received, and thereby lose all the salutary effects & great advantages resulting naturally in our favor among foreign Nations as well as among ourselves, from our real or apparent unanimity.

"Much of the strength & efficiency of any Government in procuring and securing happiness to the people, depends, on the general opinion of the goodness of the Government, as well as well as of the wisdom and integrity of its Governors. I hope therefore that for our own sakes as a part of the people, and for the sake of posterity, we shall act heartily and unanimously in recommending this Constitution (if approved by Congress & confirmed by the Conventions) wherever our influence may extend, and turn our future thoughts & endeavors to the means of having it well administered.

"On the whole, Sir, I can not help expressing a wish that every member of the Convention who may still have objections to it, would with me, on this occasion doubt a little of his own infallibility, and to make manifest our unanimity, put his name to this instrument."

He then moved that the Constitution be signed by the members and offered the following as a convenient form, viz. "Done in Convention by the unanimous consent of the States present the 17th of September (1787). In Witness whereof we have hereunto subscribed our names."

One by one the assembled delegated signed the new Constitution. As they signed, Dr. Franklin looking towards the president's chair, at the back of which a sun was pointed, observed aloud to those sitting next to him, "I have often, in the course of the session, and the vicissitudes of my hopes and fears as to its issue, looked at that sun behind the president, without being able to tell whether it was rising or setting; at length I have the happiness to know it is a rising and not a setting sun."[249]

---

[249] The Life of Washington by Washington Irving Vol IV page 563, quotation from the Madison Papers, iii. 1624

Chapter 23

"I wish the Constitution…had been made more perfect"

Signing the Constitution of the United States[250]

Not everyone greeted with enthusiasm the new Constitution of the United States adopted on September 17, 1787, signed by most members of the Constitutional Convention and ratified over the next three years.

However, the document became widely discussed not only in the United States, but in Europe. George Washington's hand in disseminating the news of the new document and encouraging support for it through numerous letters to both American and foreign leaders is a story that is rarely told.

For example, the day after the Constitution was signed, he wrote to his good friend and former aide The Marquis de Lafayette, enclosing one of the 500 printed copies of the new Constitution, printed by Dunlap and Claypoole, with the notation:[251]

"It is the production of four months deliberation. It is now a Child of fortune, to be fostered by some and buffeted by others.

---

[250] Signing the Constitution - http://www.constitution.org/img/signing.jpg

[251] George Washington's Letter and copy of the Constitution to LaFayette-September 18, 1787 - http://etext.lib.virginia.edu/etcbin/toccer-new2?id=WasFi29.xml&images=images/modeng&data=/texts/english/modeng/parsed&tag=public&part=201&division=div1

what will be the General opinion on, or the reception of it, is not for me to decide, nor shall I say any thing for or against it: if it be good I suppose it will work its way good; if bad, it will recoil on the Framers. My best wishes attend you, and yours; and with the sincerest friendship and most Affectionate regard etc.

On September 24, 1787 Washington sent letters and copies of the Constitution to Patrick Henry and Benjamin Harrison with a gentle recommendation that they "discover the good" in it:" [252]

"Dear Sir: In the first moment after my return I take the liberty of sending you a copy of the Constitution which the foederal Convention has submitted to the People of these States. I accompany it with no observations; your own Judgment will at once discover the good, and the exceptionable parts of it and your experience of the difficulties, which have ever arisen when attempts have been made to reconcile such variety of Interests and local prejudices as pervade the several States will render explanation unnecessary. I wish the Constitution which is offered had been made more perfect, but I sincerely believe it is the best that could be obtained at this time; and, as a Constitutional door is opened for amendment hereafter, the adoption of it under the present circumstances of the Union is in my opinion desirable.

From a variety of concurring accounts it appears to me that the political concerns of this Country are, in a manner, suspended by a thread. That the Convention has been looked up to by the reflecting part of the community with a solicitude which is hardly to be conceived, and that if nothing had been agreed on by that body, anarchy would soon have ensued, the seeds being richly [*sic*] sown in every soil. I am &c.

On October 4 Benjamin Harrison former Governor of Virginia, signer of the Declaration of Independence, father of President William Henry Harrison and great-grandfather of President Benjamin Harrison replied:

"I feel myself deeply interested in every thing that you have had a hand in, or that comes from you, and am so well assured of

---

[252] George Washington sends Patrick Henry a copy of the new Constitution – http://wyllie.lib.virginia.edu:8086/perl/toccer-new?id=WasFi29.xml&images=images/modeng&data=/texts/english/modeng/parsed&tag=public&part=203&division=div1

Benjamin Harrison[253]

the solidity of your judgment, and the rectitude of your intentions, that I shall never stick at trifles to conform myself to your opinion… I cannot divest myself of an opinion, that the seeds of civil discord are plentifully sown in very many of the powers given both to the president and congress, and that if the constitution is carried into effect, the States south of the Potowmac, will be little more than appendages to those to the northward of it.…I shall only say, that my objections chiefly lay against the unlimited powers of taxation and the regulations of trade, and the jurisdictions that are to be established in every State altogether independent of their laws."[254]

In the Virginia Convention Harrison specifically objected to the Constitution not having a Bill of Rights. Patrick Henry responded to Washington, on October 19, 1787 saying:

"I have to lament that I cannot bring my Mind to accord with the proposed Constitution. The Concern I feel on this Account, is really greater than I am able to express. Perhaps mature Reflection may furnish me Reasons to change my present Sentiments into a Conformity with the Opinions of those personages For whom I have the highest Reverence." [255]

In Virginia the fate of the new Constitution, which was passed in the Federal Constitutional Convention with Virginians

---

253 Signers of the Declaration – Benjamin Harrison - http://www.cr.nps.gov/history/online_books/declaration/bio16.htm

254 Benjamin Harrison's response to Washington about the Constitution - http://wyllie.lib.virginia.edu:8086/perl/toccer-new?id=WasFi29.xml&images=images/modeng&data=/texts/english/modeng/parsed&tag=public&part=203&division=div1

255 Ibid – Patrick Henry's response to Washington about the Constitution

playing leadership roles, was hotly debated. Patrick Henry, George Mason and Benjamin Harrison led the opposition to it. Patrick Henry said he was as opposed to the proposed Constitution in 1788-89 as he was to "continued British rule in 1775-76."

Patrick Henry and George Mason, both Anti-Federalists, campaigned vigorously against the Constitution because they felt it gave the federal government too much power. The new Constitution was debated for 15 days at the Virginia Convention. Henry argued,[256]

> "If our descendants be worthy the name of Americans they will preserve and hand down to their latest posterity the transactions of the present times."

Without a Bill of Rights he believed the people's freedoms "would be turned over to the will and whims of the government."

On March 2, 1788, after hearing Massachusetts had ratified the Constitution, George Washington, wrote a letter to James Madison, saying,[257]

> "The decision of Massachusetts, notwithstanding its concomitants, is a severe stroke to the opponents of the proposed Constitution in this State; and with the favorable determinations of the States which have gone before, and such as are likely to follow after, will have a powerful operation on the Minds of Men who are not actuated more by disappointment, passion and resentment, than they are by moderation, prudence and candor."

Massachusetts had accompanied her ratification with 9 proposed amendments. Washington felt, after 8 years of trying to fight a war with the States failing to provide basic needs for his army, that the Republic would fail unless there was more central power.

On March 11, 1788, in Federalist Paper #67,[258] Alexander Hamilton observed that those writing in opposition to the powers

---

[256] Bill of Rights Institute – Patrick Henry - http://www.billofrightsinstitute.org/pdf/henry_student.pdf

[257] Washington's Letter to Madison –March 2, 1788- http://wyllie.lib.virginia.edu:8086/perl/toccer-new?id=WasFi29.xml&images=images/modeng&data=/texts/english/modeng/parsed&tag=public&part=328&division=div1

and method of selection the president in the new Constitution "seem to have taken pains to signalize their talent of misrepresentation."

Opponents of the constitution, Hamiliton noted:

> "Calculating upon the aversion of the people to monarchy had exaggerated. They have endeavored to enlist all their jealousies and apprehensions in opposition to the intended President of the United States."

In Federalist Paper #68,[259] written March 14 1788, Hamilton explained the reasons the delegates had for choosing the Electoral College system, rather than direct elections by the public or elections by state legislatures or Congress itself.

> "Nothing was more to be desired than that every practicable obstacle should be opposed to cabal, intrigue, and corruption. These most deadly adversaries of republican government might naturally have been expected to make their approaches from more than one quarter, but chiefly from the desire in foreign powers to gain an improper ascendant in our councils
>
> "How could they better gratify this, than by raising a creature of their own to the chief magistracy of the Union? But the convention have guarded against all danger of this sort, with the most provident and judicious attention. They have not made the appointment of the President to depend on any preexisting bodies of men, who might be tampered with beforehand to prostitute their votes; but they have referred it in the first instance to an immediate act of the people of America, to be exerted in the choice of persons for the temporary and sole purpose of making the appointment.
>
> "And they have excluded from eligibility to this trust, all those who from situation might be suspected of too great devotion to the President in office. No senator, representative, or other person holding a place of trust or profit under the United States, can be of the numbers of the electors. Thus

---

[258] Federalist Paper #67 – on Presidency – by Alexander Hamiliton - http://lcweb2.loc.gov/const/fed/fed_67.html

[259] Federalist Paper #68- on choosing the President – by Alexander Hamilton - http://lcweb2.loc.gov/const/fed/fed_68.html

without corrupting the body of the people, the immediate agents in the election will at least enter upon the task free from any sinister bias."

In other words, the Electoral College system was chosen to avoid corruption of the selection of president and to prevent a small group of men who were already in office from selecting one of their friends. It took more than three years for all the states, including the new state of Vermont, to ratify the new Constitution:

1. Delaware, on December 7, 1787
2. Pennsylvania ratified it on December 12, 1787
3. New Jersey on December 18, 1787
4. Georgia on January 2, 1788
5. Connecticut on January 9, 1788
6. Massachusetts on February 6, 1788
7. Maryland, April 28, 1788
8. South Carolina, May 23, 1788
9. New Hampshire, June 21, 1788
10. Virginia, June 25, 1788
11. New York, July 26, 1788
12. North Carolina, November 21, 1789
13. Rhode Island, May 29, 1790
14. Vermont, January 10, 1791

On February 7, 1788 George Washington replied[260] to Lafayette who had returned to France and was involved in events that would soon become the French Revolution. At the time Washington wrote the letter, six states, including Massachusetts had already ratified the Constitution. Massachusetts ratified it the day before.

In his letter Washington told his young friend his views of the new constitution:

"As to my sentiments with respect to the merits of the new Constitution, I will disclose them without reserve, (although by passing through the Post offices they should become known to all the world) for, in truth, I have nothing to conceal on that

---

[260] George Washington's letter to Marquis de Lafayette – February 7, 1788 - http://etext.lib.virginia.edu/etcbin/toccer-new2?id=WasFi29.xml&images=images/modeng&data=/texts/english/modeng/parsed&tag=public&part=309&division=div1

subject. It appears to me, then, little short of a miracle, that the Delegates from so many different States (which States you know are also different from each other in their manners, circumstances and prejudices) should unite in forming a system of national Government, so little liable to well founded objections.

Marquis de Lafayette[261]

"Nor am I yet such an enthusiastic, partial or undiscriminating admirer of it, as not to perceive it is tinctured with some real (though not radical) defects. The limits of a letter would not suffer me to go fully into an examination of them; nor would the discussion be entertaining or profitable, I therefore forbear to touch upon it. With regard to the two great points (the pivots upon which the whole machine must move,) my Creed is simply,

1st. That the general Government is not invested with more Powers than are indispensably necessary to perform the functions of a good Government; and, consequently, that no objection ought to be made against the quantity of Power delegated to it.

2ly. That these Powers (as the appointment of all Rulers will for ever arise from, and, at short stated intervals, recur to the free suffrage of the People) are so distributed among the Legislative, Executive, and Judicial Branches, into which the general Government is arranged, that it can never be in danger

---

[261] Marquis de Lafayette Portrait - http://earlyamerica.com/portraits/lafayett.html

of degenerating into a monarchy, an Oligarchy, an Aristocracy, or any other despotic or oppressive form, so long as there shall remain any virtue in the body of the People.

"I would not be understood my dear Marquis to speak of consequences which may be produced, in the revolution of ages, by corruption of morals, profligacy of manners, and listlessness for the preservation of the natural and unalienable rights of mankind; nor of the successful usurpations that may be established at such an unpropitious juncture, upon the ruins of liberty, however providently guarded and secured, as these are contingencies against which no human prudence can effectually provide.

"It will at least be a recommendation to the proposed Constitution that it is provided with more checks and barriers against the introduction of Tyranny, and those of a nature less liable to be surmounted, than any Government hitherto instituted among mortals, hath possessed. We are not to expect perfection in this world; but mankind, in modern times, have apparently made some progress in the science of government. Should that which is now offered to the People of America, be found on experiment less perfect than it can be made, a Constitutional door is left open for its amelioration. "

On April 28, 1788, Washington responded to a letter from Lafayette in which he observed that his former General would probably be elected as president as follows:

"Knowing me as you do, I need only say, that it has no enticing charms, and no fascinating allurements for me. However, it might not be decent for me to say I would refuse to accept or even to speak much about an appointment, which may never take place: for in so doing, one might possibly incur the application of the moral resulting from that Fable, in which the Fox is represented as inveighing against the sourness of the grapes, because he could not reach them."

New Hampshire ratified the Constitution on May 23, 1788, which achieved the necessary nine-state acceptance to put it into effect .

Jonathan Trumbull, Jr. [262]

The tenth state to ratify the new Constitution was Virginia. Following the somewhat rancorous debate over the Constitution in Virginia, on July 20, 1788 Washington commented in a letter to Jonathan Trumbull, also a former aide during the Revolution and in 1788 Connecticut's Speaker of the House:[263]

> "I am happy to hear from Genl. Lincoln and others that affairs are taking a good turn in Massachusetts; but the Triumph of salutary and liberal measures over those of an opposite tendency seems to be as complete in Connecticut as in any other State and affords a particular subject of congratulation.
>
> "Your friend Colo. Humphreys informs me, from the wonderful revolution of sentiment in favour of federal measures, and the marvellous change for the better in the elections of your State, that he shall begin to suspect that miracles have not ceased; indeed, for myself, since so much liberality has been displayed in the construction and adoption of the proposed General Government, I am almost disposed to be of the same opinion. Or at least we may, with a kind of grateful

---

[262] John Trumbull, Jr. – Biography - http://bioguide.congress.gov/scripts/biodisplay.pl?index=T000389

[263] George Washington's Letter to Connecticut Speaker of the House Jonathan Trumbull - http://etext.lib.virginia.edu/etcbin/toccer-new2?id=WasFi30.xml&images=images/modeng&data=/texts/english/modeng/parsed&tag=public&part=18&division=div1

and pious exultation, trace the finger of Providence through those dark and mysterious events, which first induced the States to appoint a general Convention and then led them one after another (by such steps as were best calculated to effect the object) into an adoption of the system recommended by that general Convention; thereby, in all human probability, laying a lasting foundation for tranquility and happiness; when we had but too much reason to fear that confusion and misery were coming rapidly upon us.

"That the same good Providence may still continue to protect us and prevent us from dashing the cup of national felicity just as it has been lifted to our lips, is the earnest prayer of My Dear Sir, your faithful friend, &c".

Conditions in Europe at in 1788 were going from bad to worse and in a very short period of time Lafayette would be using everything he learned from George Washington to try to stem the tide of terror in his own nation. On June 19, 1788 Washington wrote to Lafayette some fatherly advice that showed not only a remarkable knowledge of conditions in Europe, but almost a prophetic warning about what was would happen if the volatile situation in Europe was not addressed properly. Washington observed:[264]

"There seems to be a great deal of bloody work cut out for this summer in the North of Europe. If war, want and plague are to desolate those huge armies that are assembled, who that has the feelings of a man can refrain from shedding a tear over the miserable victims of Regal Ambition? It is really a strange thing that there should not be room enough in the world for men to live, without cutting one another's throats. As France, Spain and England have hardly recovered from the wounds of the late war, I would fain hope they will hardly be dragged into this.

"However, if the war should be protracted (and not end in a campaign as you intimate it possibly may) there seems to be a probability of other powers being engaged on one side or

---

[264] Washington's Letter of Lafayette – June 19, 1788 – on "affairs in France" - http://etext.lib.virginia.edu/etcbin/toccer-new2?id=WasFi29.xml&images=images/modeng&data=/texts/english/modeng/parsed&tag=public&part=407&division=div1

the other. by the British papers (which are our principal source of intelligence, though not always to be relied upon, as you know) it appears that the Spaniards are fitting out a considerable fleet and that the English Ministry have prohibited the subjects of their Kingdom from furnishing transports for the Empress of Russia.

"France must be too intent on its own domestic affairs to wish to interfere, and we have not heard that the King of Prussia, since his exploits in Holland, has taken it into his head [not to] meddle with other people's business. I cannot say that I am sorry to hear that the Algerines and other piratical powers are about to assist the Porte, because I think Russia will not forget and that she will take some leisure moment, just to keep her fleets in exercise, for exterminating those nests of Miscreants.

"I like not much the situation of affairs in France. The bold demands of the parliaments, and the decisive tone of the King, shew that but little more irritation would be necessary to blow up the spark of discontent into a flame, that might not easily be quenched. If I were to advise, I would say that great moderation should be used on both sides. Let it not, my dear Marquis, be considered as a derogation from the good opinion, that I entertain of your prudence, when I caution you, as an individual desirous of signalizing yourself in the cause of your country and freedom, against running into extremes and prejudicing your cause.

"The King, though, I think from every thing I have been able to learn, he is really a good-hearted tho' a warm-spirited man, if thwarted injudiciously in the execution of prerogatives that belonged to the Crown, and in plans which he conceives calculated to promote the national good, may disclose qualities he has been little thought to possess. On the other hand, such a spirit seems to be awakened in the Kingdom, as, if managed with extreme prudence, may produce a gradual and tacit Revolution much in favor of the subjects, by abolishing *Lettres de Cachet* and defining more accurately the powers of government.

"It is a wonder to me, there should be found a single monarch, who does not realize that his own glory and felicity must depend on the prosperity and happiness of his People. How easy is it for a sovereign to do that which shall not only immortalize his name, but attract the blessings of millions."

After 11 states had ratified the Constitution, Congress passed an act on September 13, 1788, setting the first nationwide election for the first Wednesday in January 1789 for people to choose electors. The electors were scheduled to meet to choose the first president on the first Wednesday in February 1789 and the first meeting of the new government was set for the first Wednesday in March in the City of New York.

On January 19, 1789 Washington wrote to Lafayette after the people had chosen electors and shortly before the electors would meet who would choose the Commander in Chief during the Revolution to also be their first president. Lafayette apparently had written concerning reports indicating the choice would be Washington and he replied: '

> "I will content myself with only saying, that the elections have been hitherto vastly more favorable than we could have expected, that federal sentiments seem to be growing with uncommon rapidity, and that this increasing unanimity is not less indicative of the good disposition than the good sense of the Americans. Did it not savour so much of partiality for my Countrymen I might add, that I cannot help flattering myself the new Congress on account of the self-created respectability and various talents of its Members, will not be inferior to any Assembly in the world. From these and some other circumstances, I really entertain greater hopes, that America will not finally disappoint the expectations of her Friends, than I have at almost any former period. Still however, in such a fickle state of existence I would not be too sanguine in indulging myself with the contemplation of scenes of uninterrupted prosperity; lest some unforeseen mischance or perverseness should occasion the greater mortification, by blasting the enjoyment in the very bud.
>
> "I can say little or nothing new, in consequence of the repetition of your opinion, on the expediency there will be, for my accepting the office to which you refer. Your

> sentiments, indeed, coincide much more nearly with those of my other friends, than with my own feelings. In truth my difficulties increase and magnify as I draw towards the period, when, according to the common belief, it will be necessary for me to give a definitive answer, in one way or another. Should the circumstances render it, in a manner inevitably necessary, to be in the affirmative: be assured, my dear Sir, I shall assume the task with the most unfeigned reluctance, and with a real diffidence for which I shall probably receive no credit from the world."

Before all the original 13 states ratified the new constitution, Washington had been inaugurated and Lafayette had been confronted with exactly the challenge Washington warned him about. Lafayette used his wealth, his military expertise, his "political capitol" as a hero in both the United States and France, his dedication, knowledge, determination and love of liberty to bring to pass in France a new government that would bring more freedom to the people while maintaining some degree of order under a Constitutional monarchy.

In the end, the noble Frenchman who helped bring freedom to the Americans, barely escaped with his life when trying to do the same for his own countrymen.

Chapter 24
France's Government Dies as America's is Reborn

On April 14, 1789, Charles Thomson arrived at Mount Vernon to inform George Washington that he had been unanimously elected President of the United States. He accepted and promised to begin his journey to New York City, where he would be inaugurated on "the day after tomorrow." The day he left Mt. Vernon, on April 16, he wrote a farewell letter to the mayor and citizens of nearby Alexandria, Virginia committing them and himself "to the protection of that beneficent Being, who, on a former occasion has happily brought us together, after a long and distressing separation. Perhaps the same gracious Providence will again indulge us with the same heartfelt felicity. But words, my fellow-citizens, fail me: *Unutterable sensations must then be left to more expressive silence: while, from an aching heart, I bid you all, my affectionate friends and kind neighbours, farewell!* [265]

The president-elect then rode by horseback to New York, being greeted, honored, and hailed as "Protector of Mothers" as he traveled through Baltimore, Maryland,[266] Philadelphia, Pennsylvania [267] and Trenton, New Jersey.[268] He was inaugurated on April 30, 1789[269] and would face very quickly a world where

---

[265] George Washington's Letter to Mayor and People of Alexandria http://etext.lib.virginia.edu/etcbin/toccer-new2?id=WasFi30.xml&images=images/modeng&data=/texts/english/modeng/parsed&tag=public&part=239&division=div1

[266] Washington Letter to the Citizens of Baltimore - http://etext.lib.virginia.edu/etcbin/toccer-new2?id=WasFi30.xml&images=images/modeng&data=/texts/english/modeng/parsed&tag=public&part=240&division=div1

[267] Washington Letter to the President and State of Pennsylvania - http://etext.lib.virginia.edu/etcbin/toccer-new2?id=WasFi30.xml&images=images/modeng&data=/texts/english/modeng/parsed&tag=public&part=242&division=div1

[268] Washington's Letter to the Ladies of Trenton at the Triumphal Arch - http://etext.lib.virginia.edu/etcbin/toccer-new2?id=WasFi30.xml&images=images/modeng&data=/texts/english/modeng/parsed&tag=public&part=243&division=div1

[269] Washington's First Inaugural Address - http://etext.lib.virginia.edu/etcbin/toccer-new2?id=WasFi30.xml&images=images/modeng&data=/texts/english/modeng/parsed&tag=public&part=244&division=div1

terror was often the favored weapon of war and decision-making.

The challenges facing George Washington, as the leader of a new nation with a small population, fragile, if growing, economy and almost no navy were immediately challenged by war in Europe, an attack of anthrax that nearly killed him, problems with Indian tribes, and a bloody revolution in France which sharply divided Americans and led to the beheading of Louis XVI of France, whose support was so vital in defeating the British. Washington's friends, the Marquis de Lafayette, Tom Paine and Thomas Jefferson quickly gave their support to those in France clamoring for "freedom, equality and justice in France." Washington, on the other hand, was cautiously observing what was going on.

Five days after Washington's inauguration, an event occurred in France that began with great hopes and ended in anarchy. The Estates General opened at Versailles to resolve a financial problem. France had such a huge national debt that it was nearly bankrupt. The problem was caused by decades of lavish over-spending by the royalty of France, wars with other nations and financial aid to the Americans to defeat Britain.

The Marquis de Lafayette, who was loved almost as a son by Washington and had been a dependable and faithful aide with his military ability, was a nobleman then living in France. He had been one of 144 members of the Assembly of Notables which met in 1787 at the request of the king's finance minister, Charles-Alexandre de Calonne, in an effort to head off national bankruptcy. However, the Assembly of Notables refused to agree to pay the suggested new taxes.

At the time, the nobility paid no taxes, nor did the clergy, which left the burden of taxation to everyone else. The clergy, or the First Estate and the Nobility, the Second Estate represented about 10% of France. The Third Estate, the workers and business owners represented 90% of the population. Colonnes suggestion that the nobility pay taxes to get rid of the deficit was refused. The nobles demanded the calling of an Estates-General, which included the clergy and the Third Estate. It had been 173 years since an Estates-General had been called.

In order to raise taxes, King Louis XVI was required by law to have the approval of the nobles or to call an Estates-General. He reluctantly agreed to call the Estates-General for May of 1789, with elections for delegates to take place from January to April 1789. While each of the "estates" in previous Estates-General meetings had equal representation and met separately, King Louis approved of the Third Estate having 600 deputies, double the deputies for the nobility and the clergy. That was not equal representation since 90% of France was of the Third Estate.

However, when the approximately 1200 deputies convened in Versailles on May 4, 1789, their very first problem to solve was the first one that confronted the 1787 Constitutional Convention in Philadelphia – how would the delegate votes be counted? Should each of the 3 estates debate and vote separately – with the majority being 2 of the 3? Or should the deputies have individual votes and a majority of the deputies voting deciding issues? If they voted separately by Estates, the nobility and the clergy would be able to outvote the Third Estate, that was 90% of France's population. If voting as individuals, the Third Estate would be able to outvote the nobles and the clergy.

In 1789 Revolutionary ferment was being fueled not only by the near bankruptcy of the nation, poor crops and oppression, but also by the achievement of American Independence. In America, and its new Constitution, there was proof, a living example, of the truth of what France's philosophers had been saying in the *Encyclopédie Francoise*. The uncouth Americans had succeeded against their king and his army. How much the more might the great French nation do the same!

The philosopher often called the "Father of the French Revolution" was Jean Jacques Rousseau who wrote on the page of his most important work, *Social Contract*[270] in 1762: "Man is born free; and everywhere he is in chains. One thinks himself the master of others, and still remains a greater slave than they. How did this change come about? I do not know. What can make it legitimate? That question I think I can answer."

---

[270] Jean Jacques Rousseau – The Social Contract - http://www.constitution.org/jjr/socon.htm

Jean-Jacques Rousseau-1712-1778[271]

Rousseau's "solution" in Chapter 6 of his "Social Contract" was to form an association which "will defend and protect with the whole common force the person and goods of each associate, and in which each, while uniting himself with all, may still obey himself alone and remain as free as before." Making the new "Social Contract" work, according to Rousseau, required "the total alienation of each associate, together with all his rights, to the whole community, for, in the first place, as each gives himself absolutely, the conditions are the same for all; and this being so, no one has any interest in making them burdensome to others."

Thus by transferring one's "natural" rights to the community, Rousseau reasoned,

"Each of us puts his person and all his power in common under the supreme direction of the general will, and, in our corporate capacity, we receive each members as an indivisible part of the whole."

This definition of "natural" rights was almost totally opposite John Locke's definition as defined in Section 6 of his Second Treatise of Civil Government which laid the foundation for the philosophy of the American Revolution. John Locke wrote:

> "The state of nature has a law of nature to govern it, which obliges every one: and reason, which is that law, teaches all mankind, who will but consult it, that being all equal and independent, no one ought to harm another in his life, health, liberty, or possessions: for men being all the workmanship of one omnipotent, and infinitely wise maker;

---

[271] Jean-Jacques Rousseau-
http://www.lucidcafe.com/library/96jun/rousseau.html

all the servants of one sovereign Master, sent into the world by His order, and about His business."[272]

John Locke 1632-1704[273]

Few really noticed at the time, or since, that the philosophy on which the French Revolution was fought was for each person to put "his person and all his power in common under the supreme direction of the general will" of the people, regardless of what they were doing while the American Revolution was fought under the auspices of a philosophy that humans were "all the servants of one sovereign master" and were "sent into the world by His order and about His Business."

With the 1787 example of the writing of the American Constitution fresh in their minds, the deputies representing the 3rd Estate were united in their demand that each deputy have a vote. Knowing that giving in to the Third Estate's demand for representative voting would lead to the Clergy and the Nobles always being outvoted, they refused to meet with the Third Estate deputies.

On June 17th, the Third Estate deputies, and a few noblemen and parish priests who supported representative voting, declared themselves the National Assembly. On June 20, the leaders of the Third Estate, finding themselves locked out of their meeting place in Versailles after the king sided with the nobles and clergy on the voting issue, moved to an indoor tennis court to discuss the matter.

---

[272] John Locke – State of Nature - http://www.swan.ac.uk/poli/texts/locke/locke01.html

[273] John Locke –Historical Background - http://plato.stanford.edu/entries/locke/

Gabriel Riquetti Mirabeau, a smallpox scarred deputy to the Estates General from Aix, a stirring orator, called for the group to swear an oath they would not leave until there was a new constitution – which is what the King said he wanted. All joined the oath by acclamation.

Gabriel Riquetti Mirabeau[274]

Although displeased at the result, King Louis XVI backed down and allowed representational voting. However, the nobles and the clergy refused to meet the unruly commoners. Mirabeau, who had become the de facto leader of the Third Estate, told the master of ceremonies on June 23rd, "Go and tell those who sent you, that we are here by the power of the people and that we are only to be driven out by that of the bayonet."

Some of the noblemen, including Lafayette, and some parish priests joined the Third Estate members in urging representational vote. King Louis XVI legalized the assembly, but then dismissed his chief minister, Jacques Necker, a Genevan banker, who had urged the calling of the Estates-General and had advocated giving 600 votes to the Third Estate, instead of an equal number to the clergy and the nobles.

This led to wild rumors that the King was about to dismiss the National Assembly. Egged on by radical orators, on July 14, 1789 mobs gathered at the Bastille, the State Prison where they thought weapons were stored. The Bastille which was built in the 1380s, had been built as a fortification for the city of Paris but by 1789 was being used as a state prison. It was a formidable structure with

[274] Portrait of Gabriel Mirabeau, Ridpath's History, Vol X14, Page 641

100 foot high towers and was surrounded by a moat more than 80 ft wide.

"Taking the Bastille, July 14, 1789[275]

The Bastille dominated Paris and had become a symbol of royal despotism to the people of France. It was to the Bastille that people were often taken after being arbitrarily arrested under a *Lettre de Cachet,* where were letters signed by the king of France, countersigned by one of his ministers and closed with a royal seal, or cachet. They, therefore, were orders directly from the king and could not be appealed to any "higher" authority. Anyone arrested under a *Lettre de Cachet* was immediately imprisoned or executed without trial.[276] The mobs not only took control of the Bastille, and freed its 7 prisoners, they completely destroyed it, and carried away the stones.

The storming of the Bastille marked the beginning of the French Revolution and today the mob attack on the Bastille based on rumor and misinformation is celebrated as a national holiday in France similar to America's 4th of July.

---

[275] Taking the Bastille, July 14, 1789 – a painting by Prieure in the Louvre, Paris
[276] Lettre de Cachet - http://encyclopedia.thefreedictionary.com/lettres%20de%20cachet

According to of the French Embassy, "The storming of the Bastille, on July 14, 1789, immediately became a symbol of historical dimensions; it was proof that power no longer resided in the King or in God, but in the people, in accordance with the theories developed by the Philosophies of the 18th century."[277]

However, the Revolution in the United States was not fought based on "Philosophies of the 18th century" but on the principles defined in the Declaration of Independence. While the Declaration questioned King George III's divine right to be king, it simultaneously validated the divine role of "our Creator" as the Source of our unalienable rights to life, liberty and the pursuit of happiness. George Washington, from his close calls with death in the French and Indian War of the 1750s and to the end of his life in 1799 never sought personal power, rejected attempts to make him King of America and never failed to give the protection of "Providence" the credit for his and his country's successes.

The unity, strong military, strong economy and a moral and virtuous people that George Washington believed were necessary to make the Constitution work and for freedom to flourish could not survive in the a nation founded on Rousseau's theories of doing away with personal, individual responsibility and substituting mob rule or "alienation."

Not all of the founding fathers understood the wisdom of and even the necessity of a Constitution based on the four principles Washington believed were required for the new nation's success. It took at least twenty years and a reign of terror in France in the name of "liberty, equality and justice" to convince the fiery Patrick Henry of the wisdom of all four of George Washington's principles.

In 1799, in his last public speech before his death, while running for the Virginia State Legislature at Washington's urging as a Federalist, rather than in his traditional anti-Federalist position, Patrick Henry warned:[278] **"United we stand, divided we**

---

[277] Embassy of France – Bastille Day 2003 - http://www.info-france-usa.org/atoz/14july03.asp

[278]Patrick Henry, 1799-Appeal for Unity http://franklaughter.tripod.com/cgi-bin/histprof/misc/henrybio.html

fall. Let us not split into factions which must destroy that union upon which our existence hangs."

After the French Revolution, near the end of his life in 1819-1820, Jefferson also realized that his opposition to various doctrines within the established Churches needed to be better clarified after the horrors inflicted on the people of France by the anti-church philosophies that held sway there. He created an 82 page document called the "Jefferson Bible" in which he literally cut and pasted into a book 83 pages from Matthew, Mark, Luke and John.

In a letter to Benjamin Rush, Jefferson wrote:

"In some of the delightful conversations with you in the evenings of 1798-99, and which served as an anodyne to the afflictions of the crisis through which our country was then laboring, the Christian religion was sometimes our topic; and I then promised you that one day or other I would give you my views of it. They are the result of a life of inquiry and reflection, and very different from that anti-Christian system imputed to me by those who know nothing of my opinions.

"To the corruptions of Christianity I am indeed opposed, but not to the genuine precepts of Jesus himself. I am a Christian, in the only sense in which he wished anyone to be: sincerely attached to his doctrines in preference to all others, ascribing to himself every *human* excellence, and believing he never claimed any other."

This is a far cry from the "wall of separation of Church and State" ascribed to him today in forbidding any discussion of or display on public buildings pertaining to religion, God or the Ten Commandments

Chapter 25
Human Rights – Claimed by Man or Given By God?

On August 26, 1789, the National Assembly of France approved a document presented by Lafayette, called "The Declaration of the Rights of Man and Citizen."[279] Lafayette's good friend and ambassador to France, Thomas Jefferson, helped write it. The document began:

> "The representatives of the French people, organized as a National Assembly, believing that the ignorance, neglect, or contempt of the rights of man are the sole cause of public calamities and of the corruption of governments, have determined to set forth in a solemn declaration the natural, unalienable, and sacred rights of man, in order that this declaration, being constantly before all the members of the Social body, shall remind them continually of their rights and duties; in order that the acts of the legislative power, as well as those of the executive power, may be compared at any moment with the objects and purposes of all political institutions and may thus be more respected, and, lastly, in order that the grievances of the citizens, based hereafter upon simple and incontestable principles, shall tend to the maintenance of the constitution and redound to the happiness of all.
>
> "Therefore the **National Assembly recognizes and proclaims**, in the presence and under the auspices of the Supreme Being, the following rights of man and of the citizen:"

Few noticed at the time, or since, that there was a very basic difference in the Declaration of Rights and the American Declaration of Independence, in spite of them both talking about "unalienable rights." In the French document the "unalienable" rights were originated by a "solemn declaration" from the National Assembly. In the Declaration of Independence, the unalienable rights were **endowed** by "our Creator."

---

[279] Marquis Lafayette and Thomas Jefferson – The Declaration of the Rights of Man and Citizen – August 27, 1789 - http://www.constitution.org/fr/fr_drm.htm

Considering the mood of France's National Assembly at the time, if any mention of God or the Creator had been in the document, it probably would not have passed. In retrospect, the difference in the basic philosophy between the two documents may explain the remarkably different results obtained in the two revolutions. .

Jean-Jacques Rousseau's philosophy not only was used to validate mob action such as destroying the Bastille but, on July 12, 1790 the National Assembly passed the Civil Constitution of the Clergy which gave the government the authority to make ecclesiastical appointments.

The supreme guiding power in Rousseau's "Social Contract" is the "community," that is, human thought. The supreme guiding power, in Washington's writings is "Providence" – a power totally outside the individual or the combined power of humans, as he pointed out in his first Thanksgiving Proclamation[280] on October 3, 1789:

"Whereas it is the duty of all Nations to acknowledge the providence of Almighty God, to obey his will, to be grateful for his benefits, and humbly to implore his protection and favor, and Whereas both Houses of Congress have by their joint Committee requested me "to recommend to the People of the United States a day of public thanks-giving and prayer to be observed by acknowledging with grateful hearts the many signal favors of Almighty God, especially by affording them an opportunity peaceably to establish a form of government for their safety and happiness."

> "Now therefore I do recommend and assign Thursday the 26th. day of November next to be devoted by the People of these States to the service of that great and glorious Being, who is the beneficent Author of all the good that was, that is, or that will be. That we may then all unite in rendering unto him our sincere and humble thanks, for his kind care and protection of the People of this country previous to their becoming a Nation,

---

[280] George Washington's 1st Thanksgiving Proclamation- Oct. 3, 1789 - http://etext.lib.virginia.edu/etcbin/toccer-new2?id=WasFi30.xml&images=images/modeng&data=/texts/english/modeng/parsed&tag=public&part=368&division=div1

for the signal and manifold mercies, and the favorable interpositions of his providence, which we experienced in the course and conclusion of the late war, for the great degree of tranquillity, union, and plenty, which we have since enjoyed, for the peaceable and rational manner in which we have been enabled to establish constitutions of government for our safety and happiness, and particularly the national One now lately instituted, for the civil and religious liberty with which we are blessed, and the means we have of acquiring and diffusing useful knowledge and in general for all the great and various favors which he hath been pleased to confer upon us.

"And also that we may then unite in most humbly offering our prayers and supplications to the great Lord and Ruler of Nations and beseech him to pardon our national and other transgressions, to enable us all, whether in public or private stations, to perform our several and relative duties properly and punctually, to render our national government a blessing to all the People, by constantly being a government of wise, just and constitutional laws, discreetly and faithfully executed and obeyed, to protect and guide all Sovereigns and Nations (especially such as have shown kindness unto us) and to bless them with good government, peace, and concord. To promote the knowledge and practice of true religion and virtue, and the encrease of science among them and Us, and generally to grant unto all Mankind such a degree of temporal prosperity as he alone knows to be best".

Shortly after the storming of the Bastille, Marquis de Lafayette had been appointed as commander of the National Guard, the only effective military force in France. On October 14th, after a summer of serious illness, Washington wrote to Lafayette, "The revolution, which has taken place with you, is of such magnitude and of so momentous a nature that we hardly yet dare to form a conjecture about it. We however trust, and fervently pray that its consequences may prove happy to a nation, in whose fate we have so much cause to be interested and that its influence may be felt with pleasure by future generations."[281]

In early 1792, Washington appointed Gouvernor Morris as ambassador to France, taking Thomas Jefferson's place, who he had appointed as Secretary of State. Morris did not have as hopeful a view of the revolution in France as Jefferson had. He reported to Washington soon after his arrival in Paris that the Jacobin clubs, headed by radical revolutionists such as Maximilien Robespierre, were in control of the government and that Lafayette, in trying to stop their excesses had completely lost his authority.

Morris observed, "Were he to appear just now in Paris, unattended by his army, he would be torn to pieces."

Naturally, Morris' reports greatly concerned Washington, which annoyed Jefferson. "The fact is that Gouverneur Morris, a high-flying monarchy man, shutting his eyes and his faith to every fact against his wishes and believing everything he desires to be true, has kept the President's mind constantly poisoned with his forebodings."[282]

Tuileries Palace – built in 1500s[283]

---

[281] Washington's Letter to Lafayette – Oct. 14, 1789 - http://etext.lib.virginia.edu/etcbin/toccer-new2?id=WasFi30.xml&images=images/modeng&data=/texts/english/modeng/parsed&tag=public&part=386&division=div1

[282] The Life of Washington – Vol 5 – page 184-185 – by Washington Irving

[283] Tuilieries Palace - http://www.georgianindex.net/Napoleon/Tuileries/Tuileries.html

However, it soon was evident that Morris, not Jefferson, was right. As Washington Irving put it, in describing the overthrow of the French Monarchy:

"On the 20th of June bands from the Faubourg St. Antonine, armed with pikes and headed by Santerre, marched to the Tuileries, insulted the king in the presence of his family, obliging him to put on a *bonnet rouge,* the baleful cap of liberty of the revolution. Lafayette, still loyal to his sovereign, hastened to Paris, appeared at the bar of the Assembly, and demanded, in the name of the army, the punishment of those who had thus violated the constitution, by insulting, in his palace, the chief of the executive power. His intervention proved of no avail, and he returned with a sad and foreboding heart to his army."[284]

Tuileries, with its huge palace and spacious gardens, was attacked by Jacobin incited mobs on August 10, 1792. The Swiss guards were killed and the king and queen, who had been captured trying to flee France, and take to Tuileries, fled to the National Assembly chambers for safety. Robespierre and the Jacobins, then in total control, suspended the king's authority. Washington Irving said of the situation: "It was at once the overthrow of the monarchy, the annihilation of the constitutional party, and the commencement of the reign of terror."

Lafayette, who had headed the Constitution Party, was denounced by the Jacobins, his army refused to obey when ordered to halt the violence and he fled France, only to be captured and imprisoned by the Austrians. Eventually, his wife Adrienne and his daughters were able to be with him in Olmütz prison. His son, George Washington Lafayette managed to get to the United States. He lived at Mt. Vernon during Washington's second term in office.

It usually took one to two months, sometimes longer, for letters to be delivered from Europe, so Washington did not know at the time what was happening in Paris on a daily or weekly basis. However, on June 21, 1792, having recently received the news from Gouverneur Morris that the "newfangled statesmen" of revolutionary France should not be relied on, Washington wrote a worried letter to Lafayette that was almost prophetic:

---

[284]The Life of Washington -- page 185 –Washington Irving's description of overthrow of French monarchy

"Since the commencement of your revolution our attention has been drawn, with no small anxiety, almost to France alone… How great! How important, therefore, is the part, which the actors in this momentous scene have to perform! Not only the fate of millions of the present day depends upon them, but the happiness of posterity is involved in their decisions.

Marquis Lafayette with wife and daughters at Louts prison[285].

"You who are on the spot cannot, I presume, determine when or where these great beginnings will terminate, and for us, at this distance to pretend to give an opinion to that effect would at least be deemed presumptuous. We are however, anxious that the horrors of war may be avoided, if possible, and the rights of man so well understood and so permanently fixed, as while despotic oppression is avoided on the one hand, licentiousness may not be substituted for liberty nor confusion take place of order on the other. …

"I assure you, my dear Sir, I have not been a little anxious for your personal safety, and I have yet no grounds for removing that anxiety; but I have the consolation of believing that, if you should fall it will be in defence of that cause which

[285]Lafayette with wife and daughters in Olmütz prison - http://ww2.lafayette.edu/~library/special/exhibits/olmutz/olmutz.html

your heart tells you is just. And to the care of that Providence, whose interposition and protection we have so often experienced, do I cheerfully commit you and your nation, trusting that he will bring order out of confusion, and finally place things upon the ground on which they ought to stand."

"The affairs of the United States still go on in a prosperous train. We increase daily in numbers and riches, and the people are blessed with the enjoyment of those rights which can alone give security and happiness to a Nation." [286]

Unfortunately, the revolution in France that Thomas Jefferson, the Marquis de Lafayette and most other Americans once dreamed would bring the kind of peace and prosperity that the United States was beginning to experience quickly became a nightmare. Instead of unity, virtue, morality, a strong economy and military, other philosophies dominated the revolution in France.

Maximilien Robespierre

[286] Washington's Letter to Lafayette – June 10, 1792 - http://etext.lib.virginia.edu/etcbin/toccer-new2?id=WasFi32.xml&images=images/modeng&data=/texts/english/modeng/parsed&tag=public&part=58&division=div

The Jacobins, led by Maximilien Robespierre, became the dominant group when the wars started by the Girondins failed to generate revolution in other European nations. Robespierre, who was said to sleep with a copy of Jean-Jacque Rousseau's *Social Contract* at his side, instituted a reign of terror to France and called it "justice." In Robespierre's, "The Principles of Political Morality," he explains his view that that terror is required give virtue power: [287]

"If the spring of popular government in time of peace is virtue, the springs of popular government in revolution are at once *virtue and terror:* virtue, without terror is fatal; terror, without which virtue is powerless. Terror is nothing other than justice, prompt, severe, inflexible; it is therefore an emanation of virtue; it is not so much a special principle as it is a consequence of the general principle of democracy applied to our country's most urgent needs."

In June of 1792 the revolutionaries in control of the French Assembly were the Girondins, who were mostly professional men, lawyers or journalists, well educated and moderately rich. They favored political, but not social revolution, seeking personal advantage more than liberty for all. It was, in fact, the Girondins who represented many arms makers that declared war on Austria and Prussia April 20, 1792.

In mid-June 1792 King Louis XVI dismissed the Girondin ministry and tried to re-establish the monarchial order. This move was greeted with mob action. Over 20,000 people, under the leadership of a beer brewer named Santerre, took control of the streets of Paris, stormed the legislative assembly where Santerre delivered a speech and then converged on the Tuileries where they screamed insults and threats to the king and his family.

It was at this point that France's national anthem, the *Marseillaise*[288] was written by a French soldier named Claude Joseph Rouget de Lisle. The stirring music and words that urged the people to take up arms against those

---

[287] Maximilien Robespierre – On the Principles of Political Morality - http://www.fordham.edu/halsall/mod/1794robespierre.html -

[288] Marseillaise Hymn by Claude Joseph Rouget de Lisle - http://members.iinet.net.au/~jenks/Marseill.html

With luxury and pride surrounded,
The vile insatiate despots dare,
Their thirst for gold and power unbounded,
To mete and vend the light and air!

In August 1792, as historian John Clark Ridpath put it[289] while first a few and then thousands sang the *Marseillaise,* a rush was made for the Tulieries. Ridpath described the scene: "Louis and his family fled to the halls of the National Assembly. The Swiss guards were cut down without mercy. The mob burst through the gates of the palace and roared along the magnificent corridors. The palace was sacked, and none escaped save a few who made their way to the Assembly. The later body itself swayed towards the mob. Had it not done so, the legislature would perhaps have shared the same fate with the royal family."

The mob also raided an abbey, convent, and a seminary, slaughtering 267 priests. For five days the mobs roamed Paris, unchecked by the National Guard that, under the now imprisoned Lafayette and his National Guard that had held back the gangs of killers. Three thousand persons, mostly nobles and clergy, were seized in their own houses by night and dragged off to imprisonment and death. Princess Lamballe, a friend of the Queen Marie Antoinette, was seized, taken before the tribunal, condemned and beheaded. The executioners place her head on a pike, and exhibited it before the windows of Temple prison, where Marie Antoinette was being held. Four thousand people in the hospital of Bicêtre were captured and slaughtered.

On September 22, 1792 the Jacobins declared themselves the National Convention and promptly abolished royalty in France.

Gouverneur Morris wrote to Washington on October 23rd telling him "The king is accused of high crimes and misdemeanors; but I verily believe that he wished sincerely for this nation, the enjoyment of the utmost degree of liberty, which their situation and circumstances will permit. He wished for a good constitution, but , unfortunately, he had not the means to obtain it, or if he had, he was thwarted by those about him. What may be his fate God

---

[289] Ridpath History, Vol XIV, page 653

only knows, but history informs us that the passage of dethroned monarchs is short from the prison to the grave."[290]

Louis XVI on trial before the Convention[291]

By December the National Convention, the French Army and the mobs seemed to be working in unison. On December 10th, the king was put on trial in the Convention and charged with encouraging foreign enemies of France. The Convention then passed a resolution to change international law by authorizing every French general to proclaim the abolition of monarchy and the sovereignty of the people in all the countries the French army entered in war. "Liberty, Equality, Fraternity" was adopted as the motto of the French nation; and it was ordered that whatever power should refuse to accept the principles of the motto would be regarded as an enemy.

Gourverneur Morris wrote to Washington:[292]

---

[290] Life of Washington, by Washington Irving – page 188

[291] Ridpath History, Volume XIV, Page 659 – French Revolution –Louis XVI on Trial at Convention

[292] Life of Washington, by Washington Irving – page 190-191- quote from Life of Morris, ii. 248

> "Towns fall before them (the French army and mobs) without a blow and the Declaration of Rights produces an effect equal at least to the trumpets of Joshua. ...We must observe the civil, moral, religious and political institutions. These have a steady and lasting effect, and these only ...Since I have been in this country, I have seen the worship of many idols, and but little of the true God. I have seen many of those idols broken, and some of them beaten to dust."

In fact, a new calendar, dated from September 22, 1792 when the Jacobins took control, was created, wiping out the Christian era and replacing it with a new French Era. Sundays and all religious celebration days were eliminated and The Age of Reason was proclaimed. Laws were passed seeking to obliterate religion. By 1793, by decree from the Convention, atheism the order of the day. The dead had to be buried in twenty-four, or at the latest forty-eight, hours, and the only inscription over them had to be, "death is an eternal sleep."

Morris went on to say:

> "I have seen the late constitution, in one short year, admired as a stupendous monument of human wisdom, and ridiculed as an egregious production of folly and vice. I wish much, very much, the happiness of this inconstant people. I love them. I feel grateful for their effor5ts in our cause, and I consider the establishment of a good constitution here as the principal means, under Divine Providence, of extending the blessings of freedom to the many millions of my fellow-men, who groan in bondage onn the continent of Europe. But I do not greatly indulge the flattering illusions of hope, because I do not yet perceive that reformation of morals, without which liberty is but an empty sound."

The trial of Louis XVI lasted until January 15, 1793 and by a unanimous vote the king was found guilty as charged. At that point the entire Convention hotly debated his fate. On January 20th a vote was taken. Of the 721 votes, 366 voted for execution.

Philip of Orleans, who had joined the radicals, changed his name to *Egalite,* from the motto of the Revolution, voted without hesitation for the guillotining of his cousin. Thomas Paine, who by then also was a delegate in the French Convention, voted against the king's execution.

The execution took place 21st of January. On his way to the scaffold, the people on the street were silent and the king showed no fear. While awaiting execution, Louis XVI tried to address the people. All that was heard was "I die innocent. I pardon my enemies and I hope that my blood will be useful to the French, that it will appease God's anger..."

King Louis XVI, January 21, 1793, - Beheaded in the Public Square in Paris[293]

No more was heard as the Jacobins ordered the beating of drums to drown out his voice. When the blade dropped, the executioner lifted the severed head by the hair and cried, "Long Live the Republic!"

Louis XVI's and Marie Antoinette's 8 year old son, then the next heir to the throne of France, was forcibly taken from his mother, imprisoned above her where she could hear him cry but could not comfort him and where he was starved and abused until he died.

---

[293] Ridpath History- Vol. XIV, Page 662- Louis XVI on the Scaffold

Chapter 26
As France Disintegrates, Washington Declares Neutrality

Washington's Cabinet –(Seated) Henry Knox, Thomas Jefferson, (back turned) Edmund Randolph, Alexander Hamilton and George Washington

After being elected unanimously by the Electoral College for a second term, George Washington was inaugurated on March 4, 1793. His cabinet, with Alexander Hamilton, Secretary of Treasury, Henry Knox, Secretary of War, Thomas Jefferson, Secretary of State and Edmund Randolph, Attorney General was hopelessly split. Hamilton and Knox, who fought at Washington's side for most of the Revolution favored, as did Washington, a stronger, more dependable and effective executive. Jefferson and Randolph, who were involved in politics during the war, feared a strong central government and executive and at times accused the Federalists of secret monarchist tendencies.

Following news of the beheading of the king, which did not reach America until after the inauguration, the Girondist Revolutionary government of France appointed Edmund Genet minister to the United States, charged with the mission of collecting money from the American government to repay loans made by the beheaded king. Gouverneur Morris wrote a letter[294] to Thomas Jefferson also warning him that France's Executive Council had furnished Genet with three hundred blank commissions for privateers to be secretly given to Americans appointing them as privateers to make war on British ships. Such action, of course, would bring the United States into the war between France and Britain, which the French had declared in April of 1793.

Edmund Genet, Minister from France

Genet arrived in Charleston, South Carolina on April 8, 1793 and was received like a celebrity, wined and dined even by governors of the States. Governor Thomas Mifflin of Pennsylvania gave a toast to "the ruling power of France – may the United States of America, in alliance with them, declare war against England."

Genet lingered in Charleston, in effect setting up a French War Department on American soil, taking advantage of Charleston's port and its closeness with the West Indies to outfit privateers to disrupt British trade in the area, while whipping up pro-French sentiment among the Americans. On April 18th, President Washington sent 13 questions[295] to his divided cabinet concerning the issue and asking if a "minister from the Republic of

---

[294] The Life of George Washington, by Washington Irving, Vol. 5 page 195- Letter from Gouverneur Morris to Thomas Jefferson - 1793

[295] Questions Submitted to the Cabinet by President Washington – April 18, 1793 - http://etext.lib.virginia.edu/etcbin/toccer-new2?id=WasFi32.xml&images=images/modeng&data=/texts/english/modeng/parsed&tag=public&part=321&division=div1

France" should be received, whether treaties signed with the previous government were valid under the new revolutionary government and whether the war France declared against Britain was "offensive or defensive."

On April 22, 1793, Washington issued his Proclamation of Neutrality[296] which warned "the citizens of the United States carefully to avoid all acts and proceedings, whatsoever, which may in any manner" contravene a "conduct friendly and impartial towards the belligerent powers." At that point, France had declared war on Austria, Prussia, Sardinia, Great Britain and the United Netherlands.

Washington's Proclamation of Neutrality was angrily attacked by many angry pro-French Americans. Years later the anger and hysteria was described by John Adams, who was Vice-President in 1793, when he scolded Thomas Jefferson for failing to react "when ten thousand people in the streets of Philadelphia, day after day, threatened to drag Washington out of his house and effect a revolution in the government or compel it to declare war in favor of the French Revolution and against England."[297]

Hamilton's analysis of the situation at the time bears repeating. In May of 1793, Hamilton was pretty much alone in the level of his concern over the direction the French Revolution was taking, and was warning it could not succeed. He also was the lone, public voice in the cabinet in support of President Washington. He wrote: [298]

> "It cannot be without danger and inconvenience to our interests to impress on the nations of Europe an idea that we are actuated by the same spirit which has for some time past fatally misguided the measures of those who conduct the affairs of France, and sullied a cause one glorious, and that might have been triumphant.
>
> "The cause of France is compared with that of America during its late Revolution. Would to Heaven that the

---

[296] President George Washington's Proclamation of Neutrality- April 22, 1793 - http://etext.lib.virginia.edu/etcbin/toccer-new2?id=WasFi32.xml&images=images/modeng&data=/texts/english/modeng/parsed&tag=public&part=326&division=div1

[297] Alexander Hamilton, by Ron Chernow, page 439

[298] The Life of George Washington, Vol. 5 – Page 199

comparisons were just! Would to heaven we could discern, in the mirror of French affairs, the same decorum, the same gravity, the same order, the same dignity, the same solemnity, which distinguished the cause of the American Revolution! Clouds and darkness would not then rest upon the issue as they now do. I own I do not like the comparison.

"When I contemplate the horrid and systematic massacres of the 2n and 3d of September; (1792), when I observe that a Marat and a Robespierre, the notorious prompters of those bloody scenes sit triumphantly in the convention, and take a conspicuous part in its measures – that an attempt to bring the assassins to justice has been obliged to be abandoned; when I see an unfortunate prince, whose reign was a continued demonstration of the goodness and benevolence of his heart, of his attachment to the people of whom he was the monarch, who, though educated in the lap of despotism, had given repeated proofs that he was not the enemy of liberty, brought precipitately and ignominiously to the block without any substantial proof of guilt, as yet disclosed – without even an authentic exhibition of motives, in decent regard to the opinions of mankind; when I find the doctrines of atheism openly advanced in the convention, and heard with loud applauses; when I see the sword of fanaticism extended to force a political creed upon citizens who were invited to submit to the arms of France as the harbingers of liberty; when I behold the hand of rapacity outstretched to prostrate and ravish the monuments of religious worship, erected by those citizens and their ancestors; when I perceive passion, tumult, and violence usurping those seats where reason and cool deliberation ought to preside, I acknowledge that I am glad to believe there is no real resemblance between what was the cause of America and what is the cause of France; that the difference is no less great than that between liberty and licentiousness.

"I regret whatever has a tendency to confound them and I feel anxious, as an American, that the ebullitions of inconsiderate men among us may not tend to involve our reputation in the issue."

In June of 1793, writing as "Pacificus"[299] Alexander Hamilton directly addressed the four major objections to President Washington's Proclamation of Neutrality:

1. That the proclamation was without authority.
2. That it was contrary to our treaties with France.
3. That it was contrary to the gratitude which is due from this to that country, for the succors afforded to us in our own revolution.
4. That it was out of time and unnecessary.

Jefferson, Madison and other anti-Federalists argued the Constitution did not permit the President to make such a declaration. Hamilton, argued that the second article of the Constitution, section 1, "establishes this general proposition that the EXECUTIVE POWER shall be vested in a President of the United States of America." He also pointed out that since the "legislature have the right to declare war, it is on the other hand, the duty of the executive to preserve peace, till the declaration is made."

James Madison, as Helvidius,[300] at the urging of Thomas Jefferson, responded to Hamilton, argued "the powers of making war and treaty being substantially of a legislative, not an executive nature."

Washington also wrote letters to the people in various communities, including the "Freeholders and other Inhabitants of Salem, Massachusetts,"[301] the "Merchants and Traders of Baltimore," and the "Merchants and Traders of Philadelphia" explaining why he declared neutrality: "Placed in the situation I am by the free voice of my fellow Citizens, it becomes a duty, pleasing as it is strong, to pursue such measures as appear best calculated to promote their true interests. Under this impression I issued the late proclamation, declaring the neutrality of the United

---

[299] Alexander Hamilton in Pacificus-on Article 2, Section 2 - http://www.uiowa.edu/~c030162/Common/Handouts/ConLaw/Pacificus.html

[300] James Madison as Helvidius on Presidential Authority - http://press-pubs.uchicago.edu/founders/documents/a2_2_2-3s15.html

[301] President Washington's Letter on Neutrality to Citizens of Salem - http://etext.lib.virginia.edu/etcbin/toccer-new2?id=WasFi32.xml&images=images/modeng&data=/texts/english/modeng/parsed&tag=public&part=365&division=div1

States in the present contest between France and other European powers.

"In making this declaration, I was persuaded that I spoke the wishes of my countrymen, without violating any political or moral obligation. And the evidences of satisfaction which have been exhibited on this occasion, as well as the assurances of good citizens to use their influence in preserving the peace and prosperity of our infant republic, afford a new proof of that liberal and enlightened sentiment which has been so often and so honorably manifested by them on great occasions."

As George Washington and his supporters struggled with angry, pro-French citizens, thought to be a majority of the population at the time, decisions were being made by the French that began to convince many Americans that their President had made a wise decision to stay out of the Wars instigated by the French revolutionary government. The arrogant French minister, Edmund Genet, while Washington was at Mount Vernon in July 1793, announced to Alexander J. Dallas,[302] the secretary of Pennsylvania, that he rejected the notion of American neutrality and planned to go above Washington's head and appeal directly to the American people, asking their assistance to rig French privateers in American ports.

Thomas Jefferson, as leader of the anti-Federalist group, was helping or at least not actively discouraging Edmund Genet in trying to get Americans involved in the war between France and England. While President Washington was at Mount Vernon trying to resolve difficulties in his personal affairs due to the death of his plantation manager, Genet began to equip another privateer, *The Little Sarah,* in Philadelphia, then the nation's capital, in an effort, it appeared, to incite the pro-French element in the country to support him. Washington had sent orders to stop *The Little Sarah* from sailing from the nation's capital to attack British ships. Genet had disregarded America's prohibition against equipping privateers and had already equipped and sent to sea eight privateers. The eight privateers, with two French frigates, had captured about fifty British merchantmen, some of them within the jurisdiction of the United States.

---

[302] Alexander Hamilton by Ron Chernow, page 441

At a cabinet meeting held on July 8, 1793, without Washington, both Alexander Hamilton and Henry Knox, according to Jefferson's own notes, "should (the *Little Sarah)* attempt to depart before the pleasure of the President shall be known concerning her, military coercion (would) be employed to arrest and prevent her progress." Both wanted a battery set up on Mud Island to prevent the ship from leaving the area. Only Jefferson opposed it. [303]

Three days before , on July 5, Jefferson had an apparently secret meeting with Genet who asked for letters from Jefferson to support the French minister's plans to urge inhabitants of Kentucky, Louisiana and Canada to "undertake the expedition against New Orleans, and then Louisiana to be established into an independent State, connected in commerce with France and the United States; that two frigates shall go into the river Mississippi, and co-operate against New Orleans. The address to Canada was to encourage them to shake off English yoke, to call Indians to their assistance, and to assure them of the friendly dispositions of their neighbors of the United States." Jefferson noted that Genet said he communicated "these things to me, not as Secretary of State, but as Mr. Jefferson."[304]

Jefferson told Hamilton and Knox that Genet had assured him the *Little Sarah* would not be ready to sail until after Washington's return. It was, and it sailed to join the French attacks on British merchant ships. By July 12th, Washington was back in Philadelphia, a cabinet meeting was called, and Alexander Hamilton moved that the Government of France be requested to recall Genet. Knox added that Genet in the meantime be suspended from his functions. Jefferson urged that Genet's

---

[303] Anas – Thomas Jefferson, July 7, 1793 - #364 – Cabinet Meeting with Alexander Hamilton and Henry Knox regarding Genet's arming of *The Little Sarah* - http://etext.lib.virginia.edu/etcbin/toccer-new2?id=JefBv012.sgm&images=images/modeng&data=/texts/english/modeng/parsed&tag=public&part=1&division=div1

[304] Anas- Thomas Jefferson's notes – July 5, 1793 - #362 -His Secret Meeting with Genet - http://etext.lib.virginia.edu/etcbin/toccer-new2?id=JefBv012.sgm&images=images/modeng&data=/texts/english/modeng/parsed&tag=public&part=1&division=div1

"correspondence be communicated to his Government, with friendly observations."

The issue dragged on until November when Genet began bypassing the President because, he claimed, Washington did not have the constitutional authority to receive foreign ministers or to issue the neutrality proclamation. He also claimed to have recruited over 2000 men in his expeditions to capture New Orleans. Finally, Jefferson returned commissions to Genet that were not addressed to the President.

Then, after a cabinet meeting on November 18th while at dinner, Washington himself finally proposed requesting the recall of Genet and again, Jefferson opposed it: [305]

In his December 3, 1793 State of the Union address to Congress,[306] Washington specifically urged Congress to address the problem "Where individuals shall within the United States, array themselves in hostility against any of the powers at war; or enter upon Military expeditions, or enterprizes within the jurisdiction of the United States; or usurp and exercise judicial authority within the United States; or where the penalties on violations of the law of Nations may have been indistinctly marked, or are inadequate; these offences cannot receive too early and close an attention, and require prompt and decisive remedies."

It was a very difficult time. Not only was Washington intent on avoiding becoming involved in Europe's raging battles, he also faced "war on our frontiers," the possibility of insurrection of those supporting France and almost a non-existent military. On December 5, 1793 Washington wrote to the Senate and the House of Representatives a letter concerning "the present situation of the several nations of Europe, and especially of those with which the U.S. have important relations" specifically addressing the unacceptable behavior of Genet, France's minister:

---

[305] The Anas – by Thomas Jefferson – November 18, 1793 - #405 - http://etext.lib.virginia.edu/etcbin/toccer-new2?id=JefBv012.sgm&images=images/modeng&data=/texts/english/modeng/parsed&tag=public&part=1&division=div1

[306] George Washington's 5th State of the Union address to Congress –December 3, 1793 - http://etext.lib.virginia.edu/etcbin/toccer-new2?id=WasFi33.xml&images=images/modeng&data=/texts/english/modeng/parsed&tag=public&part=147&division=div1

"It is with extreme concern I have to inform you, that the proceedings of the person whom they have unfortunately appointed their Minister plenipotentiary here, have breathed nothing of the friendly spirit of the nation which sent him; their tendency on the contrary, has been to involve us in War abroad, and discord and anarchy at home."[307]

[307] George Washington's letter to Congress – Dec. 5, 1793 - http://etext.lib.virginia.edu/etcbin/toccer-new2?id=WasFi33.xml&images=images/modeng&data=/texts/english/modeng/parsed&tag=public&part=150&division=div1

Chapter 27
Washington Defends Freedom in a Reign of Terror

Marie Antoinette, Queen of France, Condemned at Tribunal[308]

By the time Edmund Genet was actually recalled by France, the Girondin Government he had been called to represent had disappeared under the blade of the guillotine. Had he returned to France, Genet would have been executed by the Jacobins who in the meanwhile had not only seized total control of the Convention but had executed most of the Girondin leaders. Robespierre had

[308] Ridpath's History, Vol. 14, Page 667 – Marie Antoinette Sentenced to death by guillotine.

pushed through the *Law of Suspects*[309] in September 1793 called for the arrests of those deemed to be:

> "Suspects (that) are (i) Those who, either by their conduct or their relationships, by their remarks or by their writing, are shown to be partisans of tyranny and federalism and enemies of liberty; (ii) Those who cannot justify, tinder the provisions of the law of 21 March last, their means of existence and the performance of their civic duties; (iii) Those have been refused certificates of civic responsibility (certificats de civisme); (iv) Public officials suspended or deprived of their functions by the National Convention or its agents, and not since reinstated, especially those who have been, or ought to be, dismissed by the law of 14 August last; (v) Those former nobles, including husbands, wives, fathers, mothers, sons or daughters, brothers or sisters, and agents of émigrés, who have not constantly manifested their loyalty to the Revolution; (vi) Those who have emigrated during the interval between the 1 July 1789 and the publication of the law of 8 April 1792, although they may have returned to France during the period of delay fixed by the law or before."

It was used to imprison over 200,000 people on vague charges of "conspiring against the liberties of France. Washington generously allowed Genet to remain in America. He married Cornelia Clinton, daughter of New York's Governor George Clinton and became a farmer.

On the 14th of October, Marie Antoinette, formerly queen of France, now addressed as "the widow Capet" was sentenced to death. She wrote a last letter to her late husband sister, Elizabeth, who was in the Temple Prison and would soon follow her sister-in-law to guillotine: "I have just been condemned, not to a shameful death, which can only apply to felons, but rather to finding your brother (Louis XVI) again............I seek forgiveness from all whom I know for every harm I may have unwittingly caused

---

[309] Robespierre's *Law of Suspects* – Sept. 17, 1793 - http://www.historywiz.com/primarysources/lawofsuspects.htm

them.............Adieu, good, gentle sister......I embrace you with all my heart as well as the poor, dear children...." [310]

At 10 AM on October 16, 1793, Marie Antoinette went quietly and bravely to be publicly beheaded as 30,000 people shouted "*Vive la Republique! A bas la Tyrannie!*" (Long live the Republic! Down with Tyranny!) Edmund Burke, an Irish born statesman and philosopher wrote of her execution: [311]

> "It is now sixteen or seventeen years since I saw the queen of France, then the dauphiness, at Versailles; and surely never lighted on this orb, which she hardly seemed to touch, a more delightful vision. I saw her just above the horizon, decorating and cheering the elevated sphere she had just begun to move in, glittering like the morning star full of life and splendor and joy. 0, what a revolution! and what a heart must I have, to contemplate without emotion that elevation and that fall! Little did I dream, when she added titles of veneration to those of enthusiastic, distant, respectful love, that she should ever be obliged to carry the sharp antidote against disgrace concealed in that bosom; little did I dream that I should have lived to see such disasters fallen upon her, in a nation of gallant men, in a nation of men of honor, and of cavaliers! I thought ten thousand swords must have leaped from their scabbards, to avenge even a look that threatened her with insult.
>
> "But the age of chivalry is gone; that of sophisters, economists, and calculators has succeeded, and the glory of Europe is extinguished forever."

News of the beheading of Marie Antoinette arrived in Philadelphia on January 9, 1794. Vice-President John Adams wrote to his wife Abigail,

> "The news of this evening is that the queen of France is no more. When will savages be satisfied with blood? No prospect of peace in Europe, therefore none of internal harmony in America. We cannot well be in a more

---

[310] Marie Antoinette's last letter to her sister-in-law - http://www.austrian-mint.com/e/mahist.html

[311] Edmund Burke – on the execution of Marie Antoinette - http://www.fordham.edu/halsall/mod/1793burke.html

disagreeable situation than we are in all Europe, with all Indians and with all Barbary rovers. Nearly one half of the continent is in constant opposition to the other and the President's situation, which is highly responsible, is very distressing."

"The anti-federalists and the Frenchified zealots have nothing now to do that I can conceive of, but to ruin his character, destroy his peace, and injure his health. He supports all their attacks with firmness, and his health appears to very good."[312]

To further complicate matters, Britain had instructed its Navy that all vessels laden with produce of any colony belonging to France, or carrying supplies to any French colony be detained. The harvests had failed in France and Britain hoped to starve the French to end the war. Captures of American vessels began to take place.

Meanwhile, Robespierre tried to explain his view of the purposes of what was happening to France, its people and its culture in a speech on February 5, 1794.[313] In effect, he blamed every problem that existed in France on a "base and corrupt government," of "A king, a proud senate, a Caesar, a Cromwell; of these the first care was to cover their dark designs under the cloak of religion, to covenant with every vice, caress every party, destroy men of probity, oppress and deceive the people in order to attain the end of their perfidious ambition." To justify the death not only of Marie Antoinette but approximately 17,000 others, Robespierre said, "To punish the oppressors of humanity is clemency; to forgive them is cruelty."

In March, Robespierre eliminated rivals for power among the Jacobins by having his men seize and imprison Jacque Rene Hébert, who led the most violent of the Jacobin factions, and Georges Danton, the most popular of the Jacobin leaders. They were guillotined and In May 7, 1794 Robespierre in effect attempted to make Deism France's state religion. Deism rejects revelation and miracles and defines God based entirely on human

---

[312] The Life of Washington – by Washington Irving – Vol. 5 page 240

[313] Maximilien Robespierre - On the Principles of Political Morality-Feb. 5, 1794- http://www.fordham.edu/halsall/mod/1794robespierre.html

reason and nature. In a speech called Cult of the Supreme Being[314] Robespierre explained his new civic religion:

> "Is it not He whose immortal hand, engraving on the heart of man the code of justice and equality, has written there the death sentence of tyrants? Is it not He who, from the beginning of time, decreed for all the ages and for all peoples liberty, good faith, and justice?
>
> "He did not create kings to devour the human race. He did not create priests to harness us, like vile animals, to the chariots of kings and to give to the world examples of baseness, pride, perfidy, avarice, debauchery, and falsehood. He created the universe to proclaim His power. He created men to help each other, to love each other mutually, and to attain to happiness by the way of virtue."

By July 1794, a list of other members of the Convention that Robespierre intended to execute was found and those on the list on the night of July 27th captured and imprisoned him. On the following morning, Robespierre was beheaded at the guillotine on the public square. The prisons of Paris that contained 10,000 people suspected of "anti-revolutionary sentiments" were opened and inmates went free.

Churches were reopened, decrees were passed allowing the return of nobles and priests. Businesses had failed during the Reign of Terror and jobs and food were scarce.

During the summer of 1794, America's minister to France, Gouverneur Morris had been recalled, at France's insistence after the American Government demanded Edmund Genet be recalled. James Monroe was appointed in Morris's place and he arrived in France about the time Robespierre was beheaded.

While Washington's neutrality policy, from an historic perspective, had allowed America to grow stronger and avoid the cost of another war, at the time there was a growing criticism of Washington by those who had gotten caught up in the philosophies of Edmund Genet and the notions of "democratic" mob action as the "right" of citizens when disgruntled. In 1791 Congress passed

---

[314] Maximilien Robespierre – Cult of the Supreme Being – May 7, 1793 - http://www.worldfuturefund.org/wffmaster/Reading/Communism/robespierrereligion.htm

an excise tax on whiskey, which farmers in Western Pennsylvania strongly objected to and were determined to ignore.

Washington wrote from German Town, Pennsylvania to Governor Henry Lee of Virginia about the problem on August 26, 1794 describing both its origin and the threat to the Constitution it suggested: [315]

> "As the Insurgents in the western counties of this State are resolved (as far as we have yet been able to learn from the Commissioners, who have been sent among them) to persevere in their rebellious conduct until what they call the excise Law is repealed, and acts of oblivion and amnesty are passed; it gives me sincere consolation amidst the regret with which I am filled, by such lawless and outrageous conduct, to find by your letter above mentioned, that it is held in general detestation by the good people of Virginia; and that you are disposed to lend your *personal* aid to subdue this spirit, and to bring those people to a proper sense of their duty.
>
> "On this latter point I shall refer you to letters from the War office; and to a private one from Colo. Hamilton (who in the absence of the Secretary of War, superintends the *military* duties of that department) for my sentiments on this occasion.
>
> "It is with equal pride and satisfaction I add, that as far as my information extends, this insurrection is viewed with universal indignation and abhorrence; except by those who have never missed an opportunity by side blows, or otherwise, to aim their shafts at the general government; and even among these there is not a Spirit hardy enough, yet, *openly* to justify the daring infractions of Law and order; but by palliatives are attempting to suspend all proceedings against the insurgents until Congress shall have decided on the case, thereby intending to gain time, and if possible to make the evil more extensive, more formidable, and of course more difficult to counteract and subdue.

---

[315] George Washington to Gov. Henry Lee on the Whiskey Rebellion - http://etext.lib.virginia.edu/etcbin/toccer-new2?id=WasFi33.xml&images=images/modeng&data=/texts/english/modeng/parsed&tag=public&part=370&division=div1

"I consider this insurrection as the first *formidable* fruit of the Democratic Societies; brought forth I believe too prematurely for their own views, which may contribute to the annihilation of them.

"That these societies were instituted by the *artful* and *designing* members (many of their body I have no doubt mean well, but know little of the real plan,) primarily to sow the seeds of jealousy and distrust among the people, of the government, by destroying all confidence in the Administration of it; and that these doctrines have been budding and blowing ever since, is not new to any one, who is acquainted with the characters of their leaders, and has been attentive to their manoeuvres. I early gave it as my opinion to the confidential characters around me, that, if these Societies were not counteracted (not by prosecutions, the ready way to make them grow stronger) or did not fall into disesteem from the knowledge of their origin, and the views with which they had been instituted by their father, Genet, for purposes well known to the Government; that they would shake the government to its foundation.

"Time and circumstances have confirmed me in this opinion, and I deeply regret the probable consequences, not as they will affect me personally, (for I have not long to act on this theatre, and sure I am that not a man amongst them can be more anxious to put me aside, than I am to sink into the profoundest retirement) but because I see, under a display of popular and fascinating guises, the most diabolical attempts to destroy the best fabric of human government and happiness, that has ever been presented for the acceptance of mankind."

A month later, on September 25, 1794, Washington issued a proclamation[316] announcing the first federal action under the new Constitution to call out the state militias of New Jersey, Pennsylvania, Maryland and Virginia to put prevent "the serious consequences of a treasonable opposition (that) has been employed

---

[316] Proclamation –George Washington – Sept. 25, 1794 - http://etext.lib.virginia.edu/etcbin/toccer-new2?id=WasFi33.xml&images=images/modeng&data=/texts/english/modeng/parsed&tag=public&part=390&division=div1

in propagating principles of anarchy." Behavior tolerated and glorified in France as "freedom" and "democracy" was not to be permitted under a Constitutional Republic. As Washington prepared to ride at the head of the gathering militia, he received a letter from his old friend General Daniel Morgan, whose aide-de-camp was Washington's nephew, Lawrence Lewis, his sister's son. Washington responded to General Morgan:[317]

> "I am perfectly in sentiment with you, that the business we are drawn out upon, should be effectually executed; and that the daring and factious spirit which has arisen (to overturn the laws, and to subvert the Constitution,) ought to be subdued. If this is not done, there is, an end of and we may bid adieu to all government in this Country, except Mob and Club Govt. from whence nothing but anarchy and confusion can ensue; for if the minority, and a small one too, are suffered to dictate to the majority, after measures have undergone the most solemn discussions by the Representatives of the people, and their Will through this medium is enacted into a law; there can be no security for life, liberty or property; nor if the laws are not to govern, can any man know how to conduct himself with safety for there never was a law *yet made*, I conceive, that hit the taste *exactly* of every man, or every part of the community.
>
> "Of course, if this be a reason for opposition no law can be executed at all without force and every man or set of men will in that case cut and carve for themselves; the consequences of which must be deprecated by all classes of men who are friends to order, and to the peace and happiness of the Country; but how can things be otherwise than they are when clubs and Societies have been instituted for the express purpose though clothed in another garb by their diabolical leader Genet whose object was to sow sedition, to poison the minds of the people of this Country, and to make them

---

[317] Washington's Letter to General Daniel Morgan – Oct. 8, 1794 - http://etext.lib.virginia.edu/etcbin/toccer-new2?id=WasFi33.xml&images=images/modeng&data=/texts/english/modeng/parsed&tag=public&part=403&division=div1

discontented with the Government of it, and who have labored indefatigably to effect these purposes."

The stark contrast between what was happening in France and what was happening in the United States in 1794 is a study in two systems of government that are dramatically opposite. One was based on "democracy" and the notion that there was no greater law or standard than human reason. The other was based on a Constitutional republic and a standard that there is a greater law or standard than human reason.

That greater law than the combined opinions of the majority was first clearly recognized when Jefferson's deistic phrase "that all men are created equal and independent; that from that equal creation they derive rights inherent and unalienable" was crossed out in the ensuing debates and the words "that all men are created equal that they are endowed by their Creator with certain unalienable rights;" [318]

In the 21st century, the debate between the two is as fresh and as polarizing as it was in 200 years ago. In his defense of the British soldiers after the Boston Massacre, John Adams addressed the issue: Shall the United States of America be ruled by laws passed by representatives elected by the people, or shall it be ruled by men - a monarch or a mob?

---

[318] Journals of Congress – June 22, 1776 – page 481-492 – Declaration of Independence - http://memory.loc.gov/cgi-bin/ampage?collId=lljc&fileName=005/lljc005.db&recNum=75&itemLink=r%3Fammem%2Fhlaw%3A@field%28DOCID%2B@lit%28jc0051%29%29%230050001&linkText=1

Chapter 28
Defending Freedom in a 21st Century Reign of Terror

In the 1780s the most divisive issue facing the founding fathers was slavery. The issue involved the question of the ownership of human beings. Can the notion that humans are endowed by their Creator with certain unalienable rights to life, liberty and the pursuit of happiness ever be compromised to maintain a system in which humans are sometimes the property of others and thereby are not actually "persons?" Nearly one hundred years of political effort to find a compromise on the slavery issue eventually failed.

The battle over "Federalism" and "States Rights" or "Individual Rights" has also flared up again and again, sparked largely by two opposing views of slavery. In 1857 Chief Justice C.J. Taney of the US Supreme Court ruled in *Scott vs Sandford* that Dred Scott,[319] a slave, "was not a 'citizen' within the meaning of the Constitution of the United States." Taney pointed out that "The only two provisions (of the Constitution) which point to them and include them treat them as property."

Taney wrote:

> "The words "people of the United States" and "citizens" are synonymous terms, and mean the same thing. They both describe the political body who, according to our republican institutions, form the sovereignty and who hold the power and conduct the Government through their representatives. They are what we ´familiarly call the "sovereign people," and every citizen is one of this people, and a constituent member of this sovereignty.
>
> "The question before us is whether the class of persons described in the plea in abatement compose a portion of this people, and are constituent members of this sovereignty? We think they are not, and that they are not included, and were not intended to be included, under the word "citizens" in the Constitution, and can therefore claim none of the rights and privileges which that instrument provides for and secures to

---

[319] Scott vs Sandford – US Supreme Court - http://supct.law.cornell.edu/supct/search/display.html?terms=Dred%20Scott&url=/supct/html/historics/USSC_CR_0060_0393_ZO.html

citizens of the United States. On the contrary, they were at that time considered as a subordinate and inferior class of beings who had been subjugated by the dominant race, and, whether emancipated or not, yet remained subject to their authority, and had no rights or privileges but such as those who held the power and the Government might choose to grant them.

In the 21st Century an almost identical modern debate is taking place on whether the unborn are people or, in effect, the property of the mother, based on *Roe vs Wade*, a decision by the U.S. Supreme court[320] in January 1973

Justice Blackmun ruled that while "unborn children have been recognized as acquiring rights or interests by way of inheritance or other devolution of property, and have been represented by guardians ad litem;" the "perfection of the interests involved, again, has generally been contingent upon live birth. In short, the unborn have never been recognized in the law as persons in the whole sense."

If the unborn are not "persons" under the Constitution, are they, then, property of the mother who can dispose of them as she can other property? Are human embryos, created by in vitro fertilization, the "property" of the parents? Can they, then, sell, trade or contribute those embryos for scientific experimentation or research?

After birth, at what point do children acquire "personhood" thereby having the right to life, liberty and the pursuit of happiness? When do they have the right to choose their own religion? Does the State or the Federal Government have the right to remove a child from a home that it considers abusive, or do personal rights of parents to control and "possess" their children prevent that from happening? Do the children of illegal aliens, brought to the United States as children, have the right to a free education or to possess a driver's license when they reach the age where education is required by law or when the state allows others their age to drive?

---

[320] Roe v Wade – U.S. Supreme Court - http://frwebgate1.access.gpo.gov/cgi-bin/waisgate.cgi?WAISdocID=26533816843+4+0+0&WAISaction=retrieve

Another debate involving the judiciary took place during the 2004 election over who actually has the constitutional authority to choose Federal judges, including Supreme Court Justices - the president, or the Senate? What is the proper balance between an independent judiciary and a tyrannical judiciary? And, what are the Constitutional limits and the balance of power to which the judiciary is subject? Should a minority in the Senate be able to block judicial appointments of the President by filibustering so the nominee is never voted on by the entire Senate?

In May of 2003, Supreme Court Chief Justice William Rehnquist expressed his view[321]on the need for an independent judiciary while warning that although "a judge may not be impeached for judicial acts" that does not mean "that Congress cannot change the rules under which judges operate."

John Ashcroft, Attorney General from 2001-2005, and previously a U.S. Senator from Missouri, while Chairman of Senate Subcommittee on the Constitution, gave a talk on "Judicial Despotism" in which he recalled the warning by Patrick Henry, who opposed the ratification of the Constitution calling it a "resolution as radical as that which separated us from the Crown." In New England, opponents of the new Constitution worried about liberties lost, rights eroded, and judicial power left like a "boundless Ocean."[322] Alexander Hamilton responded to such concerns with his famous phrase, "Here, Sir, the people govern."

Ashcroft observed, "Can it still be said that 'the people govern?' Or have people's lives and fortunes been relinquished to renegade judges, a robed, contemptuous intellectual elite fulfilling Patrick Henry's prophesy, that of turning the courts into 'nurseries of vice and the bane of liberty?

"Consider how far the federal judiciary has strayed. In 1987, the federal courts assumed the right to tax the American people. District Judge Russell Clark ordered a tax increase to 'remedy vestiges of segregation' in the Kansas City, Missouri school system. The decree—and two billion tax dollars –turned

---

[321] Chief Justice William Rehnquist-May 5, 2003 - http://www.supremecourtus.gov/publicinfo/speeches/sp_05-05-03.html

[322] Attorney General John Ashcroft – March 6, 1997 - http://www.lermanet.com/cos/senashcroft.htm

the city's school district into a gold-plated Taj Mahal complete with editing and animation labs, vivariums and greenhouses, temperature-controlled art galleries, and model UN wired for language translation." However, student achievement did not change.

An issue that has been hotly debated in the 21st century during President George W. Bush's first term was his response to the second terrorist attack on the World Trade Center. On September 11, 2001, four Commercial airliners were hi-jacked and two of them flown into the World Trade Center, on into the Pentagon and a fourth terrorist attack was thwarted by passengers as it headed towards Washington, DC. Some have argued that, without a declaration of war by the U.S. Congress, American troops should not have been sent to Iraq and Afghanistan. Some believed the war on Terror was unjustified and even illegal since Congress did not declare war.

However, in the past 225 years the United States has sent troops abroad to fight eight major foreign wars and at least 31 minor foreign wars, plus the Civil war in which the largest percentage of casualties per capita were suffered. Congress declared war in only five of those wars. The first Naval War America fought was with France when John Adams was president from 1798-1800. America's second war was with the Barbary pirate States in Northern Africa in 1801, when Thomas Jefferson was president. Jefferson dispatched "a squadron of frigates into the Mediterranean"[323] to stop the Barbary Pirates from seizing American Ships and capturing or killing American seamen."

Jefferson not only did not ask for Congressional approval for his action, he didn't even advise Congress of his action until his first State of the Union Address.[324] Hijacking an airplane is a violation of piracy laws, however, in modern language people who hi-jack airplanes and kill people are called "terrorists," not "pirates." Should Jefferson, under the Constitution, have first declared war on the Barbary Pirates? Do modern American

---

[323] Library of Congress – America and the Barbary Pirates - http://memory.loc.gov/ammem/mtjhtml/mtjprece.html

[324] Thomas Jefferson's 1st State of the Union Address – http://wikisource.org/wiki/Thomas_Jefferson's_First_State_of_the_Union_Address

Presidents, as some claim, require approval by the United Nations to pursue and capture modern-day "pirates?"

In John Adams administration, the pro-French sentiment led finally to Congressional passage of the much discussed Alien and Sedition Acts[325], which some current commentators have compared with the Patriot Act.[326] The Patriot Act, passed after the terrorist attacks of September 11, 2001 killed more than 3000 people, was designed to "unite and strengthen" America against acts of terrorism.

What constraints are permissible, in the Constitution, to prevent agents of a foreign power, such as Edmund Genet or supporters of modern terrorists such as Osama bin Laden from, fostering a "factious spirit to overturn the laws, and to subvert the Constitution" as Washington put it?

Another issue that surfaced again in the 21st century has been how the President of the United States should be elected. This issue which caused a lively debate in the Federal Convention of 1787, again was debated in the 2000 Presidential Election when Democrat Al Gore received 48,971,067 popular votes to Republican George Bush's 48,779,508 popular votes, Bush became president with 255 electoral college votes to Al Gore's 246 electoral votes. Some argued that the Constitution was outdated and undemocratic and should be amended to abolish the Electoral College.[327]

The 1787 Convention debated whether State Legislatures, the Congress, the people, the Senate or an Electoral College should choose the President of the United States. The founding fathers, finding fault with all other methods, selected the Electoral College, which has brought presidents into office that did not receive votes of the majority of the American people, but did represent the majority of the States. Again, this is largely over federal versus states' representation and sovereignty.

---

[325] Alien and Sedition Acts of 1798 - http://www.lexrex.com/enlightened/laws/alien_sedition.html

[326] The Patriot Act of 2001 –HR 3162 - http://thomas.loc.gov/cgi-bin/query/z?c107:H.R.3162.ENR:

[327] 2000 Presidential Election – George W. Bush and Al Gore - http://www.tompaine.com/feature2.cfm/ID/3856

In 1824 Andrew Jackson received 155,872 votes to John Quincy Adams' 105,321 votes, but John Quincy Adams became president when the election was thrown into the House of Representatives because none of the four Democratic Republican candidates received a majority in the Electoral College. In 1876 Democrat Samuel Tilden received 4,284,757 votes to Republican Rutherford B. Hayes' 4,033,950, but Hayes became president when he received one more Electoral College vote than Tilden. In 1888 Democrat Grover Cleveland received 5,540,050 popular votes to Republican Benjamin Harrison's 5,444,337 votes, but Harrison became president with a majority of the Electoral votes.

The Electoral College was chosen by the founding fathers after nine other suggestions for choosing the president were rejected.[328] The president, it was decided, needed to represent the majority of the States, not necessarily the majority of the total population. In fact, the popular vote in presidential elections was not even recorded from 1789 to 1824

Should a minority in the Senate, through filibustering,[329] (the minority using obstructive tactics) be able to prevent the majority from being able to vote to approve or reject a President's nominee? What did the founding fathers have in mind when they gave the President the right to appoint but the Senate the right of advice and consent in selecting judges and others? Would some other plan considered and rejected in 1787, such as having the Senate make appointments rather than the President, be more acceptable today? How would that work in practice with a nearly evenly divided Senate?

During the debates in the States on ratification of the Constitution, James Madison, John Jay and Alexander Hamilton wrote the Federalist Papers,[330] to explain to the people what the

---

[328] Cato Institute – Keep the Electoral College - http://www.cato.org/dailys/12-21-00.html

[329] Spectrum - Filibuster Aims to Stop Judges - http://thespectrum.com/news/stories/20030303/opinion/1097352.html

[330] The Federalist Papers http://www.yale.edu/lawweb/avalon/federal/fed.htm

Constitution[331] contained and why they thought it was important.[332]

There has never been a greater need than today for the people of the United States of America to understand and discuss the reasons why and how the Constitution was written in 1787 the way it was. What does it mean, should it be changed and how does it best protect our safety, property, happiness and perhaps survival in the 21st Century?

For the first time in history the people not only of America, but also the world, can access the "original source" information on the writing of our founding documents. Those documents have been, and are now being, used as sources for the creation of new governments all over the world. What are the principles in the Constitution that have worked so well for America? Why have other nations that appear to copy the same principles in the Constitution of the United States of America so often failed to succeed?

George Washington believed a **strong, well armed, supplied and trained military; Unity among the people, without factional, ethnic or religious hostility; a strong and free economy; and a virtuous and moral people** were needed for America to maintain its freedom. Washington believed those four principles are the four pillars upon which life, liberty and the pursuit of happiness rest.

On returning from riding at the head of the militia to Western Pennsylvania to put down the rebellion of those who refused to pay the Federal excise tax on whiskey, Washington addressed Congress about the matter, saying: [333]

> "It has demonstrated that our prosperity rests on solid foundations; by furnishing an additional proof, that my fellow citizens understand the true principles of government and liberty: that they feel their inseparable union: that

---

[331] The Constitution of the United States - http://lcweb2.loc.gov/const/const.html

[332] About the Constitution of the United States- http://lcweb2.loc.gov/const/abt_const.html

[333] George Washington's 6th Address to Congress –Nov. 19, 1794- Report on the Whiskey Rebellion - http://etext.lib.virginia.edu/etcbin/toccer-new2?id=WasFi34.xml&images=images/modeng&data=/texts/english/modeng/parsed&tag=public&part=15&division=div1

notwithstanding all the devices which have been used to sway them from their interest and duty, they are now as ready to maintain the authority of the laws against licentious invasions, as they were to defend their rights against usurpation.

"It has been a spectacle, displaying to the highest advantage, the value of Republican Government, to behold the most and least wealthy of our citizens standing in the same ranks as private soldiers; pre-eminently distinguished by being the army of the Constitution; undeterred by a march of three hundred miles over rugged mountains, by the approach of an inclement season, or by any other discouragement. Nor ought I to omit to acknowledge the efficacious and patriotic co-operation, which I have experienced from the chief magistrates of the states, to which my requisitions have been addressed.

"To every description, indeed, of citizens let praise be given. But let them persevere in their affectionate vigilance over that precious depository of American happiness, the Constitution of the United States. Let them cherish it too, for the sake of those, who from every clime are daily seeking a dwelling in our land. And when in the calm moments of reflection, they shall have retraced the origin and progress of the insurrection, let them determine, whether it has not been fomented by combinations of men, who, careless of consequences, and disregarding the unerring truth, that those who rouse, cannot always appease a civil convulsion, have disseminated, from an ignorance or version of facts, suspicions, jealousies, and accusations of the whole government.

"Having thus fulfilled the engagement, which I took, when I entered into office, 'to the best of my ability to preserve, protect, and defend the constitution of the United States,' on you, Gentlemen, and the people by whom you are deputed, I rely for support."

When the people choose their representatives, whether to their local school board, their town, county, state or nation, they have a responsibility to support the laws passed by those representatives. If they do not like the laws, they can vote them out of office. The Constitution in 1794, and in 2005, does not allow a group, such as the Whiskey makers in Western Pennsylvania in 1794, to defy the law and to threaten those enforcing the law. Washington concluded his speech, by appealing to Congress and the nation to recognize the importance of unity, morality and respect for law:

> "Let us unite, therefore, in imploring the Supreme Ruler of nations, to spread his holy protection over these United States: to turn the machinations of the wicked to the confirming of our constitution: to enable us at all times to root out internal sedition, and put invasion to flight: to perpetuate to our country that prosperity, which his goodness has already conferred, and to verify the anticipations of this government being a safe guard to human rights."[334]

On January 20, 2005, two hundred and eleven years later, President George W. Bush made remarkably similar points in his Second Inaugural Address,[335] appealing, as did Washington, for all Americans "to recall the deep commitments that unite our country" in a troubled time. He said:

"America's vital interests and our deepest beliefs are now one. From the day of our Founding, we have proclaimed that every man and woman on this earth has rights, and dignity, and matchless value, because they bear the image of the Maker of Heaven and earth. Across the generations we have proclaimed the imperative of self-government, because no one is fit to be a master, and no one deserves to be a slave. Advancing these ideals is the mission that created our Nation. It is the honorable achievement of our fathers. Now it is the urgent requirement of our nation's security, and the calling of our time."

---

[334] Ibid

[335] George W. Bush – 2nd Inaugural Address - http://www.whitehouse.gov/news/releases/2005/01/20050120-1.html

Chapter 29
God and Government in the 21st Century

While George Washington and George W. Bush both have expressed the view that God has an important role to play in the creation of good government, not everyone agrees. It was an issue that was hotly debated when the *Declaration of Independence* was written by Thomas Jefferson in 1776 and in 1789 when Jefferson, as Ambassador to France, and Lafayette, and a member of the French Assembly during the French Revolution, collaborated in writing the Declaration of the Rights of Man and Citizens..

Marble Frieze of Moses in Supreme Court Chambers[336]

It is again being debated in 2005, this time at the U.S. Supreme Court and worldwide in the media. The American Civil Liberties Union in a press release on March 2, 2005[337] stated that "The relationship between individuals and their God, which is at the core of the Ten Commandments, is and should remain a private matter. It is not the government's business." The group claims that freedom of speech is upheld by prohibiting any reference to the Ten Commandments on public property. However, the issue had to be heard by the U.S. Supreme Court which meets in a building where representatives of Moses and the Ten Commandments are everywhere – as the litigants enter the building, as they walk through the doors inside the building and as they argue their case beneath a frieze of Moses holding the tablets upon which the Ten Commandments were written, according to the Bible.

---

[336] Marble Frieze of Moses holding Ten Commandments –Supreme Court Chambers - http://www.law.com/jsp/article.jsp?id=1109597692160

[337] ACLU – Press Release – March 2, 2005 – On Ten Commandments - http://www.aclu.org/court/court.cfm?ID=17602&c=286

Declaration Committee 1776 - Thomas Jefferson, Roger Sherman, Benjamin Franklin, John Adams, Robert Livingston[338]

The debate over the role of a "Creator" or "God" began with the writing of the *Declaration of Independence* in June of 1776, when Thomas Jefferson's rough draft was presented to the Declaration Committee composed of Jefferson, John Adams, Benjamin Franklin, Roger Sherman and Robert Livingston. It was further modified during debate in the Continental Congress. The phrase in the *Declaration* that announces the very reason for proclaiming Independence: "We hold these truths to be self-evident, that all men are created equal, that they are endowed by their Creator with certain unalienable rights that among these are Life, Liberty and the Pursuit of happiness..." was not written by Jefferson.

Jefferson wrote: "We hold these truths to be sacred and undeniable; that all men are created equal and independent, that from that equal creation they derive rights inherent and inalienable, among which are the preservation of life, and liberty, and the pursuit of happiness." Jefferson, a deist, did not credit the "Creator" for granting unalienable rights. He believed in God, but did not believe in revelation – that God was interested in or involved with or talked to man.

---

[338] Declaration Committee- 1776- Jefferson,, Sherman, Franklin,, Adams, Livingston

So, what, actually IS an "inalienable" or an "unalienable" right? According to the 1848 Webster unabridged dictionary there were several meanings for the word "alienate." The first was "to convey or transfer property or a title to another." The second meaning was to "withdraw from or be estranged from God." Jefferson's "inalienable" right was a right that was human in origin, such as a title or an inherited property. An "unalienable right" was a right that bound human beings to God. One cannot transfer either life or liberty to another person, therefore it is an unalienable right. A title or property CAN be transferred and is an inalienable right..

Murder, which is defined as the "unlawful killing of another human being with malice aforethought" is a crime punishable by death in most cultures. However, if the intended victim of murder kills his attacker first, that is self-defense that PREVENTS a murder. That is why killing in self-defense is not even a crime.

The U.S. Supreme Court meets in chambers with a marble frieze of Moses holding the Ten Commandments. However, on May 5, 2000, Judge Jennifer Coffman ruled that a display in a rural Kentucky school consisting of excerpts from the Declaration of Independence, the Ten Commandments, the Mayflower Compact, Ronald Reagan's 1983 proclamation of the "Year of the Bible," our national motto "In God We Trust and the Kentucky state constitution[339] was a violation of the Constitution that had to be removed from the building.

Although the First Amendment to the U.S. Constitution merely bars the U.S. Congress from establishing a national church, today we seem to be moving towards banning our founding documents that mention "our Creator" and editing presidential messages that mention "God." The First Amendment prohibits CONGRESS from passing laws establishing a religion. However, it has been interpreted by the Supreme Court in such a way that it has limited free speech in public buildings such as school and courthouses.

---

[339] Kentucky State Constitution of 1891
http://www.lrc.state.ky.us/Legresou/Constitu/000.htm

The French embassy website in describing the storming of the Bastille by angry mobs in Paris on July 14, 1789, calls it "proof that power no longer resided in the king or in God, but in the people, in accordance with the theories developed by the Philosophies of the 18th century." A month later, on August 26, 1789, *The Declaration of the Rights of Man* was introduced into the French Assembly by Lafayette and approved.

The *Declaration* declared in part: "Law is the expression of the general will" and, therefore, the mob action in destroying the Bastille became "law." Inalienable rights where not endowed by our Creator, but from nature or the French people via the National Assembly or, in the case of storming the Bastille, from the "expression of the general will" of a mob. The mob storming the Bastille set in motion the Reign of Terror by the Jacobins who had seized control of the Assembly. By 1794, France declared the "end of the Christian era," atheism was adopted as the State Religion, churches were closed down and hundreds of priests were beheaded. During the Reign of Terror, more than 17,000 French men, women and children, starting with the king and queen of France, were publicly beheaded by the guillotine.

In America the Continental Congress unanimously voted to adopt the Declaration of Independence in which "our Creator" is designated as the source of our **unalienable** rights to life, liberty and the pursuit of happiness. In the early days of the Republic, that connection was repeatedly recognized. George Washington's first Thanksgiving Proclamation of October 3, 1789,[340] began:

> "Whereas it is the duty of all Nations to acknowledge the providence of Almighty God, to obey his will, to be grateful for his benefits, and humbly implore His protection and favor..."

The issue today is, in effect: Can the origin of our liberties even be debated in the 21st century in public schools? Can a public school teacher today allow students to read and discuss the meaning of the Declaration of Independence or Washington's First Thanksgiving proclamation?

[340] George Washington's First Thanksgiving Proclamation-Oct. 3, 1789

World War II Memorial – Washington, DC.[341]

The multi-million dollar World War II National memorial that opened in April 2004 edits God out of President Franklin Delano Roosevelt's December 8, 1941, speech to Congress and the nation. Called the "day of infamy" speech ,it began: [342]

> "Yesterday, December 7, 1941 - a date which will live in infamy - the United States of America was suddenly and deliberately attacked by naval and air forces of the Empire of Japan."

Roosevelt informed the people about Japan's attack and warned the nation of the dangers ahead and concluded his talk with:

> "Hostilities exist. There is no blinking at the fact that our people, our territory and our interests are in grave danger.
>
> "With confidence in our armed forces - with the unbounded determination of our people - we will gain the inevitable triumph - so help us God.
>
> "I ask that the Congress declare that since the unprovoked and dastardly attack by Japan on Sunday, December seventh, a state of war has existed between the United States and the Japanese Empire."

---

[341] World War II National Memorial Photos - http://www.wwiimemorial.com/default.asp?page=pictures.asp&subpage=

[342] President Franklin Roosevelt's "Day of Infamy" Speech- Dec. 8, 1941 - http://www.law.ou.edu/hist/infamy.html

President Franklin Delano Roosevelt[343]

However, the engraving on the World War II monument alters Roosevelt's words by leaving "so help us God" off the quote. It is left as if Roosevelt had total confidence in human efforts to solve the problems ahead. It reads: "With confidence in our armed forces - with the unbounded determination of our people - we will gain the inevitable triumph."

Has there been and is there now any connection between a nation's destiny and what its leaders believe about the origin of law and rights? Would the beheading of thousands in the French Revolution been avoided if its Declaration had recognized the unalienable right to life endowed by "our Creator?" The *Declaration of Rights*[344] described the "natural and imprescriptible" rights of man, which were recognized by the National Assembly as "liberty, property, security and resistance to oppression." There is no mention of life or the pursuit of happiness.

"Liberty" was defined as consisting of "the freedom to do everything which injures no one else; hence the exercise of the natural rights of each man has no limits except those which assure to the other members of the society the enjoyment of the same rights. These limits can only be determined by law." The definition did not include any limitation on the government from declaring the nation's religion and on July 12, 1790, France's National

---

[343] Franklin Delano Roosevelt 32nd President of the United States - http://www.usconstitution.com/FranklinDRoosevelt.htm

[344] France's Declaration of Rights of Man –written by Lafayette & Jefferson – http://www.yale.edu/lawweb/avalon/rightsof.htm

Assembly adopted the Civil Constitution of the Clergy[345]. That bill seized total control of the Church in France. All Church property was confiscated and the National Assembly reorganized the selection process of the priests, bishops and curates of the Church. On September 22, 1792, the Assembly wiped out the "Christian Era" and replaced it with the new "French Era."

As 19th historian John Clark Ridpath put it, [346]

> "A decree was passed against the Christian Religion and it was sought to obliterate the last vestige of the ancient system of belief. The doctrines which men had accepted for centuries were formally abrogated. Atheism was declared to be the faith of France. Immortality was denied. On all public cemeteries was placed this inscription: Death is an Eternal Sleep." The age was proclaimed the Age of Reason. Reason was deified. All the ceremonies of Catholicism were turned into ridicule and mockery. The churches were rifled and the treasures of silver and gold were carried with laughter and song to the bar of the Convention."

To a lesser degree, the 2004 presidential campaign also divided the American people into two groups based on their faith. A poll taken prior to the election showed 70% of Kerry's supporters were more worried about candidates who "are too close to religion and religious leaders" and 52% of Bush's supporters were more worried about public officials who "don't pay enough attention to religion and religious leaders." In the same poll 70% of the respondents expressed concern over "television, movies and popular music were lowering moral standards in this country."

However, recognizing the faith-based motivation of those who wrote and voted to adopt the *Declaration of Independence* and the *Constitution of the United States* is slowly being abandoned in the United States as others throughout the world seem increasingly interested in those very faith-based ideals.

On March 2, 2005 in an address at Anne Arundel Community College in Maryland, President George W. Bush made headlines in Middle Eastern Arab newspapers, by stating::

---

[345] France's 1790 Civil Constitution of Clergy – State seizing control of the Church - http://history.hanover.edu/texts/civilcon.htm

[346] Ridpath History – Volume XIV – Page 608 – French Revolution

"The world is speaking with one voice when it comes to making sure that democracy has a chance to flourish in Lebanon and throughout the greater Middle East. Freedom is on the march. It's a profound period of time."

"So I look forward to continuing to work with friends and allies to advance freedom — not America's freedom, but universal freedom, freedom granted by a Higher Being."

President Bush's comment about freedom being granted by a "Higher Being" was not widely reported in the United States, but the Arab News[347] headlined it and interviewed Shireen Hunter, director of the Washington-based Center for Strategic and International Studies Islam Program about it. She responded: "I admire his faith, and the fact that he didn't give himself credit shows his humility which I find rather endearing."

In this brief comment, President Bush referenced the founding principle about freedom that is a major source of resentment in the Arab world. It does not come from America. It comes from "a Higher Being" or "our Creator, or "God" or – in Arabic – Allah. It caught the attention of the Arab media because, as Shireen Hunter observed, President Bush "didn't give himself credit" for Iraq's freedom.

The entire world seems to be dividing rapidly into two camps, regardless of their numerous differences in religious doctrine: between those who believe human rights are founded on inalienable rights arising from nature or the law of the jungle and unalienable rights that are endowed by their mindful and caring Creator. Rights given by man, by law, or custom, can be taken away or altered or transferred by law and custom. They also can be advanced or withheld by organized political, social or religious groups using persuasion, .or force, including terrorism.

On the other hand, **unalienable rights** given to mankind by "our Creator" cannot be transferred, even if we want to.

We cannot transfer our life, our liberty or our happiness to another.

---

[347] Arab News –Bush Credits God, not US for Freedom Movement in Mideast- http://www.arabnews.com/?page=4&section=0&article=59917&d=5&m=3&y=2005

Osama bin Laden and Musab al Zarqawi

This dichotomy is best expressed in the words of two international leaders of the two sides on the issue – George W. Bush and Musab al-Zarqawi, the "prince" of Al-Qaida in Iraq, who was appointed by Osama Bin Laden. A week before Iraq's first free elections on January 30, 2005, Zarqawi released a tape[348] in which he pinpointed this issue:

> "We have declared a fierce war on this evil principle of democracy and those who follow this wrong ideology. Democracy is also based on the right to choose your religion and that is against the rule of God."

President George W. Bush

Two days later, on February 2, 2005, President George W. Bush in his State of the Union address articulated an opposite view:

> "We are all part of a great venture: To extend the promise of freedom in our country, to renew the values that sustain our liberty, and to spread the peace that freedom brings.
>
> "As Franklin Roosevelt once reminded Americans, 'Each age is a dream that is dying, or one that is coming to

---

[348] CNN – Musab al Zarqawi –Democracy against the Rule of God
http://www.cnn.com/2005/WORLD/meast/01/23/iraq.main/

birth.' And we live in the country where the biggest dreams are born. The abolition of slavery was only a dream -- until it was fulfilled. The liberation of Europe from fascism was only a dream -- until it was achieved. The fall of imperial communism was only a dream -- until, one day, it was accomplished. Our generation has dreams of its own, and we also go forward with confidence. The road of Providence is uneven and unpredictable -- yet we know where it leads: It leads to freedom.

"Thank you, and may God bless America."

The bottom line on this issue IS freedom. That is why the First Amendment to the Constitution was written and adopted on September 28, 1789, by the first Congress under the new constitution:

"Congress shall make no law respecting an establishment of religion, or prohibiting the free exercise thereof; or abridging the freedom of speech, or of the press; or the right of the people peaceably to assemble, and to petition the Government for a redress of grievances."

The French Assembly under the Jacobins in France in the 1790s, in the name of Freedom, seized the property of the nation's churches, took control of appointing the clergy priests and declared the end of the Christian era – all in the name of "freedom." Two hundred years later, in the name of Freedom, we are debating in the United States whether people, even presidents, should be allowed to talk about any role for Providence, a Creator or God on public property while terrorists, in the name of God, are equally determined to stop the spread of freedom, to choose one's belief in or even their definition of God.

President Bush concluded his second Inaugural address by reminding Americans of the founding principles of this nation. He said:

"When the Declaration of Independence was first read in public and the Liberty Bell was sounded in celebration, a witness said, 'It rang as if it meant something.' In our time it means something still. America, in this young century, proclaims liberty throughout all the world, and to all the inhabitants thereof. Renewed in our strength - tested, but not weary - we are ready for the greatest achievements in the history of freedom.

"May God bless you, and may He watch over the United States of America"

Arlington National Cemetery Monument to Mexico Civil War[349]

What DOES freedom mean? What does the Constitution really say? Does it really say that no public discussion or prayer or religious symbols such as crosses can occur on tax supported property such as school and courthouses and perhaps one day even tax-supported cemeteries? Should that last sentence have been edited out of President Bush's speech on tax-supported Internet sites, such as the White House website?

To be able to sort through these many conflicting voices, it is imperative that Americans really understand the freedoms guaranteed by the Declaration of Independence and the Constitution of the United States and be able to choose local, state, and national leaders and policies that will determine the course of and perhaps the very survival of our nation in the coming years.

---

[349] Arlington National Cemetery – Mexico Civil War monument - http://www.arlingtoncemetery.org/images/ANC_surroundings/PAGES/image49.html

About Mary Mostert

Mary Mostert was involved in politics before she was old enough to vote, and was writing articles for newspapers and for *The Nation* magazine at the age of 19. As a teenager in the 1940s she organized one of the first interracial youth groups in Memphis, Tennessee and was involved nationally and internationally in the race relations and peace movements.

In 1962 as executive director of the Independent Political Forum, she was one of 52 American women who met hundreds of women from other nations in Geneva, Switzerland, to petition delegates at 17 Nation Disarmament Conference to sign the first Nuclear Test-ban treaty. While the test ban treaty was opposed by the both the executive and legislative branches of government at the time, the small ad hoc "Mothers' Lobby" helped change opinion. Some six months later the Senate signed the treaty, and after the "Mothers' Lobby" picketing the White House, President John F. Kennedy signed it and it was ratified by a majority in the Senate.

In the mid-1960s Mary was one of the first female political commentators published in a major New York State metropolitan newspaper. She also ran a construction company, won architectural awards for restoration of historic buildings, served on redevelopment boards in the inner city of Rochester NY. By 1970 she had concluded that the War on Poverty programs were doing irreparable harm to the Black families they were meant to assist and left the Democratic Party. Mary ran unsuccessfully for the New York State Senate in 1972 as a Republican and has managed campaigns for candidates in both New York and California.

In 1991-92 Mary was secretary for a national, multi-racial women's group called "Positive Action NOW" in South Africa, her father's homeland. The organization sought to reduce the threat of civil war among the nation's various racial, religious and political groups by urging all sides to use the "language of peace, rather than the language of war." Mary, with her South African friend Julia Mavimbela and other women leaders in South Africa, met with President F.W. de Klerk, future President Nelson Mandela, Frank Mdlalose, chairman of the Inkatha Freedom Party, trade union leader Cyril Rhamaphosa, Dr. Andries Treurnicht chairman of the Conservative Party and most of the leaders of the nation's 19 political parties that had delegates to the Convention for a Democratic South Africa (Codesa) charged with writing South Africa's new Constitution .

Each of them was given a "constitution packet" that Mary put together. The packet included copies of the US Declaration of Independence, Constitution and Bill of Rights, the video "A More Perfect Union" on writing the Constitution, the Bill of Rights and other materials on our constitution. At a meeting of evangelical Christian church leaders in Kwa-Zulu in 1992 Mary explained the importance of the American concept that our unalienable rights to life, liberty and the pursuit of happiness come from God, not government. As a result, the wording of the group's proposed resolution to CODESA was rewritten to limit government interference in religious matters.

From 1994-2001 Mary edited radio talk show host Michael Reagan's newsletter, the Reagan Monitor, and created the Reagan Information Interchange on the internet. Her first book, *Coming Home – Families Can Stop the Unraveling of America*, reviewed as "destroying the myth that legislation can replace the efforts of the family" was published in 1996 by Gold Leaf Press.

During the 1998 Congressional campaigns, she launched a website, to provide voters with "original sources" information by providing links to websites of candidates of all political parties that were running for major state and national offices.

Her website (http://www.bannerofliberty.com) has expanded to provide links to numerous information sources and her weekly news analyses are published on many other websites.

Mary is the mother of six adult children, twenty-five grandchildren and two great-grandchildren.

Index

A

B

C

D

E

F

G

H- I

J

K

L

M

N

O

P-Q

R

S

T

U-V

W

X-Y- Z